the

Middle School

Counselor

Gary M. Miller
University of South Carolina

Joseph C. Rotter
University of South Carolina

The CARROLL PRESS
Publishers
43 Squantum Street
Cranston, Rhode Island 02920

About the Authors –

DR. GARY M. MILLER is an Associate Professor in the Counselor Education Program at the University of South Carolina. He completed the Doctor of Philosophy degree at Case Western Reserve University and taught at Eastern Michigan University prior to joining the University of South Carolina. He has conducted research on middle school counseling and has published articles in numerous professional journals. He has recently co-edited the book *A Consumer's Guide To The Public School* with Dr. Gyuri Nemeth.

DR. JOSEPH C. ROTTER worked as a teacher and counselor in elementary and secondary school settings before moving to the University of South Carolina where he currently holds the position of Professor of Counselor Education and Rehabilitation Services. In addition to his responsibilities at the University, he consults regularly with school districts throughout the United States. He is Editor of *Elementary School Guidance and Counseling* and serves as Director of the General Electric Foundation Career Education Leadership Institute at the University of South Carolina. His current research interests are in the area of children and stress and he is available as a workshop consultant on this topic. Dr. Rotter is also co-author of three books and many articles in professional journals. He has recently co-authored *Parent Teacher Conferencing,* published by the National Education Association.

© **Copyright 1985 by Gary M. Miller and Joseph C. Rotter**

All rights reserved. No part of this book may be reproduced for inclusion in another publication or for any other commercial purpose without permission from the publisher.

Library of Congress Cataloging in Publication Data

Miller, Gary M.
The middle school counselor

Bibliography: p.
Includes index.

1. Student counselors, Training of - - United States - - Addresses, essays, lectures. 2. Middle schools - - United States - - Addresses, essays, lectures. I. Rotter, Joseph C. II. Title

LB1721.M554 1984   *373.14*   *83-24028*
ISBN 0-910328-38-2 (cloth)   *ISBN 0-910328-39-0 (paperback)*

Manufactured in the United States of America

DR. FRED H. WALLBROWN is an Associate Professor in the Department of Counseling and Personnel Services at Kent State University. He has teaching and advising responsibilities in the school psychology, counseling psychology and master degree programs in school counseling. He is the co-author/editor of two books and seventy journal articles. He is an associate editor of *Psychology in the Schools* and an editorial board member for *Measurement and Evaluation in Guidance, The Journal of School Psychology* and *The Directive Teacher.* He is a Fellow of Division 1, General Psychology Division 16, School Psychology of the American Psychological Association and is a Diplomate in School Psychology from the American Board of Professional Psychology.

DR. KAREN K. PRICHARD is currently an Assistant Professor in the Department of Guidance and Educational Psychology at Southern Illinois University, Carbondale, Illinois. Dr. Prichard teaches in the areas of counseling and school psychology. In addition to teaching, she provides counseling to adolescents and adults at the University's Clinical Center. Dr. Prichard's research interests are in the areas of career development and children's social skills.

DR. MARY BALLOU is a faculty member in the Department of Counseling, Rehabilitation and Special Education at Northeastern University. She directs the Counseling Psychology program and conducts a private practice in therapy and consultation. Dr. Ballou has recently completed a manuscript for the book, *Mental Health: A Feminist Perspective.* In addition, she has completed an extensive research project examining "Discrimination Against Women, People With Disabilities and Ethnic Minority Members."

DR. RICHARD E. HULT, Jr., (author of Chapter Two) is an Associate Professor in the Department of Educational Research and Psychology in the College of Education at the University of South Carolina at Columbia. He has conducted research in several areas of child and adolescent development particularly focusing upon moral reasoning ability, identity status and family interaction patterns. He has published in several professional journals including *The MIddle School Journal* and the *Journal of Psychology.*

DR. NANCY WILSON (author of Chapter Eight) is coordinator of elementary guidance services in Lexington School District No. 4, Swansea, South Carolina. She also serves as an adjunct instructor at the University of South Carolina in counselor education and as a staff member of the General Electric Foundation Career Education Leadership Institute.

CREDITS

Chapter Three, pages 33-34. Reprinted with permission from the United Nations Declaration of the Rights of the Child, 1959.

Chapter Three, pages 34 and 40. Reprinted by permission of Field Newspaper Syndicate from *Ann Lander's Column* by Ann Landers, 1975 and 1976.

Chapter Three, page 36. Reprinted with permission from *School Counselor,* ASCA position statement, "Student rights: a right to due process." 1978, pages 25 and 335.

Chapter Three, pages 37-39. Reprinted with permission from Jean E. Mizer, "Cipher in the Snow," *National Education Association Journal,* 1964, 53, pages 8-10.

Chapter Three, page 42. Reprinted with permission from Child Welfare League of America, Inc., 1974.

Chapter Three, pages 43-46. Reprinted with permission of the Council for Exceptional Children from D.F. Kline, *Child abuse and neglect: A primer for school personnel.* 1977.

Chapter Four, page 61. Adapted with permission from "Key competency areas for middle school teaching" and "Key competencies for middle school teachers," University of Florida Middle School Project, 1972.

Chapter Seven, pages 101-102. Reprinted with permission from "Learning Disabilities Checklist." The New York Institute for Child Development, Inc., 1976.

Chapter Nine, pages 136-137. Reprinted with permission from D. Dinkmeyer and J. Carlson, *Consulting: Facilitating human potential and change processes.* Copyright ©1973 by Charles E. Merrill.

Chapter Nine, pages 142-143. Adapted with permission from E.L. Barnette and D. Turner, "And now a word from . . .," *Elementary School Guidance and Counseling,* 1976, 10, pages 177-183.

Chapter Nine, pages 144-145. Reprinted with permission from J.C. Rotter, J. McFadden and G. Kannenburg, *Significant influence people: A SIP of discipline and encouragement.* Copyright ©R & E Associates, Inc., 1981.

Chapter Eleven, pages 169-177. Reprinted with permission from *Career Guidance Model,* New York State Education Department, Bureau of Guidance, 1977.

Chapter Eleven, pages 175-176. Reprinted with permission from S.G. Weinrach, "The busy counselor's guide to the evaluation of career information materials." *The School Counselor,* 1974, 22, pages 53-57.

Appendix C, pages 204-217. Reprinted with permission from Ms. Delores McCord, Career Counselor, Valencia Community College, Orlando, Florida.

Appendix D, pages 218-240. Reprinted with permission from Department of Guidance and Counseling, Detroit Public Schools, "Guidance Program Model for Middle School." Detroit Public Schools, 1979.

CONTENTS

Preface ix

Chapter One   **Background of the Middle School** 1
Gary M. Miller

Chapter Two   **Developmental Characteristics
of Middle School Students** 14
Richard E. Hult, Jr.

Chapter Three   **Children's Rights** 32
Joseph C. Rotter

Chapter Four   **Individual Counseling** 58
Fred H. Wallbrown and Karen Kidd Prichard

Chapter Five   **Group Approaches** 69
Gary M. Miller

Chapter Six   **Crisis Intervention** 80
Mary Ballou

Chapter Seven   **The Handicapped Child** 95
Joseph C. Rotter

Chapter Eight   **The Counselor's Work With Special Populations:
Education for Choice** 104
Nancy H. Wilson

Chapter Nine   **Consulting** 122
Joseph C. Rotter

Chapter Ten   **Psychological Assessment** 152
Gary M. Miller

Chapter Eleven   **Career Development** 165
Gary M. Miller

Chapter Twelve   **Research and Trends** 181
Gary M. Miller

CONTENTS — *continued*

Appendix   193

    Appendix A   **Role of the Middle School Counselor** 195
    Appendix B   **Letter to Parents** 197
    Appendix C   **Career Information Systems** 204
    Appendix D   **Guidance Program Model** 218

Index   241

Dedication

to

Derek Matthew Miller
Kevin Joseph Miller

Jonathan Rotter
Jeffrey Rotter

our children who we hope, as they seek their education and their places in life, will do so with excitement, openness and a willingness to explore their potentials and their worlds.

LIST OF ILLUSTRATIONS

Figure 1:1   Representative Aims, Reasons and Features
of Middle School Programs 7

Figure 3:1   Kline Flow Chart 41

Systems of Consultation 123

Figure 9:1   The Consultation Process: Four Models 125

Consultation Practices at Work 128

Exercise 1   Who Influences the Behaviors of Children . . 138-139

Exercise 2   Identifying Your Current Significant
Influence People and The Effects They
Have on Your Behavior 139-140

Exercise 3   What Encouragement and Discouragement
Responses Do You Use When Influencing
the Behavior of Children? 140

Exercise 4   How Do You Process A Problem from
Beginning to End? 141

A Sip of Discipline and Encouragement 144-145

Table 9:2   Framework for Identification of
Forms of Rejection 146

Table 9:3   Forces Relevant to the Facilitation and
Hindrance of Innovation and Diffusion
of Teaching Practices 147-148

Table 10:1   Test Review Card Front 156

Table 10:2   Test Review Card Back 157

Figure 10:3   Loesch Testing Flow Chart 158-159

Figure 10:4   Suggested Testing Programs 160

List of Illustrations — *Continued*

Figure 11:1   Vocational Development Stages and Social Factors
of Middle School Students 167

Figure 11:2   New York State Career Guidance Model . . . 169-171

Figure 11:3   Reviewer's Rating Sheet 175

Figure 11:4   Career Film and Filmstrip Evaluation
Checklist 176

Figure 11:5   Career Literature Evaluation Checklist 178

Table 12:1   Nature of Counselor Certification for
Middle School Counselors 183

Table 12:2   Highest Ranking Counselor Functions as Viewed
by Middle School Principals 184

Table 12:3   South Carolina Principals' Rankings of
Ten Highest Counselor Functions 185

Table 12:4   Combined Principals' Rankings of Ten Highest
Counselor Functions 186

Table 12:5   Combined Rankings of Ten Highest
Middle School Counselor Functions 187

Table 12:6   Percentage of Middle Schools Reporting
Components and Services 188

Table 12:7   Middle School Guidance Services 189

PREFACE

Within recent years a new organizational structure has emerged in public education. Middle schools have been developed for the purpose of meeting the special physical, psychological and educational needs of children in the preadolescent age range. Numerous educational patterns have been suggested for middle schools, yet little has been written about the specific guidance and counseling components for young people in these schools.

The purpose of this book is to present information specifically related to the middle school counselor and the middle school counseling program. It contains twelve chapters, each highlighting specific information about middle schools and middle school counseling.

Chapter One provides an overview of the middle school movement in the United States. Chapter Two focuses on the children who attend middle schools with an emphasis on their unique needs as individuals. The rights of children are presented in Chapter Three. Individual counseling is discussed in Chapter Four while group approaches with middle school children are offered in Chapter Five. The focus of Chapter Six is on crisis intervention and the strategies a counselor may wish to consider.

Chapter Seven explores the counseling challenges of handicapped children in the middle school environment. Special populations are discussed in Chapter Eight. The consulting function of the counselor is examined in Chapter Nine. Tests and psychological assessment approaches are described in Chapter Ten. Chapters Eleven and Twelve provide information on career development and research trends in middle school counseling.

The intended audience for this book includes both educators and students in pre-service and in-service preparation, practicing middle school counselors and middle school administrators who are responsible for guidance programs.

Our special thanks go to the various authors who contributed chapters to this book: Dr. Richard E. Hult, Jr. of the University of South Carolina; Dr. Fred Wallbrown of Kent State University; Dr. Karen Kidd Prichard of Southern Illinois University at Carbondale; Dr. Mary Ballou of Northeastern University; Dr. Nancy Wilson of Lexington School District No. 4, in Swansea, South Carolina and Ms. Iwana Guess Ridgill, a graduate student at the University of South Carolina for proofreading and editorial suggestions.

In addition, we wish to thank Ms. Lela Anastasion and Ms. Jeanne Farrar for typing many of the chapters and Ms. Carolyn Schrameck of the Carroll Press for supportive and patient editorial attention in the development of this book.

GARY M. MILLER
JOSEPH C. ROTTER

Columbia, South Carolina
April, 1985

Chapter One

BACKGROUND of the MIDDLE SCHOOL
GARY M. MILLER

Introduction

To understand the development of the Middle School as an educational entity one must first consider its forerunner, the Junior High School. A historical perspective on the development of the Junior High School and its evolution into the Middle School, took place within a sixty year time period.

The Junior High School Movement: Initial Development

In his speech to the National Educational Association in 1888, President Eliot of Harvard voiced some concerns about the age at which students were entering colleges and universities. He encouraged the secondary schools to absorb the last two grades of the elementary school and thus lower the ages of entering freshmen. In addition to President Eliot, others began voicing concerns about the existent educational patterns.

The Committee of Ten (National Educational Association, 1895) was appointed by the National Educational Association in 1891 for the purpose of studying the uniformity of educational programs and the admissions requirements for college. Representatives from major colleges and secondary schools from throughout the United States participated in the discussion.

Dr. Charles W. Eliot, the President of Harvard, chaired the committee and the conference they developed was organized around the nine specific subject areas of (1) Latin, (2) Greek, (3) English, (4) Other Modern Languages, (5) Mathematics, (6) Physics, Astronomy, and Chemistry, (7) Natural History (Biology, including Botany, Zoology, and Physiology), (8) History, Civil Government and Political Economy, (9) Geography (Physical Geography, Geology, and Meteorology). From this grouping, nine separate conferences, with a total of ninety participants met throughout the country to examine each of the subject areas.

The report prepared by the Committee of Ten in 1892 was published in 1894. This was the first serious study of the relationship of high school courses and college requirements.

1

In terms of academic offerings, the Committee of Ten in 1893 proposed that courses in some mathematics areas, sciences and foreign languages be introduced earlier than the six-year high school. In 1899 the Committee on College Entrance Requirements cited a need for a six-year program beginning with the seventh grade. They viewed this as the turning point into adolescence and saw the six-year program as appropriate for youths. Support for their early suggestion was given by the Commission on Economy of Time in Education in 1913.

During the early 1900's other situations also influenced the movement toward junior high schools. Psychologists voiced concerns about adolescent youths. It was felt that adolescents did not belong in the elementary grades, but needed an educational situation more appropriate to their needs, interests and learning abilities. Consequently, schools needed to be developed to accommodate these students. Psychologists such as G. Stanley Hall documented the differences in developmental and learning needs of youths in early adolescence. There was an increasing realization that young people between the ages of 12 and 14 had needs that differed sharply from those of students in elementary and secondary schools.

Studies by Thorndike (1907), Ayres (1909) and Strayer (1911) reported that some youths were dropping out of school at the end of the eighth grade. Although they had a basic elementary education they often lacked the more specialized skills to find employment. This concern about drop-outs stimulated efforts toward the development of vocational education courses for students. It was believed that the junior high school, rather than the elementary school would be the appropriate place to introduce such courses.

Another influence in the development of junior high schools was the increased number of students in high schools. During the period of 1890 to 1920 the public school enrollment for youths in the 14-17 age group increased from 3.4 to 24 percent (Koos, 1929). This increase in enrollment created administrative and space problems that were best relieved by developing a new grade organization.

Support for developing junior high schools also came from the awareness that most teachers were prepared for secondary level teaching. Being specialists in subject matter areas, it was believed that they could better educate the adolescents in junior high schools than the more generally prepared elementary school teachers.

Lastly, extra-curricular activities could be included in the junior high school. Many of these activities seemed inappropriate for the upper elementary grades, yet could be easily incorporated in this new educational structure.

The date 1909 is generally viewed as the year when the first junior high school opened in Columbus, Ohio. However, it was not a Midwest phenomena, for in 1910 both Berkeley, California and Concord, New Hampshire opened junior high schools.

Early Purposes

One of the earliest clarifications of the purpose of the junior high school was developed in 1927 by Leonard Koos. He presented specific functions: (1) decrease in the time spent studying elementary school subjects; (2) meeting individual differences of students by presenting them a variety of courses and activities; (3) increasing the self-exploration and guidance of students via home-room guidance programs; (4) preparing students for vocations by starting vocational courses including home economics, shop courses, and business courses. He hoped that the three year junior high school would provide one additional year of vocational preparation of students prior to their leaving school at the end of the ninth grade. Vocational courses and guidance assistance given to the pupils would be helpful for students leaving school, but would also help persuade the students to remain and enter high school.

The objectives cited by Koos vary little from a later statement of the junior high school's functions developed by Bossing and Cramer (1965). Their statement addressed eight specific areas. Working with adolescents to help them with their unique needs and their individual differences represented the first function stated by Bossing and Cramer (1965). They also noted the need to assist students in the development of basic learning skills which would impact their school and future learning. The preparation for democratic living, being a responsible citizen, preparing for family life, appreciating the moral and ethical principles of society, concerning one's self with the conservation of our limited natural resources and being able to participate in our economic system represented the third function presented in 1965. Three functions focusing on the personal development of the junior high school pupils included: provision of programs to meet the personal interests and creative abilities of the adolescents; guidance and counseling programs for the students; promotion of the mental and physical fitness of these young people.

These sets of objectives represent the early and more recent attempts by educators to support the junior high school as a viable educational entity. They attempted to focus on the student, the curriculum and the services for students. Both the 1927 and 1965 objectives referred to guidance-oriented activities in the junior high school.

Emerging Concerns

Problematic issues developed as the junior high schools evolved. These schools functioning as a transition between the self-contained elementary school and the highly-specialized, departmentalized high school represented one concern. Students entering seventh grade experienced a more difficult time in making the transition to the junior high schools, than the ninth graders going into high schools.

The issue of the certification of teachers for junior high schools represented another area of concern. The typical types of certification, 7-12 or 9-12, represented more of a secondary school orientation. Few efforts were made to develop any specific requirements for preparing teachers of students in this transition period.

College entrance requirements posed another problem. Since most colleges and universities required four years of high school preparation, the ninth grade was forced to become a part of the high school organizational plan. The elimination of the ninth grade from the junior high school destroyed the concept of the three-year junior high school.

Other concerns emerged that created some disenchantment with the junior high school concept. One in particular was that the junior high school did not really develop as a separate educational enterprise, but was merely a downward extension of the high school. Concerns such as these prompted Vars (1966) to state:

> . . . let us recognize that the junior high school has been an albatross around our necks from the beginning, and we are well rid of it. (p. 112)

The Middle School: The Students

Educators became increasingly concerned about the viability of the junior high school as noted in the previous section. Combined with these concerns were new concepts regarding the development of adolescents and their needs. The efforts of Margaret Mead and Robert J. Havighurst help to highlight some of the reasons for the development of middle schools housing either grades 5-8 or 6-8.

In examining the development of pre-adolescents, Mead (1965) observed a downward trend in the ages at which young people were dating. She also noted an increased emphasis on the vocational choice process as well as increased incidents of criminal acts. Decisions regarding one's religious affiliation were occurring at younger ages, as was the lavish spending of money by pre-adolescents which she observed during the decade of the 1950's-1960's.

Each of these areas in which changes were noted placed added pressures on young people. It appeared they were entering the adult world at too rapid a pace. Mead (1965) commented:

> . . . the greatest tragedy of our present day adolescents are the
> millions that are condemned by social circumstances to learn very
> little at school and to live a life in which their potentialities are
> practically unrealized. (p. 89)

Havighurst (1965) viewed the junior high school aged youth as
being more complex, more knowledgeable about society and human
nature, more sophisticated and more knowledgeable about art and
music than previous adolescents. He noted that:

> The serious nature of life comes home to the junior high school
> youth more frequently and earlier than it did to his parents. At the
> same time he sees a complex and difficult world, in which the dis-
> tance from childhood to adulthood seems so great as to be almost
> unbridgeable. (Havighurst, 1966, p. 2)

To assist young people in dealing with the issues of life, Havighurst
believed schools could help by encouraging and promoting community service by adolescents. He also suggested more emphasis be placed
on teaching about current heroes and their effects. Lastly, he believed
adolescents needed to analyze current social issues and strive toward
reaching positive solutions to them.

Rationale

The issues noted above confront the pre-adolescent and it is students in this group, ages 10-14, for whom the middle school has developed. Alexander, Williams, Compton, Hines and Prescott (1968)
noted the term "middle" is most appropriate as the students are between childhood and adolescence and the schools are in the "middle"
in terms of serving young people who are between childhood and
adolescence. Another point of view is that the "middle" school is
between the elementary and secondary school years. Regarding the
cognitive aspects of middle school education, Curtis (1968) documented the need for middle schools: to help students master individual learning skills; to help them understand how to participate in and
contribute to society; and to promote students' explorations based
on their needs and desires.

In 1965, Alexander and Williams presented an initial rationale
for middle schools which focused on both academic and personal
developmental needs of the students. They believed the middle
school program should first meet the needs of pre-adolescents. The
promotion of the intellectual aspects of the curriculum and development of usable skills for continuous learning were also stressed. Regarding the personal development aspects of the middle school, the
health and physical education program was to meet the needs of the
students. They were to be encouraged to examine their values, reacting to the roles they would play in society. The teachers were not
overlooked in this statement, for the authors sought to promote the

unique talents and interests of the teachers in their efforts to facilitate the learning of the students.

Broad (1966) sought a separate status for the middle school. Regarding the teaching-learning aspects of the middle school he indicated that some team teaching coupled with subject specialty instruction should be incorporated. The middle school should be designed to provide for the transition from the elementary school to the secondary high school. This could be best implemented by a gradual shift from the self-contained classroom to the more specialized one in the later years of the children's middle school experiences. He suggested that additional facilities should be available to students in order to promote their learnings in laboratory-type settings. From a psychological and sociological perspective, guidance services should be provided. The students from throughout a school district would come together as a unit one year earlier, thus promoting interrelationships within the school district. Another benefit of such an educational effort would result as the high school courses became more unified in the grades 9-12. A final influence of the middle school would be the impact upon the preparation of teachers to work in middle schools. Revisions in teacher preparation programs at the pre-service level as well as with in-service efforts would result. Also, State Departments of Education would need to develop new criteria for certifying teachers for middle schools. The impact of this movement, then, had multiple implications for many aspects of education.

In 1968 Compton wrote that the middle school was a definite break from the traditional efforts seen in many school organization plans. A positive articulation with the elementary school was seen as a critical component. Her promotion of team teaching and skills laboratories coincided with Broad's (1966) concepts for middle school educational efforts. Compton (1968) included providing opportunities for students to engage in independent studies and various activities for personal development. To provide for these two aspects, it would be necessary to have sufficient flexibility in the programs and schedules of the students. Homeroom guidance activities conducted by a teacher prepared in the field of guidance and counseling represented another dimension of Compton's (1968) middle school concept. Compton also saw the need to have administrators, teachers and staff who understood the pre-adolescent age group and who were prepared to offer the educational activities appropriate to these youths.

The benefits of such new and diverse programs to the students attending middle schools has been clearly highlighted by Gastwirth (1967) and Turnbaugh (1968). The former saw the need for the

Figure 1:1
REPRESENTATIVE AIMS, REASONS, and FEATURES of MIDDLE SCHOOL PROGRAMS

Aims as accepted in The Emergent Middle School (2)	Reasons as perceived by 110 Middle School Principals (3)	Features summarized by the NEA Research Bulletin (4)
To serve the educational needs of the "in-between-agers" in a school bridging the elementary school for childhood and the high school for adolescence.	To provide a program specifically designed for students in this age group. (2)	A span of at least three grades to allow for the gradual transition from elementary to high school instructional practices.
To provide optimum individualization of curriculum and instruction for a population characterized by great variability.	To provide more specialization in grades 5 and/or 6. (9)	Required special courses, taught in departmentalized form such as industrial arts, home economics, foreign language.
In relation to the foregoing aims, to plan, implement, evaluate, and modify, in a continuing curriculum development program, a curriculum which includes provision for: (a) a planned sequence of concepts in the general education areas; (b) major emphasis on the interests and skills for continued learning; (c) a balanced program of exploratory experiences and other activities and services for personal development of values.	To try out various innovations. (7) To use plans that have been successful in other school systems. (9)	Guidance program as a distinct entity to fill the special needs of this age group. Limited attention to interschool sports and activities.
To promote continuous progress through and smooth articulation between the several phases and levels of the total educational program.	To better bridge the elementary and the high school. (3)	Emerging departmental structure in each higher grade to effect gradual transition from the self-contained classroom to the departmentalized high school.
To facilitate the optimum use of personnel and facilities available for continuing improvement of schooling.	To eliminate crowded conditions in other schools. (1) To move grade 9 into the high school. (5) To remedy the weaknesses of the junior high school. (6) To utilize a new school building. (8) To aid desegregation. (10)	Flexible approaches to instruction-team teaching, flexible scheduling. Faculty with both elementary and secondary certification.

Permission to reproduce this table was granted by Dr. Jack E. Blackburn and the *High School Journal*.

middle school to aid in the transition from pre-adolescence to adolescence. The middle school was conceived as an institution designed to promote the students' sense of self-identification as persons. Turnbaugh (1968) wrote of the intellectual development of youth in this age group as being one of the concerns of the middle school. He also concentrated on the personal-social development of enrollees. The middle school was viewed as in institution wherein the pressures of academics, athletics and societal forces were to be minimized. The academic aspect of this is somewhat in agreement with Compton's (1968) perception of academic evaluation, which would be based on the individual's progress and not contingent upon the achievements of one's peers.

Turnbaugh (1968) also saw the need for wholesome and appropriate outlets of expression, based again on the needs of each person. Turnbaugh's idea of reducing the isolation of students from each other in regard to age, race, and socio-economic group appears to be in agreement with the earlier idea expressed by Broad (1966) of bringing diverse students together in a middle school one year earlier than the usual first year of high school.

Blackburn (1969) highlighted the concern of the middle school for the total education of pre-adolescents. A concern noted in Blackburn (1969) was the apparent over-emphasis on departmentalized, subject-matter offering. Blackburn (1969, p. 147) provides a good summary of the aims, reasons, and features of the middle school. (See Figure 1:1, page 7.)

Development of Middle Schools

The evolution of junior high school structures into middle school units did not commence until the 1960's. A comprehensive survey by Cuff (1967) examined many aspects of middle schools during 1965-66. Of the 50 states surveyed only 29 reported having middle schools. At this time 499 middle schools were in existence and 55 percent of them had a grade range of 6-8. Four principal reasons for their development included: (1) integration, (2) population shifts in school districts, (3) the retirement of outdated school plants and (4) an attempt to resolve the problems that plagued the junior high schools.

Through the efforts of Alexander and Kealy (1969), a survey was conducted in 1966-1967. They found 1,101 middle schools in operation, most with either a 5-8 or 6-8 grade range. The rationale for their development differed from Cuff's (1967) findings for there was now a focus on the needs of children in this age group, a need for continuity of educational programs and a need for more flexibility in curriculum.

In 1969, Pumerantz surveyed states' recognition of the middle school concept. During the 1967-68 school year, Connecticut was the only state having legislation defining the middle school. Five other states indicated that middle schools had been recommended or endorsed, but no legislation had been passed for them. There were 44 states not defining the middle school concept through law. A total of 88 percent of the states surveyed did not recognize the middle school concept, nor did they offer any suggestions or recommendations to their local school districts regarding middle school organization plans.

The most recent national survey of middle schools conducted in 1977 by Brooks (1978a, b.) documented the increase in middle schools throughout the country. In 1977 there were 4,060 middle schools in operation, almost four times the number in existence a decade earlier (Alexander and Kealy, 1969). There was little change in the rationale for starting these schools. They focused upon bridging the elementary-secondary school gap, tailoring programs to meet the needs of youth and eliminating the over-crowded conditions in the elementary or high schools.

This rather rapid increase in the number of middle schools reported by Brooks (1978a) as school districts began to weigh the benefits gained from their efforts with junior high schools. Apparently the need to concentrate specifically on the pre-adolescent years as unique in the total development of the child gained greater recognition.

Future Trends

In 1978 Alexander reacted to the research studies of Brooks (1978a, 1978b) and itemized some goals still to be achieved in the middle schools. He believed every student should be known as an individual, and that at least one adult in the school should accept responsibility for that student's guidance. Achieving full mastery of skills relating to continued learning, together with a commitment to their use and improvement, represented a second goal. Decision-making and problem-solving skills needed to be developed by each student along with a useful body of fundamental knowledge. As a final goal, opportunities to explore and develop interests in numerous aspects of life needed to be developed, for these could benefit the student in aesthetic, leisure and career interests.

In examining the number of varied goals, concepts and justifications for the middle school, the reader will note how often guidance and guidance-related activities emerged. Writers concerned about the needs of middle school youth were aware of the role guidance might play in the total educational plan.

The Middle School Counselor

Background

The role of the middle school counselor, like the middle school itself, has had an interesting evolution. Schertzer and Stone (1981) clearly present a record of the development of guidance services in the public schools. At the same time that junior high schools were being considered and developed at the start of the twentieth century, efforts toward developing guidance services were also emerging. In fact, 1907 was the year when Jessie B. Davis, as principal of the Grand Rapids High School in Grand Rapids, Michigan introduced a weekly guidance period as part of an English composition class. This period focused on "vocational and moral guidance," and represented the first documented effort at providing guidance services to students in a school setting (Mathewson, 1962, p. 72).

Specific influences have been identified by Traxler (1957) as promoting the guidance movement. Each of these diverse influences interacted in such a manner as to accent the needs of people for assistance in dealing with issues in their lives. The spread of philanthropy and humanitarianism represented one influence. Concern for the welfare of others and donations to socially-oriented causes did much to provide help to those seeking it. Concern about the moral lives of people resulted in a call for individuals to help youth. Because many youth were in the public schools, guidance activities in this setting were encouraged.

The increased awareness of the mental health movement and positive steps toward mental health was the third influence on the guidance movement. Those concerned about the mental health of children encouraged teachers to be more sensitive to the psychological issues confronting their students. Eventually, specialists would be sought to work with children in the school setting. A growing awareness of the unique differences in children and the need to identify and know them as individuals became an ever-increasing concern of educators. Guidance programs were seen as ways to promote efforts in this direction.

Assessment of individuals through the use of various standardized instruments represents another influential factor in the development of the guidance movement. The effort toward systematic approaches to gathering data to help the individual in the learning process was accepted and viewed as a part of the guidance activities in the schools.

Support from the federal government in various ways helped the guidance movement. From the vocational education acts such as the George-Reed Act in 1929, the George-Ellezey Act in 1934, the George-Dean act in 1936, and the George-Barden Act in 1946, came support for vocational education activities as well as the development of guidance units in various state education departments. Beginning with the National Defense Education Act of 1958, through more recent legislation for career education, one can see the continuing support for guidance at the federal level.

Carl R. Rogers developed the approach to therapy commonly known as the client-centered approach. From his theoretical position emerged research which supported this revolutionary approach to helping people with issues they faced. His focus on *the person in the process of helping* assisted counselors in developing a person-oriented rather than a problem-oriented approach to the counseling process. Throughout the years, Rogers' theory has undergone some modifications but its emphasis on the person has remained a major influence on the guidance movement.

In examining some of the background information about the guidance movement one must remember that counselors were first employed in secondary schools and then eventually in elementary schools. At the present time there seems to be an increase of approximately one thousand elementary counselors per year in the public schools (Shertzer and Stone, 1976, p. 92). As of 1976, approximately 10,770 counselors were employed in public elementary schools, including grades K-6. This is a ratio of one counselor for every six elementary schools in the United States (Myrick and Moni, 1976). Data on the status of middle school counselors is unclear for little has been reported regarding these counselors.

Role of the Middle School Counselor

The parallel progress of the evolution of middle schools from junior high schools and the emergence of interest in guidance programs for youth has taken a relatively short period of time when one considers the history of public education in the United States.

With the evolution of the middle school, the need for guidance professionals educated to assist students at this level became obvious. Consequently, the American School Counselor Association Governing Board officially recognized a position paper developed by Mary K. Ryan in 1972-73. With input from counselors, this paper was modified and presented in 1974. With slight editorial changes, the final document, "The Unique Role of the Middle/Junior High School Counselor," was published in 1978. The document in its entirety is reprinted in Appendix A.

The middle school counselor has to work with many publics. As the statement clearly articulates at the same time helping to focus on the specific nature of the counselor's responsibilities. It is obvious that changes may occur, however, the basic ideas surrounding the role of the middle school counselor are strong and appropriate.

REFERENCES

Alexander, W.M. & Williams, E.L. School's for the middle school years. *Educational Leadership.* 1965, *23*: 217-223.

Alexander, W.M. & Kealy, R.P. From junior high school to middle school. *The High School Journal.* 1969, *53*: 151-153.

Alexander, W.H., Williams, E.L., Compton H., Hines, V.A. & Prescott, D. *The Emergent Middle School.* New York: Holt, Rinehart & Winston, Inc., 1968.

Alexander, W.M. How fares the middle school movement? *Middle School Journal.* 1978, *9*(3): 3-21.

American School Counselor Association Governing Board. The unique role of the middle/junior high school counselor. *Elementary School Guidance and Counseling.* 1978, *12*, 203-205.

Ayres, L.P. *Laggards in Our Schools.* New York: The Russell Sale Foundation. Charities Publication Committee, 1909.

Blackburn, J.E. Middle schools: dreams and realities. *The High School Journal.* 1969, *53*: 145-150.

Broad, P. The middle school: trends toward its adoption. *The Clearing House.* 1966, *40*: 331-333.

Brooks, K. The middle school – A national survey. *Middle School Journal.* 1978[a], *9*(1): 6-7.

Brooks, K. The middle school – A national survey. *Middle School Journal.* 1978[b], *9*(2): 6-7.

Compton, M.F. How do you prepare to teach transescents? *Educational Leadership.* 1973, *31*: 214-216.

Compton, M.F. "The middle school: Alternative to the status quo." *Theory Into Practice,* 1968, *7:* 108-110.

Cuff, W.A. "Middle schools on the march." *National Association of Secondary School Principals Bulletin.* 1967, *51:* 82-86.

Curtis, T.E. "The middle school in theory and practice." *National Association of Secondary School Principals Bulletin.* 1968, *52: 135-140.*

Gastwirth, P. "Questions facing the middle school." *Clearing House.* 1967, *41:* 472-475.

Mathewson, R.H. *Guidance Policy and Practice.* (3rd ed.) New York: Harper & Row Publishers, 1962.

Myrick, R.D. & Moni, L. "A status report of elementary school counseling." *Elementary School Guidance and Counseling.* 1976, *10*, 156-164.

National Education Association. *Journal of Proceedings and Addresses Session of the Year 1894.* St. Paul: National Educational Association, 1895.

Pumerantz, P. "State recognition of the Middle School." *National Association of Secondary School Principals Bulletin,* 1969, *53:* 14-19.

Shertzer, B. & Stone, S.C. *Fundamentals of Guidance,* 4th ed. Boston: Houghton Mifflin Company, 1981.

Strayer, G.D. *Age And Grade Census of Schools And Colleges: A Study of Retardation And Elimination* (United States Bureau of Education Bulletin No. 5, 1911. Whole Number 451). Washington, D.C.: U.S. Government Printing Office, 1911.

Thorndike, E.L. *The Elimination of Pupils From School* (Department of Interior: Bureau of Education Bulletin No. 4, 1907. Whole Number 379). Washington, D.C.: U.S. Government Priinting Office, 1908.

Traxler, A.B. *Techniques of Guidance.* New York: Harper & Brothers, 1957.

Turnbaugh, R.E. Middle school, a different name or a new concept? *The Clearing House.* 1968, *43:* 86-88.

Vars, G.F. Junior high or middle school? which is best for the education of young adolescents? *The High School Journal.* 1966, *50:* 109-113.

Chapter Two

DEVELOPMENTAL CHARACTERISTICS
of MIDDLE SCHOOL STUDENTS

RICHARD E. HULT, Jr.

The middle school years constitute one of the most significant transition periods in the human life cycle. Young people between the ages of ten and fourteen experience dramatic changes in every aspect of growth and development. Although interactions are complex and boundaries imprecise, these important changes and events which mark the end of childhood and the prelude to maturity may be understood to occur in several dimensions. In this chapter, the major physiological, cognitive and social characterisitics of middle schoolers are examined in relation to key developmental tasks and implications for practitioners.

Although the scientific study of early adolescence has only in recent years received significant attention, many theories have emerged in efforts to explain the multifaceted character of this period. The primary role of any such theory is to facilitate a more accurate understanding and allow for a more coherent interpretation of the many observations made of adolescent behavior.

Some theories have become useful in providing a better understanding of specific dimensions of development. A select number of the more significant of these theories are examined later in this chapter. Other theories help us interpret adolescent behavior in more general terms. Robert Havighurst's developmental task theory is one of the most notable and provides a framework for understanding the middle school adolescent.

Havighurst (1972) defines a developmental task as a set of skills, knowledge, functions and attitudes which an individual needs to acquire during a phase of life in order to become successful during and after that period. The accomplishment of developmental tasks serves to ensure the satisfaction of both individual and societal needs. Each task is structured by biological functions as well as social and cultural sanctions. Together, these sanctions loosely determine a time frame during which an individual should accomplish or work out a given

14

task. The following represents Havighurst's revised set of adolescent developmental tasks described in his 1972 volume. The age periods within which each task becomes most relevant have been analyzed by Thornburg (1975) and these are also presented.

Havighurst's Developmental Tasks and the Age Periods
of General Resolution

	Developmental Task	Approximate Age Period of Resolution
1.	Forming more mature relationships with agemates of both sexes	10 - 15½
2.	Achieving a masculine or feminine social role	10 - 17
3.	Accepting one's physique and using one's body effectively	11½ - 18
4.	Achieving emotional independence from parents and other adults	12½ - 23
5.	Developing conceptual and problem-solving skills	10 - 17
6.	Preparing for marriage and family life	15½ -
7.	Preparing for a career	14½ - 23
8.	Acquiring a set of ethics as a guide to behavior	13½ -
9.	Developing social intelligence	17 -

While all of the above have some importance for the emerging adolescent the first five tasks are particularly relevant. These and other developmental patterns will be considered further.

Physical Development in Early Adolescence

Among the primary tasks of the emerging adolescent are the recognition and acceptance of one's physical body and the development of skills for using the body effectively. A fundamentally related task is the formation of a satisfactory gender identity which consists of self perceptions as an adequate male or female figure. Throughout the life cycle, body self concept and gender identity generally remain important components of self definition. During early adolescence these issues become highly significant but often complicated.

The dramatic physical growth changes which occur during the 10-15 year age period are governed by the body's preparation for and attainment of puberty - the time of life when sexual maturity begins. All facets of the young person's life become dominated by such pubertal changes as increases in body height, breadth, depth, heart size, lung capacity, bone length and the presence of powerful hormones secreted by the endocrine glands. Educators and counselors should note that the emotional outbursts and extreme mood changes often displayed by emerging adolescents is due in part to temporary hormonal imbalances caused by these hormone secretions.

The Growth Spurt

Growth of height and weight is clearly the most noticeable dimension of the puberty growth spurt. These changes are largely controlled by underlying skeletal and muscular development. Bones increase in density and hardness as well as in width and length. Although the extension of the long bones in the arms and legs becomes most prominent, less obvious but dramatic changes occur in such structural areas as the shoulders, ribs and pelvis as well as in the extremity areas of the wrists, ankles, feet and hands.

This period of skeletal growth changes generally follows a sequence in which the extremity areas grow and reach maturity first followed by the limbs and then hip width, chest and shoulder breadth and finally trunk length respectively. Because adult size is achieved first in the face, hands and feet, the young adolescent often experiences anatomical incongruity and awkwardness in physical activities. Teachers and counselors should note that such experiences may contribute significantly to the middle school adolescent's feelings of embarassment, confusion and perhaps inadequacy. These feelings may become manifest in withdrawal or acting out behavior as well as in a decline in achievement motivation. Wherever possible, it is important that emerging adolescents be encouraged and supported in their efforts toward developing new physical skills and accepting the dramatic bodily changes which they experience.

Variability in Growth

There is considerable variability in physical growth development among early adolescents. For some, to be thirteen means having achieved sexual maturity and an adultlike stature. For others, thirteen may still be a physical age of childhood. The extent of developmental age variation during this period is noted by Joan Lipsitz (1980).

Most schools sort children according to chronological age. To be thirteen means that you are probably in the eighth grade and are studying a curriculum deemed appropriate for eighth graders. From a developmental standpoint however, to be told that someone is thirteen is to be told almost nothing about that person (except, of course, probable grade placement). (p. 20)

General sex differences do exist regarding the onset and extent of the growth spurt. For girls, the average age at which the growth spurt is initiated is approximately ten years with peak velocity occurring at a mean age of 11.8 years and a sharp decline in growth rate after age 12.5. The average age of menarche is 12.9 years. For boys, the growth spurt occurs about two years later from age 12 to 14.5 with the apex in velocity at about 13.

For both sexes, cell numbers increase dramatically during the period of 10.5 to 16 years. Muscle cell number increases approximately 100 percent with males showing a comparatively greater development of lean tissue and a corresponding decline in fat tissue. However, because their growth spurt begins earlier, girls generally have larger and better developed muscle tissue during the 10 to 13 year age period; and, at this time, girls often surpass boys in physical performance.

Taking account of the sex difference and within gender variability in maturation, it is not uncommon to observe a six year difference in physical age between early developing girls and late maturing boys. Middle school teachers and counselors should note that the years of early adolescence for later developing boys are often particularly difficult. These boys may experience acute feelings of inferiority not only in physical stature and athletic skill but also in social and academic competence as well. In such cases, "acting out" and "class clowning" may become compensatory behaviors for peer approval.

Secular Trends in Physical Maturation

There is a significant body of research data indicating that young adolescents today are reaching sexual maturity earlier and ultimately achieving greater physical stature when compared to adolescents of similar racial and ethnic origins in previous generations. In his comprehensive study, Tanner (1962) reported that from the period between 1830 and 1960, girls have been experiencing menarche by about three to four months earlier each decade. In Norway, the average age at menarche in 1840 was more than 17 years and by 1950 it had decreased to about 13.4. The same study reported that, on the average, girls at menarche in the United States were slightly over 14 years of age in 1910 and under 13 in 1955. While comparable data on boys is limited, the available findings suggest a similar trend (Kiil, 1939).

With regard to secular change in increased height and weight, Jones and Jones (1957) report that American girls between the ages of 12 and 18 were, on the average, about 10 pounds heavier and two inches taller in 1932 as compared to 1892. During this same period, the average height increase for 16 year old boys was 3 inches. Although several reasons have been advanced to explain these changes, improved medical care and nutrition are likely the most significant factors.

Conflict between parents and young adolescents often centers on dating privileges and curfew hours. Middle school educators should keep in mind that the parents of today's emerging adolescents were, for the most part, slightly less advanced in physical maturation during their own age period of 10-13 and likely did not experience quite the same feelings in matters of sexual curiosity and need for greater autonomy as compared to their sons and daughters of today.

Cognitive Development in Emerging Adolescence

Since intelligence remains one of those elusive and difficult to define concepts, any discussion of it carries elements of controversy with it. Although important for developmental studies, space does not allow for consideration of the merits and problems of intelligence testing. The selected focus of the following discussion is on the general patterns of and changes in mental functioning during late childhood and early adolescence. What is particularly emphasized is the multifacted nature of cognitive development during this period.

We have already noted that emerging adolescence is a time period during which individual differences become pronounced in physical development and it should be understood that the same holds true for cognitive development as well. The model which perhaps best accounts for individual differences and the complexity of mental growth is that advanced by J.P. Guilford (1956, 1959, 1967, 1968).

Guilford's Model of Intelligence

According to Guilford, intelligence consists of three different areas of functioning. These three are cognitive operations, contents and products and each has several components which combine to yield one hundred and twenty different mental abilities.

The operations or processes represent the major forms of human thought. These consist of cognition, memory, divergent production, convergent production and evaluation.

Cognition refers to general awareness and concentration abilities involved in taking account of changes in the environment as well as labeling different elements in the environment.

Memory refers to the ability to store and retrieve information.

Divergent production is defined as the ability to generate hypotheses for possible problem solution — an ability closely linked with creativity.

Convergent production refers to logical deduction abilities exercised when a given amount of information is sufficient to determine a unique answer. Convergent production also involves those abilities used in concept formation requiring the grouping of disparate elements within general categories.

Evaluation refers to general interpretation skills. These include the ability to assess the results of problem solving decisions and to make new decisions when necessary. These five basic processes constitute the formal structure of human intellect and are utilized differently depending on the contents of thought.

Guilford identified four kinds of content which include the following:

Figural content is perceptual information based primarily on the images and critical features of visual and auditory data. This is a general category of perceptual information which includes the content of perceived objects and events.

Symbolic content is information from symbols such as numbers, letters and various arrangement of lines which denote specific meanings. For example, the disciplines of science and mathematics utilize such symbols as (+, −, =) to refer to specific meanings.

Semantic content is information from words and sentences.

Behavioral content is nonverbal information derived from human interactions; such as, moods, thoughts and desires of other human beings based on the perception of behavior.

Thus, depending on a child's native endowment and environmental circumstances, he or she will differentially apply his or her cognitive operations to four areas of content. Guilford refers to the results of these unique applications as the products of thought and he suggests there are six such products.

Units are individual items of information.

Classes are sets or categories of units.

Relations are the connecting links between classes or between units.

Systems are complex organizations of classes such as exist in well developed ideas or theories.

Transformations refer to changes or revisions of information in units or classes.

Finally, *implications* refer to expectations or predictions based on given information.

Collectively, these products of the intellect represent the unique profile of knowledge and competencies of an individual.

The value of Guilford's model for our study of early adolescence is that it is sensitive to the many ways in which intellectual development can become manifest. We observe that some children develop cognitive skill more rapidly for the symbolic content of mathematics while others develop greater abilities for the semantic content of words and sentences. Although symbolic and semantic content areas are generally regarded as the basics of an academic curriculum, teachers, coaches and counselors may become instrumental in fostering intellectual development in several areas. Some students may demonstrate interest in the figural content of music, the visual arts or the mechanical sciences. Through appropriate curriculum experiences students apply such operations as cognition, memory and evaluation to the contents of tonal images in music and the visual forms of art work and mechanical design. Students also benefit from the application of cognitive operations or processes to the behavioral content experienced in athletic competition as well as in various contexts of social interaction. The supportive curricula and teaching methodologies for middle school students are those which are adequately flexible to promote the development of cognitive competencies in several content areas without sacrificing proper emphasis on the basics.

As we have noted, individual differences characterize any adequate description of mental development during the middle school years. Some students show dramatic overall increases in mental age during the eleven to fourteen year period. Others develop more slowly and show accelerated trends in mental growth during the mid-teens. During periods of acceleration, students demonstrate marked improvement in their ability to apply all cognitive processes. Their increasingly sophisticated use of divergent and convergent thinking as well as evaluation skills become evident in the transition shift from concrete operational thinking to formal operational thinking.

Piaget's stage theory provides another useful perspective for understanding both the generalities and variability of intellectual development. Since the thinking levels of most middle school students are located either in the stage of concrete reasoning, or in the stage of formal thought or, indeed, in some combination of the two, it is important to describe the abilities developed in each of these stages.

Concrete Operational Thinking

According to traditional Piagetian theory, children generally reach the level of concrete logical reasoning at age six or seven and this period extends to approximately age eleven or twelve at which time formal operational thinking begins. However, since many variables may alter the chronological age period when a given stage of development becomes dominant, no Piagetian stage can be strictly equated with a given age period. This is particularly emphasized for the later stages of concrete and formal operations since such factors as previous experience and cultural demands play an increasingly important role in determining the course of cognitive growth. Concrete operational thought is typically the dominant mode of functioning for fifth and sixth graders and is very common for seventh, eighth and even ninth graders.

With the development of concrete operations, several logical abilities emerge and become exercised in the child's problem solving activitiy. Elkind (1967) suggests that the major tasks of this stage involve mastering classes, relations and quantities. *Mastering classes* requires that the child become able to arrange objects or entities into *hierarchical classifications* and to understand class *inclusion relationships*. This involves understanding part-whole, whole-part and part-part relationships.

Questions which reveal such classification skills include: "Are there more boys or more children in the classroom?" The child who has not yet attained concrete operational thinking might answer more children, more girls or more boys since the youngster does not understand the class relationships of the problem. The concrete operational thinker can simultaneously, keep track of the whole and the parts of the whole and hence can respond correctly and explain the answer. In this problem, children is the whole which is made up of boys and girls, each a part of the whole.

The major logical and mathematical operators which mediate the child's thinking are represented by the following symbols: $<, >, +, -, =$. The concrete operational child understands that all children = all boys + all girls, all children − all boys = all girls, and all children − all girls = all boys. Moreover provided that there are at least some boys and some girls in the class, the child knows that all boys < all children and all girls < all children.

In mastering classification skills, the concrete operational thinker also becomes able to perceive and understand part-whole combinations. This means that the child can logically grasp the fact that one and the same person, object or entity can belong to more than one class at the same time. For example, the child realizes that a person may be both a Catholic as well as an American but that neither are all Catholics, Americans; nor are all Americans, Catholics.

With respect to *mastering relations,* the child learns that certain terms acquire meaning only in relation to others. For example, by applying the logical operators > (more than) and < (less than), the child can make comparisons of objects and logically arrange a series with respect to a given characteristic such as size, height or weight. In learning to arrange the label objects in a series according to size, the child learns that such terms as large, larger and largest are relational to one another. In this way the child uses fewer absolute categories and increasingly more relational concepts as the relative properties of the environment become better understood.

In *mastering quantities* the concrete operational child learns that certain properties of a given quantity of matter remain the same despite changes which may take place for that quantity. This general ability, which Piaget refers to as *conservation,* is demonstrated by a child when he or she notes that such properties as the amount, weight or mass of a quantity of matter are not altered even though the shape or distribution of the matter may change. Additional properties which the concrete operational child acquires conservation for are: number, length and area.

Concrete operational thinking thus involves the application of certain logical operations (addition, subtraction, equivalence, etc.) to concrete elements of perception and thought (i.e., objects, entities, etc.). Within this process the child's thinking becomes structured by several rules:

Commutativity - No matter in what order the elements of a set are combined, the results will be the same. (e.g., $a + b = b + a$).

Associativity - No matter how the elements of a set are combined the results are the same (e.g., $(a+b)+c = a+(b+c)$).

Identity - For each element in a set there is an identity element such that $a - a = 0, a = a$.

Reversibility - For every operation in a set there is an inverse operation which cancels the effects of the first operation $(a + b = c; b = c - a; a = c - b)$.

Composition - Any two elements of a set which are combined produce a third element of the set $(a + b = c)$.

The period of concrete operations characterizes a stage of intellectual development in which thought becomes logically structured by rules allowing information to be gathered, organized and used in problem solving. However, there are important limitations in the thinking of the concrete operational student. First, thought and problem solving primarily focus on what is real, observable and what is immediately present. In working with middle schoolers at this level, it is important that teachers and counselors make use of adequate concrete illustrations and examples for effective communication.

Also, because of restricted ability to consider abstractions, the concrete thinker generally does not approach a problem with the idea that there may be several possible solutions to it. Rather, he or she is predisposed to accept or believe in the first explanation presented or the first conclusion reached on his or her own. Often such conclusions are based on only small segments of the total evidence available. The concrete thinker thus has difficulty weighing evidence and considering the merits of arguments. Problems often must be repeated or presented in several ways for students to understand their scope and complexity. Patience and understanding are important ingredients of effective teaching and counseling which attempt to improve these logical skills in middle school students.

Formal Operational Thinking

According to Piaget (1969), the most mature level of human intelligence is reached at the stage of formal operational thought when logical reasoning becomes applied to abstract forms or ideas. He states:

> The great novelty that results consists in the possibility of manipulating ideas in themselves and no longer in merely manipulating objects. In a word, the adolescent is an individual who is capable (and this is where he reaches the level of the adult) of building or understanding ideal or abstract theories and concepts. (p. 23).

The transition to formal thought requires the attainment of several dimensions of abstract reasoning. One of the most significant features of adolescent formal thinking is the ability to form hypotheses and mentally follow through on the logical implications of these hypotheses. The adolescent understands that an hypothesis is only one "possible" way of explaining an event or solving a problem and to examine the merits of an hypothesis one must examine what the hypothesis implies. In hypothetical deductive reasoning, possibility thus becomes more important than concrete reality and the formal thinker becomes increasingly more able to compare systematically and consider many possibilities in making a decision on a given problem. This is reflected in the adolescent's ability to reason about and make judgments on the truth or falsity of propositions (statements about reality which are true or false) as well as make judgments about the validity of arguments and theories based on the available evidence. The formal reasoning adolescent thus becomes a more sophisticated critic of teachers and counselors often asking for a justification of such statements.

The formal thinker's ability to consider possiblities is also demonstrated in solving combinational logic problems. To solve such problems effectively requires that the subject develop a comprehensive plan. One of the classic problems which Inhelder and Piaget (1968) developed to examine the way adolescents generate combinational systems involved combinations of chemicals. In this episode, five bottles of colorless liquid labeled 1, 2, 3, 4 and G are shown to the subject. The experimenter then shows the subject two glasses of clear fluid. One glass contains 2 while the other contains a combination of 1 + 3. Next, the experimenter adds drops of an unknown combination of the five liquids to each glass and demonstrates that a certain combination will produce a yellow colored liquid in one of the glasses. The subject is then asked to create the yellow colored fluid using any combination the the five liquids. In attempting to solve this problem, the concrete thinker tries random combinations of liquids and has difficulty keeping track of the results. Such efforts generally are unrewarded. In contrast, the formal operational adolescent uses a plan or strategy to systematically test for all the possible combinations of the liquids understanding that eventually one such combination must work. As each possible combination is tested, the system allows the adolescent to keep track of which combinations have been tried and which remain to be tried. As such strategies for creating abstract comprehensive plans become established as mental structures, the adolescent shows increasingly less dependence on concrete experience in solving problems.

Closely related is the formal thinker's ability to understand and use the concept of probability in making decisions. This involves appreciating the difference between random and non-random events as well as understanding that, for certain cases, an observed event reflects the proportion of each kind of element to a larger pool of elements. For example, if one draws an ace from a full deck of cards then the next card drawn is less likely to be an ace. That is, the probability of any event is always a ratio of the number of possible occurrences of the specific events in question to the total number of all possible events. Understanding probability allows the adolescent to make more accurate predictions about future events. This becomes clearly important for decision making with respect to career, marriage and adult role taking in general.

The Transition from Concrete to Formal Thought

Although the traditional age periods for concrete and formal thought have been identified respectively at 7-11 years and 12 years and beyond, there is a growing body of research which suggests that a significant majority of young adolescents do not attain formal operational skills at least until the mid teens. Lawson and Renner (1974) administered a battery of six Piagetian tasks to a total of 588 students ranging from the seventh to the twelfth grade in twenty-five schools in Oklahoma. The results indicated that the majority of students remain concrete operational even through the twelfth grade. The percentage of concrete thinkers ranged from 83 percent in the seventh grade to 66 percent in the twelfth. On a larger scale, Shayer, Kuchemann and Wylam (1976) studied the transition from concrete to formal thinking in British students between the ages of 7 and 14 years of age. Approximately 2000 subjects were selected in each year group for a total sample population of about 10,000. The findings indicated that most adolescents in the 12 to 14 year age period demonstrated a pronounced development in concrete operational thinking. Only 20 percent of the sample showed even the earliest development of formal thought. Similar results were obtained by Neimark (1975) who examined the longitudinal development of formal operations. None of the oldest of Neimark's subjects (15-year olds) had entirely achieved formal thought.

According to research studies on the development of the human brain and central nervous system, there may be important biological reasons for the above findings. Despite the developmental variability among young adolescents, what is particularly noteworthy from the results of several of these studies is that, for many adolescents, the age interval of 12-14 years appears to be a comparatively slow period for nervous system development as well as for increases in mental functioning. This is in contrast to the previous interval of 10-12 years and the subsequent period of 14-17 years where significant increases in both brain growth and mental development have been reported. In general, girls demonstrate these developmental patterns somewhat earlier than boys and experience their most dramatic adolescent period of brain growth and mental development during the 10-12 year period. For boys, the most significant gains in mental development occur during the 14-17 year period. (Cornell and Amstrong, 1955; Eichorn and Bayley, 1962; Epstein, 1974a, 1974b, 1978; Epstein and Toepfer, 1978).

Students who have scored high on intelligence tests and have done well academically in elementary school generally develop a high self concept of academic ability. However, research suggests that many of these bright students often flounder in the middle school years showing decline in test performance, achievement and self concept (McCall et al. 1973; Toepfer, 1979). Conrad Toepfer (1979) has argued that a major reason for this is that middle school curricula and teaching strategies for bright students presume high levels of formal reasoning than these students have actually attained. The result is a "turn off" effect where students become discouraged by and alienated from school and look elsewhere for more gratifying experiences. Depending on the circumstances, this "turn off" effect may lead middle schoolers to display more aggressive, withdrawal, or regressive behavior which may become expressed in the form of underachievement in school, juvenile delinquency, high sexual activity, drug and alcohol abuse or even suicide. Because the decision making powers of the middle schooler are not well established, it is important to remember that the emerging adolescent years in general (and perhaps the 12-14 year interval in particular) constitute a period of high vulnerability. Middle schoolers need encouragement. In planning instruction and communication strategies, teachers and counselors should recognize that a middle school student may be very bright (in terms of I.Q. test performance) but not necessarily formal operational.

Emotional and Social Development in Early Adolescence

During the elementary school years two important needs which emerge in the child's life are: the need to receive and express love, affection, and friendship; and the need to experience a sense of competence with respect to academic and behavioral skill development. Both of these needs remain important but become more complicated in early adolescence due to the dramatic growth changes which occur and developmental tasks which become significant. This concluding section examines the major social and emotional characteristics of emerging adolescents in relation to these needs and developmental changes.

Emotional characteristics

The range of emotional experiences for the middle schooler is significantly greater than that of the elementary school child. Not only does the emerging adolescent experience the basic emotions of joy, anger, fear, love and hate but also such feelings as elation, depression, ecstasy, grief panic, jealousy, pride, embarassment and anxiety. Moreover, the emotional experiences of the young adolescent become more energized and intense and this intensity often translates into a general mood of physical restlessness. Emerging adolescents are beginning to understand that life holds many new possibilities for them and they are generally enthusiastic for new experiences. However, this increased energy and enthusiasm often lacks direction. An important feature of a healthy middle school environment is the availability of several constructive activities in which students can become involved. In addition to music, athletics and dances, these might include science or chess club activities where interests and skills can be focused and developed.

Feelings of ambivalence define an important emotional characteristic of middle schoolers. The emerging adolescent is in a state of transition — leaving the world of childhood innocence for the exciting, yet high-risk world of adolescence and adulthood. At times, the middle schooler may feel reluctance about growing up. He or she may show nostalgia for the kind of love and protection experienced in earlier parent-child relationships. At other times the middle schooler may demonstrate feelings of hostility toward parents and adults in efforts to achieve more emotional independence. Parents also experience ambivalence about their son or daughter growing up and must make adjustments to new role changes. Hence, it is not uncommon to find the quality of parent and emerging adolescent relationships to be characterized by increased conflict and tension.

Social Development

The social development of the emerging adolescent is closely linked to three developmental tasks previously noted. These are: forming more mature relationships with age-mates of both sexes; achieving a masculine and feminine social role; and achieving emotional independence from parents and other adults.

Hurlock (1955) has identified three important "social worlds" of the young adolescent. One is the family within which personal interaction between brothers, sisters and parents continues to be important for the satisfaction of basic needs for love and affection and the development of social and sex role skills. The second is the school which involves social interaction between teachers and other adults as well as peers. Peer interaction and peer conformity reach a high level during the 10-14 year age period when group standards for dress, language and behavior styles become very influential. The third social world consists of closed and intimate friendships usually with one or two peers of the same sex. The function of these "best friendships" during early adolescence is the sharing of private thoughts, hopes and anxieties. This is an important context for the first experience of intimacy and the development of accompanying social skills.

In view of the developmental tasks most relevant during early adolescence, it is not surprising that peer interaction is the dominant social activity for middle schoolers. For the most part, social interaction is with the same sex peers during the 10-12 year period, while during the later middle school years (ages 12-14) interaction between the sexes increases. In this transition, the criteria for peer status often change and posing problems for some middle schoolers. Boys and girls who have been well accepted by peers of the same sex during middle childhood may find less peer acceptance in early adolescence. Physical maturity and attractiveness as well as social and leadership abilities are important standards determining popularity and group acceptance. Those who are judged not to meet one or more of these standards may be avoided or even ridiculed (Mitchell, 1974). Such experiences make the period of early adolescence difficult for some middle schoolers. Peer standards are the reference by which the middle school student largely evaluates himself or herself. Peer rejection is thus devastating to self esteem; and, in order to gain peer recognition, some are willing to experiment with drugs, become class clown, become sexually active or even commit acts of delinquency.

In working with middle school students, it is important that teachers and counselors recognize the reasons for many of the negative behaviors which students display. Some may show high enthusiasm for school work and other activities for a period of time then lapse into a period of alienation and negativism. Others may show negative behavior more consistently. A middle school student may become emotionally elevated or "turned on" to certain school activities as a function of feeling competent, accepted and encouraged. The same student may also become "turned off" as a function of perceived self incompetence, social rejection, and feelings of discouragement.

These patterns are due to a number of factors. Because the emotional experiences of middle schoolers are intense and fluctuating, mood changes can be dramatic. It should be remembered that heightened anxiety may interfere with the emerging adolescent's ability to concentrate well on academic tasks which in turn lowers academic performance and self esteem.

A major source of anxiety concerns sexual behavior. The basic need to receive and express love and affection is complicated in early adolescence by the intense passion for sexual expression. Cultural signs on how these feelings of passion are to be managed are unclear. Pornography continues to be sold in the local drugstores while parents often communicate the notion that any form of sexual expression in the middle school years is forbidden. While sex education programs remain important both in the elementary and middle schools, the middle school counselor must be prepared to deal with students' conflicts over matters of sexual behavior.

Adding to the emerging adolescent's feelings of confusion is the phenomenon which David Elkind (1967) refers to as egocentrism. This is the individual's failure to differentiate between what others are thinking about and his own mental preoccupations. As young adolescents spend a great deal of time looking at themselves in the mirror, they often become preoccupied with certain perceived physical inadequacies such as ears or a nose which is thought to be too large or skin which is thought to be ugly. Because the young adolescent is so convinced of these obvious deficiencies, he or she imagines that others also fully attend to and find these physical characteristics to be repugnant. Because of this egocentrism, emerging adolescents may become overly defensive and misinterpret the remarks of teachers and counselors sensing a personal attack is being made on them because of these self perceived inadequacies.

Negative behaviors are compensatory in nature. When the basic needs for love and affection and the experience of mastery and competence are not adequately met, students become discouraged. Some attempt to boost ego strength by putting others down or becoming overly agressive or disruptive. Others may withdraw to protect themselves from failure or show immature forms of behavior in efforts to gain attention.

Yet, even while some negative behavior is almost inevitable, the middle school years remain a potentially very rich period of development. The middle school teacher and the middle school counselor can be very instrumental in realizing this potential in positive ways. Recognizing the notable individual difference in development among middle schoolers, attention should be given to each student's progress and particular talents. In general, the supportive middle school environment requires that teachers and counselors provide:

> an effective structure for teaching and learning in a variety of settings;

> appropriate maturity demands for moral and social skill development; and

> effective communication and personal encouragement.

REFERENCES

Cornell, E.L., & Armstrong, C.M. Forms of mental growth patterns revealed by reanalysis of the Harvard growth data. *Child Development, 26,* 1955, 169-205.

Eichorn, D.H., and Bayley, N. Growth in head circumference from birth through young adulthood. *Child Development,* 33, 1962, 257-271.

Elkind, D. Egocentrism in adolescence. *Child Development,* 28, 1967, 1025-1034.

Epstein, H.T. Phrenoblysis: Special brain and mind growth periods: I, Human brain and skull development. *Developmental Psychobiology,* 3, 1974, 207-216.

Epstein, H.T. Phrenoblysis: Special brain and mind growth periods: II, Human brain and skull development. *Developmental Psychobiology,* 3, 1974, 217-224.

Epstein, H.T., and Toepfer, C.F. A neuroscience basis for reorganizing middle grades education. *Educational Leadership,* 36, 1978, 656-660.

Guilford, J.P. The structure of intellect. *Psychological Bulletin,* 53, 1956.

Guilford, J.P. Three faces of intellect. *American Psychologist,* 14, 1959.

Guilford, J.P. *The nature of human intelligence.* New York: McGraw-Hill, 1967.

Havighurst, R.J. *Developmental tasks and education,* 3rd edition. New York: McKay, 1972.

Hurlock, E.B. *Adolescent development,* 2nd edition. New York: McGraw-Hill, 1955.

Inhelder, B., and Piaget, J. *The growth of logical thinking.* New York: Basic Books, 1958.

Jones, H.E., and Jones, M.C. *Adolescence.* Berkeley: University Extension, University of California, 1957.

Kiil, V. Stature and growth of Norwegian men during the past 200 years. *Skr. norske Vidensk Aknd.,* 6, 1939.

Lawson, A.E., and Renner, J.W. A quantitative analysis of responses to Piagetian tasks and its implication for curriculum. *Science Education,* 58, 1974, 544-559.

Lipsitz, J.S. The age group. In *Toward adolescence: The middle school years.* Seventy-ninth Yearbook of the National Society for the Study of Education. Edited by M. Johnson. Chicago: University of Chicago Press, 1980.

McCall, R.B., Appelbaum, M.I., and Hogarty, P.S. Developmental changes in mental performances. *Monographs of the Society for Research in Child Development,* 38, 1973.

Mitchell, J.J. *Human life: The early adolescent years.* Toronto: Holt, Rinehart, and Winston of Canada, 1974.

Neimark, E.D. Longitudinal Development of formal operations thought. *Genetic Psychology Monographs,* 91, 1975, 171-225.

Piaget, J. *The psychology of the child.* New York: Basic Books, Inc., 1969.

Shayer, M., Kuchemann, D.E., and Wylam, H. The distribution of Piagetian stages of thinking in British middle and secondary school children. *The British Journal of Educational Psychology*, 46, 1976, 164-173.

Tanner, J.M. *Growth at adolescence*, 2nd edition. Oxford: Blackwell Scientific Publications, 1962.

Thornburg, H.D. *Development in adolescence*, Monterey, Calif.: Brooks/Cole, 1975.

Toepfer, C.F. Brain growth periodization — A new dogma for education. *Middle School Journal*, 10, 3, 1979, 18-21.

Chapter Three

CHILDREN'S RIGHTS

JOSEPH C. ROTTER

... nothing about human life is more precious than
that we can define our own purpose and shape our
own destiny.

Norman Cousins

Perhaps you wonder why a chapter in a guidance fundamentals book is devoted to children's rights. Do not dismay. Many such chapters have been written before under the guise of "The Counselor As Change Agent," or "The Counselor As Advocate." Sometimes whole chapters are devoted to the topic and then again, the subject is only implied in other books. We feel that at the heart of all guidance programs are the rights of children; their rights to social, personal, educational, psychological and ecological justice. Inequities related to dress, physical appearance, income, social skills, physical, social and psychological disabilities, sex, race, religion, language, or learning style can be overcome through the help of the counselor. So important are these rights that they cannot be glossed over or hidden beneath the jargon of the trade.

Children today suffer as much as they have in any other time. In this chapter we will address the counselor's advocacy role in acquiring and sustaining the middle school child's rights. Much has been researched and written about the abuse of the very young child however, a dearth of literature exists on the rights of the adolescent (Kalisch, 1978). Little can be found on the rights of the child in the middle. Like the beam balanced on a fulcrum that can plunge in either direction by the slightest weight, so the middle school age child teeters, depending upon the significant others in his or her life.

Indeed, the abuses to children early in life leave an indelible mark that affects behavior in later school years and often throughout life. These abuses have been written about and researched for some time. Unfortunately, the preventive approaches and remediations are in many cases still forthcoming.

Perhaps at this point a definition of the term child abuse is in order. Many definitions have been offered (Martin, 1972, Gil, 1968, Morse, Sahler & Friedman, 1970, Trace and Clark, 1974, Spinetta & Rigler, 1972, and Light, 1973) but perhaps the most widely accepted Was stated by Kempe, Silverman, Brandt, Droegemueller & Silver (1962). They define child abuse as a situation —

> . . . in which a child is suffering from serious physical injury inflict-
> ed upon him by other than accidental means; is suffering harm by
> reason of neglect, malnutrition, or sexual abuse; is going without
> necessary and basic physical care; or is growing up under conditions
> which threaten his physical and emotional survival. p. 63

This broad definition covers a myriad of conditions some of which
are not readily detectable.

The middle school counselor must be cognizant of the developmental history of the children in his/her care and ask what limitations
(physical, social, cultural, or emotional) have impeded the child's
ability to function without debilitating effects? What special considerations need to be applied to a given child based upon these limitations? What information needs to be shared with others regarding
the child's developmental history to prevent further discomfort and
provide nourishment for growth? These and other questions must be
addressed by the counselor at this critical middle school age.

The comprehensiveness of this topic of children's rights can be
summarized in the U.N.'s Declaration of the Rights of the Child
(1959). The Preamble states that:

> The child, because of his physical and mental immaturity, needs
> special safeguards and care, both before and after birth, and that
> individuals and groups should strive to achieve children's rights by
> legislative and other means. Mankind, it says, owes the child the
> best it has to give.

In ten carefully worded principles, the declaration affirms that
all children are entitled to:

1. The enjoyment of the rights mentioned, without any exception
   whatsoever, regardless of race, color, sex, religion, or nationality;
2. Special protection, opportunities, and facilities to enable them
   to develop in a healthy and normal manner, in freedom and
   dignity;
3. A name and nationality;
4. Social security, including adequate nutrition, housing, recreation, and medical services;
5. Special treatment, education, and care if handicapped;
6. Love and understanding and an atmosphere of affection and
   security, in the care and under the responsibility of their parents
   whenever possible;
7. Free education and recreation and equal opportunity to develop
   their individual abilities;
8. Prompt protection and relief in times of disaster;
9. Protection against all forms of neglect, cruelty, and exploita-
   tion;
10. Protection from any form of racial, religious, or other discrimi-
    nation, and an upbringing in a spirit of peace and universal
    brotherhood.

Finally, the General Assembly resolved that governments, non-governmental organizations, and individuals should give this declaration the widest possible publicity as a means of encouraging its observance everywhere.

And, stated so clearly through the words of a child in the Ann Landers Column (1975).

> *Dear Ann Landers:* Us kids have rights, too. Too few adults are willing to recognize this fact. I hope you will print the Bill of Rights for Kids so every parent who reads your column can see it. It's time we were treated like people.
> 1. I have the right to be my own judge and take the responsibility for my own actions.
> 2. I have the right to offer no reasons or excuses to justify my behavior.
> 3. I have the right to decide if I am obligated to report on other people's behavior.
> 4. I have the right to change my mind.
> 5. I have the right to make mistakes and be responsible for them.
> 6. I have the right to pick my own friends.
> 7. I have the right to say, "I don't know."
> 8. I have the right to be independent of the good will of others before coping with them.
> 9. I have the right to say, "I don't understand."
> 10. I have the right to say, "I don't care."
>   —A Reader Since Childhood in Las Vegas
> *Dear Reader:* Here are your Bill of Rights. Some of them I buy, especially numbers 4, 5, 6, and 9. Number 2 is off base, and number 3 I would accept — to a point. As for number 8, I don't dig it. Number 10: Of course you have the *right* to say you don't *care*, but that doesn't mean you *shouldn't* care.

This chapter will address these rights of children with emphasis on the current research on child abuse and identifying characteristics of the abused child and abusive adult along with recent litigation and legislation in this area.

The counselor's role as change agent will be emphasized in an attempt to encourage counselors to identify and address the inequities existing within the schools, homes, and the community. As Brown (1977) has suggested, one of the critical personal qualifications of the counselor must be courage — courage to confront the obvious and often the not so obvious. In essence, the counselor's advocacy role will be stressed.

In addition to the physical and psychological abuse, more specifically emphasis will be placed on the misuse of standardized instruments, classroom placement, and separation and isolation.

History of Childhood

History is laden with abusive practices toward children. Greenleaf (1978) documents the trauma experienced by children through the ages.

Children were used in medieval times as commodities to be eliminated at will. Used as objects of play, they were often tossed between buildings only to be fumbled to their death by an inept or careless adult. In the 17th and 18th centuries children were considered as cattle to be auctioned on the block and submitted to the labors of a master, beaten and battered if considered not worthy. It wasn't until the child labor laws of the 19th century that children were granted any human rights. Often these laws were construed as a means of keeping children from taking the jobs away from adults rather than protecting them from the terrors of adults.

One of the sad ironies in the history of children is that there was a Society for the Prevention of Cruelty to Animals before there was such a society for children. And it wasn't until the 1960's that children were granted freedom of speech and due process rights. Not until the 1960's were children considered people according to the U.S. Constitution.

Although the Supreme Court has granted children most of the rights enjoyed by adults, nevertheless, in practice many inequities still remain. The due process rights guaranteed to protect the child from injustices are listed by the Massachusetts Advocacy Center (1975) to include:

1. A right to notification of charges against the child in writing, stating what regulation was broken and what the proposed discipline is to be;
2. A right to be told all of the evidence against the child;
3. A right to a hearing before the child is severely disciplined;
4. A right to representation at this hearing by a lawyer, a child advocate, or someone else;
5. A right to a fair and unbiased hearing;
6. A right to question and "cross-examine" school personnel who are accusing a child of a serious infraction of school rules;
7. A right to present a "defense" and offer different descriptions of what happened;
8. A right to a written statement of both the decision and why it was decided in this particular way;
9. A right to appeal the decision to a higher school authority such as the superintendent, the school board, etc.

The American School Counselor Association approved the following position statement in 1978:

The American School Counselor Association supports the right of all students to be guaranteed the protections of due process as provided by the United States Constitution.

"No person . . . be deprived of life, liberty, or property, without due process of law." Amendment V ". . . nor cruel and unusual punishments inflicted." Amendment VIII ". . . to be informed of the nature and cause of the accusation; to be confronted with the witnesses against him; to have compulsory process for obtaining witnesses in his favor, and to have assistance of counsel for his defense." Amendment VI

The Supreme Court holds that the guarantee of due process protections requires that both the procedures followed and the laws under which they are followed be fair. Due process has come to have two meanings — one "procedural" and the other "substantive."

In order to afford each student the rights of procedural due process, the American School Counselor Association believes every school, whether public or private, should provide an opportunity for a fair review of disciplinary cases. Particularly in cases of expulsion, each student should have the right to fair procedure, that is, a right to speak to the issue and a right to call witnesses. Students under 18 must have a parent, guardian, or adult representative present. The committee hearing the charges, questions, and statements can make recommendations to the administration. If both sides are still not satisfied with the decision, it should then be taken to the Board of Education with the opportunity for another hearing.

The counselor has an obligation to see that students are aware of their right to due process protections. There should be means to inform students of the procedures and steps necessary to bring about due process.

Counselors have the responsibility to encourage school administrators to develop written policies concerning due process rights for students and to implement procedures guaranteeing this right.

Parents, labor, religion, government, and yes, education continue to espouse rights but practice something less. Van Hoose (1975) points out —

> Educators give lip service to freedom, individual rights, and democracy; but in practice they often deny these rights to students. Schools espouse democratic ideas but at the same time engage in authoritarian practices that violate all principles of individual liberty. Such practices are antithetical to most principles of education in a democratic society. (p. 279)

Recent and proposed legislation has fostered the rights of children as persons. The Family Educational Rights and Privacy Act has caused a purging of the incriminating materials in many school records. There was a time when the "problem" children in school could be identified by looking for the thickest file of records. There was and still is, in many instances, a tendency to accumulate negative material on children. The counselor should periodically investigate the school files and become active in eliminating negative generalized statements that may be incriminating. Furthermore, the counselor should conduct workshops for teachers to encourage the use of specific positive materials for such files. In addition, the counselor can help parents understand their rights in protecting their child from unconstitutional and illegal practices.

Public Law 94-142, the Education for All Handicapped Children Act, provided that all handicapped persons between the ages of 3 and 21 must have available to them a free and appropriate public education. The Child and Family Services Act when enacted will provide funds for dealing with the special rights of children. So, we have come a long way since the time when children were considered "chattels," but the counselor must remain on guard to protect and preserve these given rights of children.

Counselor's Role

The APGA Ethical Standards (1974) state that, "The member's primary obligation is to respect the integrity and promote the welfare of the counselee or client with whom he is working." If you in turn look at the developmental role of the counselor and the obligation to serve all students, then, it follows that the counselor must "respect the integrity and promote the welfare" of all students in the school.

This story by Jean Mizer (1964) emphasizes the need to take note for all children in our care.

CIPHER IN THE SNOW

by
Jean E. Mizer

It started with tragedy on a biting cold February morning. I was driving behind the Milford Corners Bus as I did most snowy mornings on my way to school. It veered and stopped short at the hotel, which it had no business doing, and I was annoyed as I had to come to an unexpected stop. A boy lurched out of the bus, reeled, stumbled, and collapsed on the snowbank at the curb. The bus driver and I reached him at the same moment. His thin, hollow face was white, even against the snow.

"He's dead," the driver whispered.

It didn't register for a minute. I glanced quickly at the scared young faces staring down at us from the school bus. "A doctor! Quick! I'll phone from the hotel. . . "

"No use. I tell you he's dead." The driver looked down at the boy's still form. "He never even said he felt bad." he muttered, "just tapped me on the shoulder and said, real quiet, 'I'm sorry. I have to get off at the hotel.' That's all. Polite and apologizing like."

At school, the giggling shuffling morning noise quieted as the news went down the halls. I passed a huddle of girls. "Who was it? Who dropped dead on the way to school?" I heard one of them half-whisper.

"Don't know his name; some kid from Milford Corners," was the reply.

It was like that in the faculty room and the principal's office. "I'd appreciate your going out to tell the parents." the principal told me. "They haven't a phone and, anyway, somebody from school should go there in person. I'll cover your classes."

"Why me?" I asked. "Wouldn't it be better if you did it?"

"I didn't know the boy," the principal admitted levelly. "And in last year's personalities column I note that you were listed as his favorite teacher."

I drove through the snow and cold down the bad canyon road to the Evans place and thought about the boy, Cliff Evans. His favorite teacher! I thought. He hasn't spoken two words to me in two years! I could see him in my mind's eye all right, sitting back there in the last seat in my afternoon literature class. He came in the room by himself and left by himself. "Cliff Evans," I muttered to myself, "a boy who never talked." I thought a minute. "A boy who never smiled. I never saw him smile once."

The big ranch kitchen was clean and warm. I blurted out my news somehow. Mrs. Evans reached blindly toward a chair. "He never said anything about bein' ailin'."

His step-father snorted. "He ain't said nothin' about anything since I moved in here."

Mrs. Evans pushed a pan back to the stove and began to untie her apron. "Now hold on," her husband snapped. "I got to have breakfast before I go to town. Nothin' we can do now anyway. If Cliff hadn't been so dumb, he'd have told us he didn't feel good."

After school I sat in the office and stared bleakly at the records spread out before me. I was to close the file and write the obituary for the school paper. The almost bare sheets mocked the effort. Cliff Evans, white, never legally adopted by step-father, five young half-brothers and sisters. These meager strands of information and the list of D grades were all the records had to offer.

Cliff Evans had silently come in the school door in the mornings and gone out the school door in the evenings, and that was all. He had never belonged to a club. He had never played on a team. He had never held an office. As far as I could tell he had never done one happy, noisy kid thing. He had never been anybody at all.

How do you go about making a boy into a zero? The grade school records showed me. The first and second grade teachers' annotations read "sweet, shy child"; "timid but eager." Then the third grade note had opened the attack. Some teacher had written in a good, firm hand, "Cliff won't talk. Uncooperative. Slow learner." The other academic sheep had followed with "dull"; "slow-witted"; "low I.Q." They became correct. The boy's I.Q. score in the ninth grade was listed at 83. But his I.Q. in the third grade had been 106. The score didn't go under 100 until the seventh grade. Even shy, timid, sweet children have resilience. It takes time to break them.

I stomped to the typewriter and wrote a savage report pointing out what education had done to Cliff Evans. I slapped a copy on the principal's desk and another in the sad, dog-eared file. I banged the typewriter and slammed the file and crashed the door shut, but I didn't feel much better. A little boy kept walking after me, a little boy with a peaked, pale face; a skinny body in faded jeans; and big eyes that had looked and searched for a long time and then had become veiled.

I could guess how many times he'd been chosen last to play sides in a game, how many whispered child conversations had excluded him, how many times he hadn't been asked. I could see and hear the faces and voices that said over and over, "You're dumb. You're a nothing, Cliff Evans."

A child is a believing creature. Cliff undoubtedly believed them. Suddenly it seemed clear to me: When finally there was nothing left at all for Cliff Evans, he collapsed on a snowbank and went away. The doctor might list "heart failure" as the cause of death, but that wouldn't change my mind.

We couldn't find ten students in the school who had known Cliff well enough to attend the funeral as his friends. So the student-body officers and a committee from the junior class went as a group to the church, being politely sad. I attended the services with them, and sat through it with a lump of cold lead in my chest and a big resolve growing through me.

I've never forgotten Cliff Evans nor that resolve. He has been my challenge year after year, class after class. I look up and down the rows carefully each September at the unfamiliar faces. I look for veiled eyes or bodies scrouged into a seat in an alien world. "Look, kids," I say silently, "I may not do anything else for you this year, but not one of you is going to come out of here a nobody. I'll work or fight to the bitter end doing battle with society and the school board, but I won't have one of you coming out of here thinking himself into a zero."

Most of the time — not always, but most of the time — I've succeeded. (pp 8-10)

Jean E. Mizer, "Cipher in the Snow," **NEA Journal,** November 1964, 53:8-10.

The long term effects of child abuse and neglect has been equated to malnutrition, leaving its indelible mark. Although the child may not be currently experiencing abuse, he/she may be destined to suffer the long term consequences. Ann Landers (1976) in her column, responds to a person in such a dilemma.

> *Dear Ann Landers:* Is there relief of kind for a person with my problems? How do other people deal with it? I can't be the only one.
>
> I am nearly 60 years old and I still cry, brawl, sob, walk the floors and wring my hands because of my miserable childhood.
>
> Never a hug or a kiss, a compliment or a kind word. It was always an order, a crack on the side of the head, a shove or a kick. We weren't spanked. We were beaten. We weren't slapped, we were pummeled.
>
> Why can't I forget? Why do parents do such things? No sweet memories. It's torture. Am I crazy?
>
> *Dear Haunted:* No, you aren't crazy, but you do need professional help to overcome the anger and resentment that has hung on much too long.
>
> You were an unloved, battered child. Most unloved and battered children had parents who were also unloved and battered. When you understand what their lives must have like you will stop grieving about your miserable childhood and look outward and ahead, instead of inward and back.

Identification and Processing

Kline (1977) offers a flow chart for processing suspected abusive treatment of children. This procedure may vary among states but some prearranged system should be followed to assure thoroughness in handling such cases. The chart indicates at the start that "employees should be alert to the possible signs or symptoms of abuse or neglect."

See page 41 for the Kline Flow Chart.

The following lists of identifying factors and dynamics of child abuse should be shared with all school personnel.

Some Dynamics of Child Abuse

There are some behavioral and attitudinal traits of parents and children which are indicative of possible child battering. Some of these traits may be present without the occurrence of battering. When there is actual battering, however, many of these traits are almost always present.

Figure 3:1. KLINE FLOW CHART

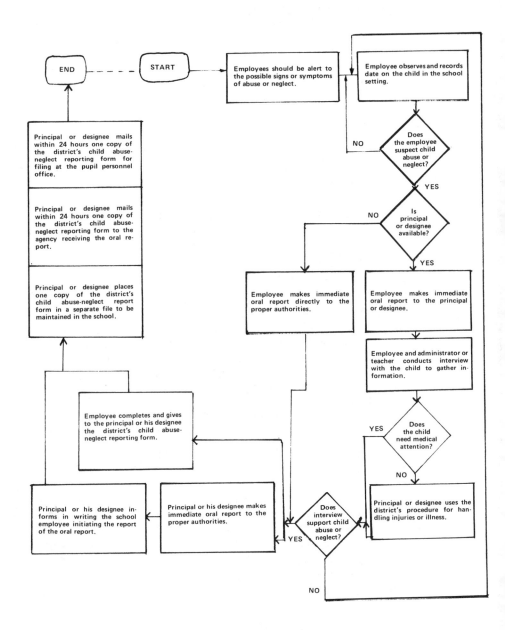

Things to look for should you have the occasion to talk with parents or observe the interaction between parent and child:

1. Frequently, the parent has a distorted view of the child. The parent may describe the child as trying to hurt or anger him or may say the child does not love him. He may see the child as basically bad, deserving severe punishment. The parent may sound paranoid about the child, indicate feelings that the child is persecuting him and often projects his feelings onto the child.

2. Frequently, the parent's expectations of the child's behavior are not appropriate to the child's age. A mother may expect adult behavior from her child.

3. There may be a lack of warmth in the relationship between parent and child. Mother or father may not perceive and relate to the child's needs. The child may not behave as if he expects his needs to be met.

4. The parent wants the child to meet *his* needs. He wants to be loved, given to by the child as if the parent were the child and the child were the parent. This theme of role reversal seems to come through in many of the symptoms.

5. There is almost always a history of battering in the background of one of the parents. The parent may feel beating kept him in line and is the right way to discipline children.

6. The parent may have high expectations of himself and the child. This may lead to the parent administering severe punishment for minimal behavior infractions. The parent's high expectations of himself has been internalized as a result of severe treatment and criticism of his parent when he was a child. This results in the parents usually reacting on a black is black and white is white basis with no recognition of gray areas. The parent may be critical of the child regardless of efforts made to please the parent. The parent seldom mentions any good quality of the child.

7. The parent may rationalize his treatment of the child, claiming it is necessary to prevent any sign of evil behavior from developing.

8. The parent may express a fear that he or she will hurt the child. They may describe an impulse to hurt or kill the child or may simply say they do not like the child. This sort of revelation would probably be rare without a strong relationship and deep trust being present. However, if it does occur, the parent is really asking for help and is at a critical turning point.

9. Frequently, the battering family is isolated in the community. There are no friends or social activities.

From: Child Welfare League of America, Inc., 1974.

Identifying the Battered or Molested Child

Physical Factors

1. *Marks and Bruises on the Body:* Some are visible, but some may be hidden from view. This is why a nurse's check is so important. Sometimes these marks and bruises may be hard to identify - especially if they are made by teeth or unusual instruments. It is particularly meaningful to note when these marks could not possibly be made by or incurred in the situation the child reports; i.e., bite marks on back due to "falling off a bike," whip marks on legs due to "falling while jumping rope," black eyes due to getting in a "fight with my cat," patches of hair missing due to "washing my hair too hard."

   A young child was seen in a nursery school to have odd marks, like bites, all over his back. When the mother was questioned she said they were indeed bites and that the child got them at the nursery school. The mother had not previously reported this to the nursery school, and the nursery school reported the situation to the Juvenile Probation Department and denied the charges. The mother then changed her story and said that they might not be bites, and she didn't know what they were. Police pictures were taken of the marks, and these pictures were shown to a group of five dentists who all stated that they were indeed the bite marks of a human adult.

2. *Serious Injuries such as Broken Bones:* Although these are most dramatically evidenced in very young children, an older battered child may often come up with a series of broken arms, fingers, head injuries, etc., or a variety of burns, ranging from minor to fatal, but consistently viewable.

3. *Distended Stomach:* Many battered children are not fed properly and appear to be malnourished. The parents often give excuses such as "he's a finicky eater," "he has a vitamin deficiency," or "the doctor doesn't know what's wrong with her." The truth of the matter is that these children are not fed at home or are fed only on scraps. They often do not come to school with lunch and steal food from other children, or they steal candy which they share to gain friends.

   Santa Clara County had a tragic and classic example of this in a fourteen-year-old girl who physically looked about seven, had not attained puberty, and who had been physically mistreated most of her life. She was also being starved to death.

   A lack of medical care for injuries can also be a significant factor and should be noted. Many parents will report that their child has "brain damage" and this, in fact, may be true. A neurological report on the child should be requested whenever possible.

It has been found that many children do sustain minimal or severe brain damage through beatings or may be permanently damaged from incidents inflicted in early childhood.

4. *Appearance of Mental Retardation:* Battered and molested children often appear retarded, especially if the maltreatment has gone undetected for a prolonged period of time. This is often an excuse their parents give to questioning people in order to shift the blame away from themselves. Many of these children mature mentally and physically to a dramatic degree when removed from the family home.

5. *Dirty Appearance:* These children are often hygienically uncared for and are forced to wear cast-off clothing. The parents may report that they are clean when they leave for school and "just get dirty on the way." They may also say that the child has "torn up all the good clothes I just got her," implying that the child is mentally retarded or disturbed. It is especially important to note when one child is treated differently from the other children in the family - in the type of clothing, lunches, number of injuries or body cleanliness. Very often only one child in the family is singled out for cruel treatment, and this situation of scape-goating is also something that should be documented.

6. *Cleanliness of the Home:* Battered and molested children do not necessarily come from poor or lower income houses or families. It is just more difficult to detect and document those cases from middle and upper class families because the parents are usually more skillful in their deceit and have more sources available to cover up their pathology. It is not uncommon, however, to find a very clean, tidy lower income home with many children, all well cared for, that also houses one battered and neglected child.

Emotional Factors:

1. *Regressive Behavior:* Battered and/or molested children usually show signs of regressive behavior. They may become very childish, cry a lot, suck their thumbs or withdraw into fantasy worlds. An abrupt change in a child's behavior should be documented and investigated. Sometimes these children give the impression of being mentally retarded when, in fact, they are not. The degree of emotional disturbance may be proportionate to the length or severity of trauma. Diagnosis is difficult if the child brings this behavior pattern with him when entering a new school. However, close observation will reveal deterioration as the child moves from grade to grade.

2. *Acting Out Aggressive Behavior:* Battered and molested children often act out their anger and hostility on others. They may become involved in delinquencies, i.e., petty thefts or trinkets

which they give to other children to form friendships. Often they will steal food and money in order to survive.

The sexually molested girl may become sexually promiscuous, and her behavior may become the talk of, not only the school, but the whole neighborhood. Often a molested girl will confide in a special girlfriend or a favorite woman teacher. These confidences may not take the direct form of information about being molested, but may involve such statements as "I'm afraid to go home tonight," "I want you to help me go live with my aunt in Stockton," etc. A wise and interested teacher can build up trust in a child and be standing by when the child holds out a desperate hand.

3. *Poor Peer Relationships or Inability to Make Friends:* Often these children do not have social skills or are too emotionally disturbed to form peer relationships. These relationships are usually frowned upon or forbidden by parents. The parents have a vested interest in keeping them emotionally isolated. The children have such a bad self-image that they cannot believe another human being could be interested in them in any way. Their built in "bad me" concept overshadows their whole existence.

Parents often move or try to move these children from school to school or environment to environment. An example of this was seen in the case of the previously mentioned fourteen-year-old girl who appeared to be age seven. Her mother withdrew her from school, stating she was going to live with relatives out of the county. Unfortunately, the school did not make contact with the "new" school, and the child was being kept at home and being mistreated. There were siblings attending school in the same district who could have provided this information, had they been asked.

4. *Deep-seated Pathological Impact:* The victims of battering and/ or child molestation often develop deep-seated psychiatric problems which have an impact on their whole future development. Evidence shows that the majority of men in prison who are classified as psychopathic or sociopathic personalities were beaten children. They have little feeling for others or guilt about their misconduct. The molested girl often becomes a prostitute. She finds it difficult to relate to men on any meaningful level and often fails to protect her own children from the same victimization.

The home life of these victims as adults is usually very unsatisfactory, and their pathology is passed on to their children . . . then to their children's children. Victims of molest are plagued with feelings of insecurity, guilt, bad self-image, depression and sexual problems. The victims of battering are filled with feelings of fear, hate, aggression, and an inability to empathize. The molested and battered child almost always needs psychiatric treatment if he is to make any kind of a positive psychological adjustment to life.

From: Child Welfare League of America, Inc., 1974.

Once child abuse or neglect is suspected then procedures such as those suggested in the chart should be followed.

The counselor might find the Child Abuse-Neglect Reporting Form to be helpful in processing such cases.

The following School Child Abuse/Neglect Checklist is offered by Kline (1977) to help determine how extensively a school is involved in child abuse and neglect prevention, identification and processing.

School Child Abuse/Neglect Checklist

Listed below are the goals toward which every school should strive in an effort to eliminate child abuse and neglect in our society. Rate your school on a scale of 1 to 5:

        1 = Not involved
        2 = Somewhat involved
        3 = Involved but needing improvement
        4 = Substantially involved
        5 = Extensively involved

1. My school has developed and implemented a policy and procedures to be followed in the identification and reporting of suspected cases of child abuse and neglect.

    1   2   3   4   5

2. My school has developed and disseminated information to the public on the school's roles and responsibilities in the identification and reporting of suspected child abuse and neglect cases.

    1   2   3   4   5

3. My school, in cooperation with the child protection agency, physicians, police, hospital personnel, lawyers, and interested and concerned parents, has helped develop an awareness within the community of the extent to which child abuse and neglect may be present.

    1   2   3   4   5

4. My school (and my colleagues) act as an advocate to ensure that services are provided for abused and neglected children and their families.

   1   2   3   4   5

5. My school provides annual inservice training for all school employees on the subject of identifying and reporting children suspected of being abused and/or neglected.

   1   2   3   4   5

6. My school ensures that all records of child abuse and neglect and considered health and safety records, are not placed in the child's educational record, and are maintained in a "central school registry" on all reports.

   1   2   3   4   5

7. As part of the inservice training provided, my school makes sure that all personnel are aware of the effects that abuse, neglect, and sexual molestation can have upon the child's academic performance and behavior in school.

   1   2   3   4   5

8. My school has helped develop an awareness among my colleagues and other school personnel that abuse of children is multidimensional and can result in a high incidence of abused and neglected children being enrolled in special education classes.

   1   2   3   4   5

9. My school has helped all personnel develop an awareness of the importance of their behavior upon the development of behavior patterns and personality characteristics of the child.

   1   2   3   4   5

10. My school offers programs for both secondary students (grades 7 through 12) and adults on appropriate child rearing and parenting behaviors.

    1   2   3   4   5

11. My school, in cooperation with other community agencies and organizations, helps provide child care services and facilities for school age parents.

    1   2   3   4   5

12. My school, in cooperation with other community agencies and organizations, helps provide child care services such as crisis

nursery facilities, preschool day care centers, and other crisis intervention services.

1   2   3   4   5

13. My school conducts a review and evaluation of the child abuse and neglect policies, procedures, programs, and services at least once annually.

1   2   3   4   5

14. My school seeks to employ new teachers and other school personnel from teacher education programs that provide preservice training in the identification, reporting, treatment, and prevention of child abuse and neglect.

1   2   3   4   5

15. My school is represented on the multidisciplinary team established in the community to help solve individual child abuse and neglect cases as well as to create a climate where abuse, neglect, and sexual molestation of children is reduced or eliminated.

1   2   3   4   5

Child Abuse-Neglect Reporting Form

Oral Report made to principal or designee: Date_____ Time_____

Child's name _____/_____/_____
                 Last name (legal)   First   Middle

Age _____Birthdate_____Sex _____

Child's address_____

Names and addresses of parents or other person(s) responsible for the child's care.

Father_____ Mother _____

Guardian or caretaker _____

Address _____ Telephone _____

Observations leading to the suspicion that the child is a victim of abuse or neglect. (Use Appendix A when answering this question.) Supply time and date of observation(s).

Additional information. Interview with the child and name of other school employees involved.

Written report made to principal or designee: Date _____ Time _____

Signature _____ Signature _____
                Initiator of the report   Observer of the interview

        To be filled out by the principal or designee:

Oral report made to: Written report made to:

Local City Police   _____   Local City Police   _____
County Sheriff   _____   County Sheriff   _____
Division of Family Services _____   Division of Family Services _____

Date_____ Time _____   Date_____ Time _____

Principal's signature _____

Distribute copies: 1. Mail to agency receiving the oral report.

                    2. Mail to the district's pupil personnel office.

                    3. Place in principal's child abuse-neglect file. (Not to be placed in the child's personal file).

With this extensive but necessary background information on children's rights and child abuse and neglect, this chapter will now address the specific concerns within the educational community.

The Hidden Curriculum

The effort on the part of many educators toward the back to basics movement has stemmed from concerns of lower academic achievement scores on standardized tests, concerns over discipline problems and perhaps a notion that children have too many rights. The first two concerns perhaps are legitimate. There is some question, however, whether going back to basics will resolve these problems. The latter concern regarding children's rights usually stems from the question: Do children have responsibilities as well as rights? The answer to this question is, of course, Yes. In fact, by providing children with rights we are teaching them, through first hand experience, models of responsible adult behavior (Massachusetts Advocacy Center, 1975).

The notion of modeling and experiencing learned behavior early in life need not be discussed here but the impact that such notions have in the school setting are significant to the concerns of this chapter.

Bloom (1976) has identified two parts to the school curriculum: the manifest curriculum, i.e., reading, writing, arithmetic; and the latent or hidden curriculum which includes values, rules, norms of behavior, interpersonal relationships, and social skills. If by going back to basics, schools ignore this hidden but powerful part of the curriculum then much trouble lies ahead for education. Long after the dates of history are forgotten the psycho-social learnings will be remembered and have lasting impact on the lives of people. Counselors must assure that this latent curriculum not be hidden but instead design programs to address this most intricate part of the learning process. As Glasser (1969) so aptly states —

> What students learn - not from what they are taught but from the way the school is organized to treat them - is that authority is more important than freedom, order more precious than liberty, and discipline a higher value than individual expression. This is a lesson which is inappropriate for a free society - and certainly inappropriate to its schools (p. 90).

Techniques to help children

Many techniques may be used within the classroom to help children. These techniques are not considered counseling but are ways of helping children know that they are important. These techniques should be used with all children and may prove especially helpful to children with low self-concepts.

> Show the child that you care about him/her.
>
> Let the child know that he/she is not alone.
>
> Encourage children to talk about their feelings.
>
> Call parents for good accomplishments of children.
>
> Encourage children to focus on their assets and accomplishments.
>
> Communicate through a smile, pat on the back or nod.
>
> Help students to set realistic goals.
>
> Attempt to change inappropriate behavior through modeling acceptable behavior.
>
> Refer students to the school counselor for help with intimate personal and social problems (Robinson, 1979).

Use of standardized instruments

So often children are victimized by the standardizations of our society. Human growth and development experts suggest that the child should be performing certain tasks or developing at given stages in order to be "normal." Nutritional experts offer daily minimum allowances for proper growth. Dentists tell children they must have straight teeth to look like everyone else and on and on we go. We have become a society of standards. In education we have abused standards so much that many school districts are being sued both by parents who claim that their child was not treated to the same standard as other children and of parents who don't want those same standards used on their child. We have implanted upon parents and children that if their child does not fall within a narrow range, (which we, by the way, have set) then their child needs special service or at least does not fit the mold. Truly evaluation is critical if we are to measure our effectiveness and improve the process of education. However, often times the true purpose of measurement is whitewashed by our need to prove that what we are doing to kids is OK. What often happens through this process of "guaranteed prediction" or "self fulfilling prophecy" is that children are indeed misplaced, misguided, mistreated, and mistaken.

If we are to continue to use standardized instruments to measure aptitude, achievement, interests and personality then the following rights as listed by Loesch (1975) must be honored:

1. Children have the right to properly conducted assessment procedures.
2. Children have the right to be assessed through the use of the most appropriate instruments and techniques available.
3. Children have the right to complete, comprehensive, and honest feedback on their assessed characteristics and performances.
4. Children have the right to an explicit explanation of their results including as extensive an analysis of the assessment data as is possible.
5. Children have the right to know how the results of the assessment procedures will be used and to whom they will be made available.
6. Children have the right to discuss the assessment process and results with an individual qualified to provide accurate information.
7. Children have the right to further or other varieties of assessment as merited or desired.
8. Children have the right to feedback that explains how the assessment data appliees to them as a unique individual. (pp. 290-296)

The counselor must play a key role in securing these rights for each child. As perhaps the most knowledgeable person within the school in the area of the use of standardized tests, the counselor needs to coordinate in-service activities for teachers, serve as consultant to principals and parents, and most essentially serve as counselor to the students who are being measured in one way or another.

Classroom Placement

As the emphasis continues on placement of the handicapped student in the least restrictive environment it is critical that placement of these children be made utilizing the best procedures available. A test score will no longer suffice for placement criteria. Unfortunately in many settings little more than test scores are used. Due to insufficient funds and lack of adequate professional staff many children continue to be placed inappropriately with long lasting academic and psychosocial effects.

In addition, again with the emphasis on the handicapped it is possible that other children within the system will go unnoticed. The counselor must maintain a role of advocate for *all* children thus protecting the rights of these children and assuring classroom placement which is in the best interest of the child and not solely at the whim or self interest of the school.

In school suspension

In school suspension programs are currently under experimentation in many schools around the country. Essentially, it is an alternative approach to kicking kids out of school. Complaints from parents and merchants, as well as recognition by many educators of the negative results of suspension *from* school, the alternative of in school suspension is now under study. Briefly, the process goes like this: The child commits some infraction against the school policy which would normally result in suspension from school for a designated period of time. Instead of sending the child home, or in many cases to the streets, a designated location within the school is identified for in school suspension. The student spends the suspension time under supervision and during the regular school day within the building completing the academic assignments as provided by his/her teachers. In addition, the adult in charge, having a small number of students in his/her care, can discuss the infractions with the child, identify possible causes, and help to prevent future problems. Thus, the program under these conditions has a remedial orientation.

If such programs are approached from the standpoint of remediation, of both the child and environment, there is some potential humanitarian usefulness. If, on the other hand, the program is punitive in nature (with the underlying notion of only getting trouble-makers out of circulation and keeping parents and merchants off the schools' backs) then it is unjustified.

Summary

The counselor's role as child advocate is, needless to say, an endless job. It behooves the counselor to become thoroughly familiar with the procedures and resources within the community in dealing with these critical issues. A child's life or potentially altered future may rest with a counselor's efforts to take appropriate action.

Glossary of Terms

Abnormal: Deviating from a standard; not average, typical, or usual.

Abused Child: The product of child abuse; any person under the age of 18 years in the charge of a caretaker who is nonaccidentally injured by an act of omission or commission.

Affective domain: A sphere of activity or influence pertaining to feelings or emotions.

Aggressive: Behavior characterized by offensive acts or attacks; action or activity carried out in a forceful manner.

Bilateral: Affecting or pertaining to both sides of the body.

Bruise: An injury that does not break the skin but causes ruptures of the small underlying vessels with resultant discoloration of tissues; contusion.

Burn: An injury produced by, or as if by, burning (described in terms of degrees — 1st, 2nd, 3rd — in accordance with their depth through the skin).

Caretaker: Anyone responsible for the health and well being of a child (a parent, guardian, foster parent, teacher, baby sitter, or any other person charged with the care of a child).

Central nervous system: The system controlling those bodily functions of, relating to, comprising, or originating in the brain and spinal cord.

Clingy: Behavior characterized by a strong tendency to physically hold onto and/or a reluctance to separate from; a strong emotional dependence.

Cognitive domain: A sphere of activity or influence pertaining to or relating to the acquisition and application of knowledge.

Commission: A willful or volitional act.

Concept: A class of members of share some properties in common.

Confined: A state existing when movement is restricted beyond accepted norms; bound, imprisoned, denied freedom, locked up.

Critical attribute: A property of every example of a concept. (If it is removed, the example becomes a nonexample.)

Descriptor: A property of a concept which may, in and of itself, be insufficient but delimits examples of the concept: pictures, words, descriptions, characteristics.

Destructiveness: Behavior resulting in damage to property, self, or others.

Different stages of healing: Injuries of differing ages.

Domain: A sphere of influence or activity.

Extended diagnosis: the use of social, emotional, economic, or other environmental factors which tend to confirm or deny suspected cases of child abuse.

Fracture: A break or rupture in the bone.

> *Chip fracture:* A break in a bone which separates a small fragment from the main body of the bone.

> *Concussion fracture:* A break in a bone resulting from impact.

> *Green stick fracture:* An incomplete fracture of the long bones, principally in the forearm; one side of the bone is broken and the other side is bent.

> *Long bone fracture:* A break in one of the elongated bones supporting a limb, e.g., femur, humerus.

> *Spiral fracture:* A break in a bone resulting from a twisting or torque.

Gross examination: Physical examination without the aid of radiologic instruments or surgical entry.

Hematoma: A swelling containing blood.

Injury: A harm, hurt, or wound that adversely affects health, looks, comfort, or success. A specific impairment of body structure or function caused by an outside agent or force which may be physical, chemical, or psychic.

Internal injury: An injury to the internal organs, e.g., bowel, kidneys, spleen, liver, heart, lungs, mesentery.

Lability: Characterized by rapid emotional or mood changes.

Lethargic: Apathetic, sluggish, a state of overpowering drowsiness or sleepiness.

Malnutrition: Faulty or inadequate nutrition; the state resulting from inadequate or improper feeding.

Marasmus: Progressive wasting or emaciation, especially a wasting in infants; failure to thrive.

Masochism: The act of inflicting harm or causing harm to be inflicted upon one's self.

Mesenter: The membrane enfolding the intestines.

Metaphysitis: The line of the junction of the shaft of a long bone (diaphysis) and the end segment of the bone (epiphysis), which during early life are separated by cartilage.

Neglectful: Giving little or no attention or regard to; careless; unattending; inadequate caring.

Nonaccidental: Occuring other than by chance; an injury which is inconsistent with the stated cause.

Omission: The act of neglecting or leaving undone; neglect of duty; failure to act.

Paralysis: Complete or partial loss of function involving motion or sensation in a part of the body.

Passive: Not reacting visibly to something that might be expected to produce manifestations of an emotion or feeling.

Performance lag: An unexplained discrepancy between observed and realistically expectable behavior.

Physical: Of or pertaining to the body.

Posturing: Remaining motionless for unusually long periods of time.

Psychological injury: That which adversely affects the emotional or intellectual well being of a child.

Psychotic: Referring to mental disorders characterized by defective or lost contact with reality.

Radiologic: Of or pertaining to the use of radioactive substances in medicine; x-ray, principally referring to x-ray diagnosis.

Retarded: Limited in intellectual or emotional development.

Retinal hemorrhage: Rupture of blood vessels in the perceptive structure of the eye.

Roentgenology: The branch of radiology which deals with the diagnostic and therapeutical use of roentgen rays.

Role reversal: A pathological pattern of behavior wherein a child assumes the parent role of providing emotional support.

(Kline, 1977)

REGIONAL and NATIONAL AGENCIES

American Humane Association
Children's Division
Post Office Box 1266
9725 E. Hampden
Denver, Colorado 80231

Child Welfare League of America, Inc.
67 Irving Place
New York, New York 10003

International Society for the Prevention of Child Abuse and Neglect
1205 Oneida Street
Denver, Colorado 80220

National Center for Child Abuse and Neglect
Office of Child Development
Post Office Box 1182
Washington, D.C. 20013

National Committee for Prevention of Child Abuse
Suite 1250
332 S. Michigan Avenue
Chicago, Illinois 60604

Parents Anonymous
22330 Hawthorne Blvd., Suite 208
Torrance, California 90505

Regional Institute of Social Welfare Research
P.O. Box 152
Athens, Georgia 30603

U.S. Senate Subcommittee on Children and Youth
443 Old Senate Office Building
Washington, D.C. 20510

REFERENCES

ASCA position statement. Student rights: a right to due process. *School Counselor*, 1977, 25, 335.

Bloom, B.S. *Human characteristics and school learning.* New York: McGraw Hill, 1976.

Brown, J. *Organizing and evaluating elementary school guidance services: why, what, and how.* Monterey, Calif.: Brooks/Cole, 1977.

Ethical Standards. American Personnel and Guidance Association, 1974.

Gil, D. In Kempe, C. and Helfer, R. (Eds.) *The battered child.* Chicago: University of Chicago Press, 1968.

Glasser, I. Schools for scandal: the bill of rights and public education. *Kappan*, 1969, 51, 190-194.

Greenleaf, B.K. *Children through the ages.* New York: McGraw-Hill, 1978.

Kalisch, B.J. *Child abuse and neglect: an annotated bibliography.* London: Greenwood Press, 1978.

Kempe, C.H., Silverman, F.N., Brandt, F.S., Droegemueller, W., & Silver, H.K. The battered child syndrome. *Journal of the American Medical Association*, 1962, 181, 17-24.

Kline, D.F. *Child abuse and neglect: a primer for school personnel.* Reston, Va.: Council for Exceptional Children, 1977.

Landers, Ann. *Ann Landers' Column.* Field Enterprises, Inc., 1976.

Landers, Ann. One kid's own bill of rights. *Ann Landers' Column.* Field Newspaper Syndicate, 1975.

Light, R. Abused and neglected children in America: a study of alternative policies. *Harvard Educational Review,* 1973, 43, 556-598.

Loesch, L. A child's guide to educational and psychological assessment. *Elementary School Guidance and Counseling,* 1975, 9, 289-297.

Making schools work. Boston: Massachusetts Advocacy Center, 1977.

Martin, H. The child and his development. In Kempe, C. and Helfer, R. (Eds.) *Helping the battered child and his family.* Philadelphia: J. B. Lippincott, 1972.

Mizer, J. E. Cipher in the snow. *National Education Association Journal,* 1964, 53, 8-10.

Morse, C., Sahler, O., and Friedman, S. A three year follow up study of abused and neglected children. *American Journal of Children,* 1970, 120, 439-446.

Robinson, L. "Child abuse and the counselor." Unpublished manuscript, University of South Carolina, 1979.

Spinetta, J., and Rigler, D. The child abusing parent: a psychological review. *Psychological Bulletin,* 1972, 77, 296-304.

Tracy, J., and Clark, E. Treatment for child abuse. *Social Work,* 1974, 19, 338-342.

United Nations Declaration of the Rights of the Child, 1959.

Van Hoose, W.H. Children's rights and the counselor. *Elementary School Guidance and Counseling,* 1975, 9, 279-286.

Other References

Burns, M. *I am not a short adult! getting good at being a kid.* Boston: Little, Brown and Company, 1977.

Chamberlain, W. A. *A planning model for the development of programs for abused and neglected children in rural areas.* Athens, Ga.: Regional Institute of Social Welfare Research, Inc. (no date).

Davis, I.L., Eckerman, C., & Jarvey, C. *Child abuse and neglect: a school community resource book.* Wisconsin Department of Public Instruction, Bulletin No. 9096, 1977.

Farson, R. *Birthrights.* New York: MacMillan Publishing Co., 1974.

Gross, B. and Gross, R. (Eds.) *The children's rights movement: overcoming the oppression of young people,* New York: Anchor Press, 1977.

Paul, L.P., Newfeld, G.R., & Pelosi, J.W. (Eds.) *Child advocacy within the system.* Syracuse, N.Y.: Syracuse University Press, 1977.

Rotter, J.C., & Crunk, W. (Eds.) Special issue on children's rights. *Elementary school guidance and counseling,* 1975, 9.

The rights of children. *Harvard Educational Review.* Reprint series No. 9, 1974.

Understanding child maltreatment: help and hope. Rockville, Montgomery County Public Schools, 1976.

Chapter Four

INDIVIDUAL COUNSELING

FRED H. WALLBROWN and KAREN KIDD PRICHARD

Would a middle school counselor by any other name be the same? In many cases the answer to this question would be "yes." Often, middle school counseling is viewed as either "upgrading" elementary school counseling techniques and strategies or "downgrading" those from the high school setting. Even though middle schools have grown to include nearly 4,060 in the United States in the last decade, higher education is just beginning to offer courses and/or areas of concentration in middle school counseling. The purpose of this chapter is to delineate some of the developmental characteristics of middle school age youngsters, describe competencies that are necessary for a counselor working in this setting, show how developmental characteristics relate to interacting with parents and teachers and to individual counseling, and then to suggest specific strategies and techniques that will enable counselors to meet the developmental needs of middle school youth.

Developmental Characteristics And Tasks

Broadly speaking, the developmental characteristics that typify middle school age students can be conceptualized as conflicts or crises between competence and ineptness, uniqueness and imitation. Many of these conflicts are cited by Perrone, Ryan and Zeran (1970). The first conflict, that between competence and ineptness, involves this age youngster's attempts to gain new skills and to perform some sort of meaningful work and the feelings of inadequacy that result from the youngster's not being able to perform to idealized standards, or from comparison to others more competent. On the one hand, youngsters are likely to experience social reinforcement from both adults and peers for skill development. Grades, praise, material rewards and the like are ways that adults encourage youth to "get better" at what they do. Being part of the "in" group at school is generally accomplished by evidencing high levels of either academic or physical skills. Additionally, mastering new skills often leads to more independence for the student and a keener sense of self-worth.

On the other hand, these youngsters are receiving messages of inadequacy both from the social environment and self. Since our society places such a great emphasis on mastery of skills, those children who because of physical or mental limitations cannot perform in the expected manner receive a great deal of negative feedback. Such feedback obviously lowers the student's self-esteem. Since no one can do everything well, even those students who are not physically or intellectually limited will experience failure when trying to master some tasks. Additionally, because students tend to measure themselves on the basis of idealized standards, they may experience feelings of inferiority when they do not meet these standards. For example, rather than judging success or failure at playing football by comparing themselves with peers, these students are likely to judge their performance based on a comparison with a star of the National Football League.

The second conflict of uniqueness versus imitation has to do with the youngster's emerging concept of self as distinct from family and the need to identify with a peer group. While these students are busy asserting their need to be free and to "do their own thing," they are at the same time experiencing a need to belong to and be accepted by a peer group. A conversation like the following is not unusual.

"Come on, Mom, you can trust me."
"Yes, I know I can, but I still don't think you should stay out so late."
"Well I don't know why not, all my friends do."

Williams (1975) suggests that this conflict can be likened to the identity crisis described by Erikson (1968). In Erikson's perspective, "crisis" does not imply impending disaster, "but a necessary turning point when development must move one way or another." (Williams, 1975, p. 13)

> (T)he lists of trait characteristics . . . include such characteristics as: turbulent, moody, restless, lethargic, other directed, inward looking, concerned with opinions of peers, rejecting of standard of adults . . . Now these are not necessarily problems — but they are crises. The point is that crises are developmental — not detrimental. (ibid.)

How well the student resolves the conflicts described above will, to a great extent, determine the progress the student makes on the developmental tasks of this age. Newman and Newman (1975) indicate that the four developmental tasks of middle school age children are physical maturation, the attainment of formal operational thinking, the attainment of membership in the peer group, and the development of heterosexual relationships. "Mastery of the tasks of later stages of development often depends on the successful acquisition of earlier and simpler skills" (Newman & Newman, 1975, p. 24). If you want more information on the developmental perspective, the following references may prove useful: Behrens and Maynard (1972) *The changing child: Readings in child development;* Elkind (1978) *A sympathetic understanding of the child birth to sixteen;* Inhelder and Piaget (1958) *The growth of logical thinking from childhood to adolescence;* Piaget (1952) *The origins of intelligence in children;* Perrone, Ryan and Zeran (1970) *Guidance and the Emerging Adolescent;* and Sund (1976) *Piaget for educators.*

We have suggested that developmentally, middle school age youth can be viewed as in a state of conflict; conflict between competence and ineptness, and uniqueness and imitation. While this stage is certainly typified by crises, these crises should be viewed as normal and part of the emerging adolescent's natural progression from childhood to adulthood. Having discussed the developmental characteristics of middle school students, the next step is to identify some personal qualities and competencies of the middle school counselor.

Qualities and Competencies

Depending on one's theoretical framework, there are a variety of counselor roles. From an existential-humanistic viewpoint, the counselor should be able to engage in human-to-human encounters or be authentic and self-disclosing. If one's viewpoint is transactional analysis, the counselor's role is that of "teacher, trainer, and resource person with heavy emphasis on involvement" (Harris, 1967, p. 239). According to Goodstein (1972, p. 274) for behavior therapy "the role of the counselor is to facilitate the development of socially appropriate behavior by systematically reinforcing this kind of client behavior."

While there are a variety of counselor roles depending on one's theoretical stance, we feel that no matter which stance is adopted, there are certain personal characteristics and competencies that should be evidenced by all middle school counselors. Personal characteristics are: 1) emotional strength to live with the emotionality of middle school children because she/he is not overly protective of own dignity and has positive view of self; 2) willingness to listen patiently and get involved with student concerns; 3) ability to admit own errors and openness to change; flexibility; and 4) respect for the worth of the individual and the individual's dignity.

Competencies of a middle school counselor are:

1. Awareness of how his/her own behavior is affected by situations and beliefs; acceptance of a variety of behavior that is different from her/his own —
   — identifies personal priorities for individual counseling, collects data regarding effectiveness of counseling, and works to bridge the gap(s) between the two
   — recognizes differences between own values and those of specific youth and specific social goals
   — identifies the feelings and reasons for those feelings that another has toward him/her
   — encourages others to express opinions different from own.
2. Responsiveness and supportiveness of peers and students —
   — analyzes interaction patterns between self and others by using systematic observation
   — seeks feedback from peers and students as a means of identifying how his/her own behavior affects others
   — organizes student activities based on student interests.
3. Understanding of the physical development process of the middle school student and organization of counseling according to that process —
   — helps students through informing them about physical development and ways of coping with their changing bodies
   — analyzes student behavior according to physiological traits.
4. Organization of counseling according to the intellectual development process of middle school students.
   — helps students identify their own cognitive strategies and how these affect their classroom work
   — uses concrete rather than abstract counseling techniques.
5. Use of strategies in individual counseling appropriate to the socio-emotional process of middle school students —
   — understands and utilizes the need for peer approval as a motivating force in the lives of students
   — facilitates students' opportunities to experience success and works to reduce those aspects of the school system that reward the few
   — answers questions relating to sex in a comfortable, complete, and unbiased fashion
   — is able to discuss and interpret present societal confusion regarding sex roles in the language of the student
   — is not personally insulted by the student's need to be independent, often shown through resentment of all authority.

These fine competency areas obviously do not encompass all aspects of what it takes to be a "good" middle school counselor. Whatever your personal values and theoretical stance dictates as "good" counseling applies in a middle school setting. That is, we do not believe that only a "certain type of person" or a certain theoretical approach is the best one for individual counseling with middle school students. However, we do believe that the foregoing "Competencies" are necessary for effective interactions with pre-adolescents. Note that an understanding of the developmental process underlies many of the competencies. Continuing in this vein, we will next discuss how such an understanding translates to the counselor's role in interacting with parents and teachers.

Interacting with Parents and Teachers

The role of middle school counselor as he or she interacts with parents and teachers is that of advocate, explainer, arbitrator, and "interfacer." As we mentioned earlier, emerging adolescence is a time of upheaval, of questioning authority, of restlessness; in short, of crises. Youths in crisis do not operate in a void; their actions and feelings interact with the larger systems of school and family. The inner turbulence these youth are experiencing often spills over and impacts on the adults in their world. As the middle school counselor, your role is often one of helping other adults in the youth's world cope with the many feelings and behaviors that may appear inappropriate by helping these adults see the emerging adolescent from a developmental framework.

As an example, let's look at the developmental task of physical maturation. As is obvious to anyone who has come in contact with middle school students, this age is marked by the beginnings of physical maturity. This rapid physical growth does not take place at the same rate in all parts of the body, however, often leading to a period of awkwardness.

As a case in point, we can think of parents who called our office to request that we see their son. They described several situations where he had broken things they valued. No matter how often he was warned to "be careful" he would drop dishes he was drying ("Probably because he doesn't like drying dishes.") or knock things off the coffee table. In a state of frustration the father said, "Everything that kid touches turns to junk."

Ross' side of the picture was that his folks "are always on my case about something; I can't seem to do anything right." Simply observing Ross in the office led to some conclusions about what the difficulty might be. Even though he was nearly 5'10" tall and had many mature physical characteristics, his fine muscle coordination had not kept pace with his large muscle growth. In other words, he was going through a pretty normal "clumsy" stage. He agreed that it might be useful for him and his parents to get together in our office to discuss the problem. During this conference, the developmental task of physical maturation was described to the parents and it was suggested that rather than deliberately breaking things, Ross was the "victim" of an uneven growth pattern. In this context, the parents were able to view Ross' behavior not as trying to get out of drying dishes by breaking them, but as an understandable stage of development. Several strategies for solving the problem were generated including having Ross do other chores that did not call for fine muscle coordination (such as emptying the trash and making beds).

In many ways the counselor's role is one of helping parents and teachers view middle school youngsters in perspective so that rather than viewing their crises as detrimental, they are viewed as developmental. Another good example of how this perspective can be helpful is in assisting teachers' understanding of the emerging adolescent's challenging authority. As we mentioned earlier, a developmental task of this age is the emergence of formal operational thinking. At this stage, pre-adolescents begin to be able to generate more alternatives and to use this to question customary ways of acting. This often leads to questioning value assumptions and/or an outright rejection of current values as useless or meaningless. In the classroom, this may often look as if the student is challenging the teacher's authority. By helping the teacher understand that this is a natural "stage" for the child, it is less likely that the teacher will view such interactions as personal attacks. This can often provide the teacher with enough "psychological distance" that by not becoming personally defensive she or he can channel this tendency in the students in productive ways such as doing a unit on values clarification.

In summary, then, we view the major task of the middle school counselor as that of assisting the adults in the pre-adolescent's world to understand the child from a developmental perspective and to provide support for these adults as they encounter youths in crisis. The next, and final, issue we'd like to address is individual counseling with middle school youth. We'll suggest a framework within which the child's needs can be assessed and how this assessment leads to specific counseling strategies and techniques.

Counseling the Individual

Many years of experience in counseling pre-adolescents has led us to the conclusion that no one theory or set of techniques is the best possible for all youth; in other words, our approach tends to be very eclectic. Through a great deal of "trial and error learning" we've developed an informal way of looking at kid's needs and developing intervention strategies to meet these needs. The works of Lazarus (1976) and Keat (1979) clearly encompass, in a much more formal way, an approach which can be labeled "pragmatic technical eclecticism" (Keat, 1979, p. 1) – an approach which we feel provides for a structured assessment as well as an eclectic approach to interventions.

This approach is known as multimodal therapy and assesses the client by looking at seven interactive modalities: *B*ehavior, *A*ffect (feelings and emotions), *S*ensation, *I*magery, *C*ognition, *I*nterpersonal relationships, and *D*rugs-Diet (Lazarus, 1973). Lazarus (1976) uses the acronym BASIC ID (the first letter of each modality above) to represent this approach and as a convenient way to remember which seven areas to assess. As Keat (1979, p. 2) points out, two important concepts are omitted in the initial BASIC ID paradigm – school and family. Therefore, he expands *S* (sensation) to include school and *I* (interpersonal relations) to include both family and community.

In the next few paragraphs, we'd like to discuss how to use the multimodal therapy approach with adolescents. Due to space limitations, our treatment of this area will be relatively cursory so we'd really recommend that you read Lazarus (1971, 1976) and especially Keat (1979) for a much more definitive look at multimodal therapy.

After establishing the necessary rapport and climate of trust with the client, you begin by assessing each of the seven modalities. Write the seven-letter acronym BASIC ID down the left hand side of a piece of paper. In the next column indicate positive and/or negative aspects of each modality, and finally, possible intervention techniques/ strategies.

To give you a clearer understanding of how this process operates, let's briefly examine the case of a 12 year old boy, Alan. His English teacher suggested we see him because he seemed very withdrawn and he refused to participate in class even though the teacher felt sure he knew the material. The teacher also indicated he seemed generally unhappy.

Based on the information provided by the teacher and that gained by interacting with Alan during the initial session, the BASIC ID profile we developed was as follows:

	Mode	Positive/Negative	Possible Interventions
B	(behavior)	Not aggressive/withdrawal	contracting with teacher, behavioral rehearsal
A	(affect)	/anxiety	relaxation training
S	(sensation-school)	likes to read/math	math tutoi
I	(imagery)	/little self-esteem	Kalb & Viscott (1976) *What every kid should know*
C	(cognition)	/dependent on mom	assertiveness training, talk to mom about more responsibilities
I	(interpersonal relationships)	/few friends	friendship training *T.A. for teens* (Freed, 1976)
D	(drugs-diet)	no drugs/overweight	exercise program at "Y," books on nutrition, talk to P.E. teacher about setting up success in gym

This profile was only our initial thinking on what seemed to be Alan's problems and possible intervention strategies. As you can see, there were some gaps and these would need to be filled in as more data were provided during subsequent counseling. Keeping in mind that one of the major developmental tasks of this age is the attainment of membership in a peer group, the fact that Alan had few, if any, friends seemed to be a likely area with which to start.

Since Alan liked to read, we suggested *T.A. for teens* (Freed, 1976) as a way for Alan to understand interpersonal transactions. We also helped him rehearse what to say when he met someone, how to find areas of common interest, and how to keep frienships by being considerate and so forth. Part of his difficulty in extending himself to others was based on his poor self-image due to his weight so we attacked this area at the same time. We asked Alan to keep a list of what foods he ate and then suggested that by cutting down on junk foods, he might be able to lose some weight. The local YMCA also offered a program for overweight youth which we encouraged Alan to join. Being overweight also caused P.E. to be the bane of his life so part of our intervention was to contact the P.E. teacher and help him set up ways that Alan could experience success in gym.

As we indicated earlier, all seven modes interact with each other and changes in one or more are likely to affect the others. With this in mind, we contacted Alan's English teacher and suggested that she draw up a contract with Alan specifying that if he volunteered an answer twice per class for a week that she would take him to the university library (something he indicated that he would really like to do).

Our rationale for this strategy was twofold: 1) by interacting with a significant adult in his world, Alan could acquire a more positive view of himself, and 2) by correctly answering questions in English he both experienced success and his peers might begin to view him in a more positive manner.

Some of Alan's difficulties also seemed to stem from a somewhat overprotective mother. When we contacted her, she agreed to come to school to discuss Alan's problems. She described Alan's behavior at home as being generally "mannerly" but that he had recently been somewhat disobedient and seemed to be questioning her authority. After explaining that this type of behavior was not unusual for a boy Alan's age (the developmental perspective again) we suggested that she might enjoy reading *Hold them close, then let them go* (Robertiello, 1975). We also indicated that we thought it would be helpful for Alan to learn assertiveness so that he could be more direct in expressing his needs rather than making angry demands. We also elicited her help in Alan's weight program.

As you can see, the difficulties we chose to attack and some of the methods or strategies we used were clearly based on a developmental perspective. Suggesting that Alan might like to read the T.A. book was based not only on his enjoyment of reading, but also on the fact that he was developing the higher cognitive processes that would enable him to understand and internalize this reading. Our concern with his interactions with his mother was based on the concept of the crisis of uniqueness and imitation — his developmental task was to begin to see himself as a unique individual and also part of a peer group. Recognizing that acceptance by a peer group is extremely important for pre-adolescents, we tried to initiate strategies that would help him gain acceptance, i.e., success in English and gym, friendship training, weight control.

There is one additional point we would like to make in regard to Alan, one which we feel has been implied in our interventions but not explicitly stated. Helping Alan also required that we engage many of the adults in his world — his mother, English teacher, and gym teacher to name a few. In many ways, then, we were engaged in helping these adults view Alan from a developmental perspective, part of the role that we feel is necessary for an effective middle school counselor. Working with these adults requires a great deal of tact and the willingness to listen to their side of the issue. Its all well and good to suggest to the gym teacher that he "should" be willing to do some individualized planning for Alan, but the realities of his world are that he has fifty boys each period, making such individualization appear somewhat unreasonable. Providing support for your peers as well as some workable ideas of how to go about what you are asking them to do is much more likely to get you what you want than attacking them for what they are not doing.

There are no doubt any number of techniques/strategies that you could generate for each of the BASIC ID modes we assessed for Alan and you may even have placed some of his problems in a different modality. As we view it, this is one of the strengths of using a multimodal approach — each counselor can use his or her own judgment and most effective strategies. If you'd like some alternatives, Chapter 11 in Keat (1979) called, "Multimodal Therapy: Getting it all together" is extremely helpful in generating possible interventions in each of the seven modes and his references are an excellent source of books for pre-adolescents and their parents.

Our intent in this chapter has been to provide a developmental framework for middle school youth. Working within this framework, we have suggested counselor competencies and how interactions with parents and teachers are translated in terms of developmental tasks. Finally, we suggested that a good way of assessing these youth and developing interventions for individual counseling is by using the multimodal or BASIC ID approach. Hopefully, we have facilitated your ability to counsel middle school youth and the adults in their world so that the inherent crises of this age are viewed as developmental, not detrimental.

REFERENCE NOTE

1.   Both the personal characteristics and competencies were adapted from "Key competency areas for middle school teaching," and "Key competencies of middle school teachers." Gainesville, Fla.: University of Florida Middle School Project, 1972.

REFERENCES and ADDITIONAL READING

Behrens, H., & Maynard, G. (Eds.) *The changing child: Readings in child development.* Glenview, IL: Scott Foresman, 1972.

Brown, J., & Brown, C. *Consulting with Parents and Teachers.* Cranston, R.I.: Carroll Press, 1982.

Dustin, R. & George, R. *Action counseling for behavior change.* 2nd ed. Cranston, R.I.: Carroll Press, 1977.

Elkind, D. *A sympathetic understanding of the child birth to sixteen.* Boston: Allyn and Bacon, 1978.

Erickson, E. *Identity: Youth and crisis.* New York: Norton, 1968.

Freed, A. *T. A. for teens.* Sacramento, CA: Halmar Press, 1976.

Goodstein, L. Behavioral view of counseling. In B. Stefflre & W. Grant (Eds.). *Theories of counseling* (2nd ed.) New York: McGraw Hill, 1972.

Harris, T. *I'm O.K – You're O.K.* New York: Avon, 1967.

Inhelder, B. & Piaget, J. *The growth of logical thinking from childhood to adolescence.* New York: Basic Books, 1958.

Kalb, J., & Viscott, D. *What every kid should know.* Boston: Houghton-Mifflin, 1976.

Keat, D. *Multimodal therapy with children.* New York: Pergamon Press, 1979.

Lazarus, A. *Behavior therapy and beyond.* New York: Wiley, 1971.

Lazarus, A. (Ed.) *Multimodal behavior therapy.* New York: Springer, 1976.

Lazarus, A. Multimodal behavior therapy. Treating the "BASIC ID." *The Journal of Nervous and Mental Disease,* 1973, *152,* 404-411.

Newman, B., & Newman, P. *Development through life: A psychological approach.* Homewood, IL: Dorsey Press, 1975.

Perrone, P.A, Ryan, T.A., & Zeran, F.R. *Guidance and the Emerging Adolescent.* Scranton, PA: International Textbook Company, 1970 (now issued by The Carroll Press, Cranston, R.I.)

Piaget, J. *The origins of intelligence in children.* New York: International Universities Press, 1952.

Robertiello, R. *Hold them close, then let them go.* New York: Dial Press, 1975.

Sund, R. *Piaget for educators.* Columbus, OH: Charles C. Merrill, 1976.

Williams, E. Transcence and identity crisis. *Transcence,* 1975, *3,* 13-17.

Chapter Five

GROUP APPROACHES

GARY M. MILLER

Introduction

The purpose of this chapter is to examine avenues by which the middle school counselor can use group approaches. Initially, the need for and use of group counseling for sharing physical and emotional concerns of middle school students will be discussed. Classroom meetings will be presented as a realistic way of helping middle school students in an educational setting. In addition, some ethical guidelines for using group approaches will be presented.

Group Counseling

Group counseling can provide a very helpful opportunity to assist students who are experiencing various types of difficulties in their lives. The process is designed to be preventive in nature with the intent being the resolution of issues before they become more serious problems for the individual. Within the group setting the student can present and discuss dilemmas arising in life and learn about different ways of resolving these dilemmas.

Dinkmeyer (1969) provided a solid rationale for group counseling. He emphasized that since children are social beings whose growth and development takes place in groups, it seems logical they would be comfortable meeting and discussing issues with their peers. Within this setting the counselor can observe the kinds of social relationships the children share with each other and learn more about these interactions than would be possible in individual counseling.

Dinkmeyer (1969) also noted that in the group setting students can identify with their peers and receive feedback regarding the issues they have presented. This feedback can be helpful in developing new strategies for dealing with specific issues.

A further clarification of group counseling has been stated by Vriend and Dyer (1973):

> The process of group counseling includes (a) labeling behavior of group members that is self-defeating; (b) helping individuals to identify their goals, stating them clearly and publicly in behavioral terms and expressing a commitment to work on goal attainment; (c) assisting each group member to understand himself and the motivations for his behavior; (d)

69

creating alternatives to the debilitating behavior; and (e) trying out new
modes of behavior both within and without the group. (p. 53)
As can be seen, group counseling can be the setting in which interaction and learnings can take place for the benefits of the students
involved.

Initial Screening

Prior to having students enter a group counseling experience it
is advised that the counselor interview each student to clarify the
purpose of group counseling and the expectations of the student as a
group member. This initial screening can be helpful to both the counselor and the student.

During the initial interview it is important to inform the student
of some of the forces that may influence the group as counseling progresses. Ohlsen (1970) has identified nine specific forces about which
the client should be aware. *Commitment to discuss one's concerns* and
to work at developing new behavior to resolve those concerns is one
factor to be considered. Without such a commitment the individual
will benefit very little from the group experience. Being a voyeur as
others talk about their concerns and issues may benefit some people,
but such members will be contributing very little to the group itself.
It is critical for students to understand what their role in the group
should be and agree to be full, participating members. Participation
can help them with their own issues and can also place them in the
role of a helper to others.

The student's purpose in wanting to enter group counseling is
the second factor noted by Ohlsen (1970). The expectations of the
client need to be clarified and defined in order to maximize the probability of the student gaining help from the group counseling experience. During the initial interview the counselor may have to assist
the person in specifying the goals to reach while engaged in group
counseling. Knowing goals can help the student establish bench
marks as he or she faces and works on issues within the group.

Ohlsen (1970) addresses *responsibility* as the third factor that
must be clarified during the initial interview prior to one's entering a
group. It must be emphasized to the student that one must take responsibility for one's actions in the group. The student needs to
understand that as a group member one needs to participate and contribute to the happenings in the group. The counselor's responsibility
as a facilitator for the group is also clarified at this time for the
student.

Another of the factors in the group setting is that of *acceptance.*
Ohlsen (1970) has noted that the student must be aware that accept-

ance of others will be encouraged in group counseling. Acceptance can be most helpful as one begins to trust in others and accept what they have to share and, conversely, to be accepted by one's peers. Through mutual sharing and discussion in the group setting the students can be helped to better understand themselves and their fellow students.

Two other factors noted by Ohlsen (1970) seem to be related. The fact that the group can become very attractive to the student and promote a *sense of belonging* needs to be mentioned to the student. The attractiveness to the group can influence one's behavior as one remains in the group. Also, one's sense of belonging to a group can increase as a factor of the group counseling experience. For some students this sense of belonging is very important and the acceptance and trust they experience in the group can contribute to a positive experience for them.

One's *sense of security* (Ohlsen, 1970) cannot be underrated in group counseling. When one feels secure in a setting there is an increased probability that discussion of the issues facing group members will be facilitated. In such a setting students will be more comfortable to share their thoughts and ideas and receive assistance from those present in the group.

Tension will also be a factor present in the group (Ohlsen, 1970). This tension can provide a dynamic force to help the student move toward a resolution of the issue he or she is confronting. When dealt with properly, the student can learn to use tensions as growth-promoting and not debilitating factors in the group.

Lastly, Ohlsen (1970) suggests the student be *aware of the group norms* that may eventually emerge. The student needs to know that as the group progresses, specific actions, behavior and interaction will be approved or disapproved by the group. An understanding of the idea of group norms can help the student gain awareness as to how some eventual ground rules may emerge in the group.

By having initial individual interviews with potential group members the counselor can help in clarifying factors and preparing the student for the upcoming group counseling experience.

The Process

Once the counseling group has convened it is helpful to have the students introduce themselves and mention to the other members the specific issues they wish to deal with in the group. A decision they should discuss at this time is whether the group will be an open or a closed group. If it is an open group, the membership changes as people resolve their issues and new members are added. If it is a closed group, the membership will remain constant until the entire group terminates. The pros and cons for each type of group should be openly discussed and resolved the group members. By promoting this decision-making, the counselor re-confirms the responsibility the group members have for their group.

The counselor's role in the group needs to be that of facilitator as well as psycho-educator (Ivey, 1976). The counselor needs to establish the conditions necessary for the group to interact, keeping in mind the time restraints. As the session opens the counselor can give a brief description of the nature and purpose of the group, clarify the amount of time each session will last and the number of sessions available. Also, the confidential nature of the sessions needs to be noted and any answers provided regarding questions by students about the group. This initial structuring can do much in defining some of the reality limits that surround the group.

The psycho-educator (Ivey, 1976) aspects emerge as the counselor models effective and appropriate interpersonal skills in the group. At times the counselor may intervene and demonstrate specific skills and have students practice these within the group.

One obvious skill the members need to have in order to help others in the group is that of listening. If the counselor becomes aware members are not listening to each other, the counselor may need to educate some of the group members in proper listening skills. It is critical that the counselor be sensitive and not judgemental in helping students improve their listening skills.

Effective confrontation is the second member skill that may need to be taught within the group. Inappropriate confrontations can result in unnecessary hurt to group members. When performed properly, confrontation provides a direct, concise personal statement to another group member as to how that person's behavior and actions are striking the other group members. Criticism should not be cutting and punitive; rather, it should be sensitive and growth-promoting. If the counselor becomes aware members are not confronting their peers in a growth-promoting fashion, then it is most appropriate for the counselor to intervene and educate members to help them confront each other positively.

Associated with confrontation is the skill of providing feedback to group members. Feedback provides the person the opportunity to gain an understanding as to how a personal behavior or mannerism may be affecting other members of the group. Johnson (1972, pp. 15-17) has provided the following specifics regarding feedback:

1.   Focus feedback on behavior rather than the person.

2.   Focus feedback on observation rather than inferences.

3. Focus feedback on description rather than judgment.

4. Focus feedback on descriptions of behavior which are in terms of "more or less" rather than in terms of "either-or".

5. Focus feedback on behavior related to a specific situation, preferably to the "here and now" rather than on behavior in the abstract, placing it in the "there and then".

6. Focus feedback on the sharing of ideas and information rather than on giving advice.

7. Focus feedback on exploration of alternatives rather than answers or solutions.

8. Focus feedback on the value of it may have to the receiver, not on the value of "release" that it provides the person giving the feedback.

9. Focus feedback on the amount of information that the person receiving it can use rather than on the amount that you have which you might like to give.

10. Focus feedback on time and place so that personal data can be shared at appropriate times.

11. Focus feedback on what is said rather than why it is said.

Again, when the counselor sees members struggling in their feedback efforts it is time to move into the psycho-educator role (Ivey, 1976). Demonstration, role-playing and reactions to the role-playing efforts of the participants can help them strengthen their feedback skills.

Providing and receiving help represents an essential skill for the group participants. Even though in the initial interview each person agreed to help and be helped, there are times when some members may falter. This final member skill emerges with the integration of positive listening, confronting and feeding back information appropriately within the group. As the members begin to interact sensitively together, showing respect, acceptance, and caring as they listen, confronting and providing feedback to each other they can become more open to others and more open to themselves, consequently allowing others to help them. The incorporation of these basic skills in a facilitative environment can promote growth and assist students in resolving the issues they are facing.

As termination of the group approaches, the counselor must be sensitive to the effect of termination on some members. It is sometimes difficult for students to see their group conclude. It is suggested that one or two meetings prior to the final meeting the idea of termination be introduced. This gives members a chance to make a final effort to resolve either their own personal issues or any issues that may have emerged within the groups. It also helps them examine what the group has meant to them as well as how they can incorporate their learnings in their lives. Termination should provide a closure for the group and also a beginning as students face their futures.

The Structured Exercise

Over the past 12 years a number of handbooks of structured group activities have become available to counselors. These must be evaluated by the professional counselor as to their efficacy for middle school children. They are only tools for use at the appropriate time and setting and can not be considered as the essence of group counseling. When considering use of such activities, the counselor must consider the well-being of the clients and the nature of the leader's role in the activity.

Trotzer (1977) has noted some specific guidelines for the counselor to consider when using structured group activities. He (Trotzer, 1977) first expresses the need for the counselor to thoroughly know the exercise and feel secure in using it. The counselor needs to be fully aware of the intent of the exercise, its process and the kinds of outcomes one can anticipate after having conducted the activity. If the exercise will not contribute to the good of the members of the group, then it should not be used.

A second concern noted by Trotzer (1977) is how comfortable and familiar the counselor may be with a specific exercise. If one is uncomfortable with the activity, group members can readily note this and may not wish to participate. This resistance can delay the progress of the group and cause members to distrust the counselor with whom they are meeting.

A guideline that seems most appropriate, especially for middle school children, is to use mainly verbal rather than physical exercises. (Trotzer, 1977). The verbally-oriented activities allow group members to discuss and participate together, avoiding some of the discomforts members may experience in a physical, non-verbal activity.

Trotzer (1977) also suggests incorporating activities that do not have a possible negative stigma attached. Using the language of the group members is the key. Excessive jargon may lead to defensiveness or misunderstandings. Be specific and clear regarding the activities that are introduced.

Obviously, the counselor must consider the maturity level of the students (Trotzer, 1977). The counselor needs to be sensitive to the abilities of each group member to engage in specific activities. Members must not feel pressured or manipulated to participate and each member should be allowed to opt out of an activity which does not seem appropriate.

One must also consider the time and space factors for group exercises (Trotzer, 1977). There must be sufficient time allowed to introduce the activity, participate in it, and discuss its impact upon group members. This last aspect is very important as students may wish to de-brief themselves after a certain experience in order to consider some of the learnings that activity may have for them. Needless to say, space is an important consideration. The counselor needs to know the physical parameters for the group and be sure sufficient space and materials are available for conducting the exercises and should plan ahead to accommodate such an effort.

Involvement is critical for any group exercise. Trotzer (1977) suggests the counselor select activities which will maximize participants involvement in the group. In addition, the rights of each participant must be respected; consequently each person is encouraged to determine the extent of his or her involvement in an exercise. Although these may appear to be contradictory guidelines, they are not. Only through self-involvement will individuals participate.

A final guideline suggested by Trotzer (1977) focuses upon the outcomes of the activity for the group. By knowing the group members, the leader should be able to anticipate some of the outcomes of exercises. However, in addition to the counselor's anticipation, it is important to determine whether one, as a counselor, and the group itself is capable of facing and dealing with specific exercise outcomes. This further stresses the need for the counselor to know the group an to provide time at the close of each activity for the members to discuss the impact and outcome of the exercise.

It is believed these guidelines can be helpful to the counselor who uses structured group exercises with students. Perhaps each counselor can develop a check list prior to presenting a structured group exercise, and perform a check-out prior to conducting the activity. It can also be helpful for the counselor to keep notes on the different exercises and use these as a reference for the introduction of them in future groups.

Classroom Meetings

Background

A relatively new concept of working with students in groups is the classroom meeting. Two works by Glasser (1965, 1969) have done much to stimulate interest in conducting group meetings within the classroom, having both students and their teachers participate. The philosophical basis for these meetings rests on the concept of Reality Therapy (Glasser, 1965). Glasser (1965) contends that people need to discover ways to fulfill their needs. Without a strong, positive relationship with other people, the individual may engage in unrealistic activities in order to fulfill his or her needs. Glasser (1965) believes that through positive interactions with others the person begins to realize his or her own worth and, as a worthwhile person, engages in satisfactory ways of behaving. By functioning in a worthwhile manner, the student becomes a responsible person who is able to fulfill specific needs without preventing or depriving others from achieving their needs. Individuals who do not know how to fulfill their needs, except at the expense of others, are viewed by Glasser (1965) as irresponsible.

Glasser (1965) stresses that responsible behavior can be taught to children and uses a four-step process in helping students become responsible. The first step in Reality Therapy (Glasser, 1965) is to have the student identify the present behavior being exhibited. This behavior is examined so the person clearly understands that it is not fulfilling present needs. Secondly, Glasser (1965) notes that the student must be encouraged to make a value judgment as to the appropriateness of the exhibited behavior, for the well being of others in the group. This evaluation of one's own behavior brings one in contact with the reality of living with others and emphasizes that the responsible person will act in an appropriate, manner with others. Once the student evaluates the behavior, a commitment for a new way of behaving is agreed upon. Here is where the counselor can function as a teacher in helping the student examine positive behavioral alternatives. The agreement is reached that the student will then act in this fashion in the future. The student is aware that there are no excuses accepted if one does not act in the new manner agreed upon. However, if the student does fail in the attempts at exhibiting new, responsible behavior the process is initiated again and each step followed to the development of a new commitment for behaving. The anachronym, IBEP, which represents Involvement, Behavior, Evaluation and Planning has been suggested by Bassin (1978).

In a later work, Glasser (1969) discusses using Reality Therapy concepts in classroom meetings with students. He believes that the classroom is the most appropriate place to meet with students to resolve problems. The teacher conducts the meetings, emphasizing problem-solving, not fault-finding or punishment, for student behaviors. The meetings may last for as little as 10 minutes with young children and progress up to 45 minutes with older children. It is believed that in their meetings students can discuss and resolve issues of importance to themselves and their peers.

In *Schools Without Failure* (Glasser, 1969) elaborates upon the Social-Problem-Solving Meetings, Open-Ended Meetings, and the Educational-Diagnostic Meetings. The intent of the Social-Problem-Solving Meetings is to ". . . attempt to solve the individual and group educational problems of the class and the school." (Glasser, 1969, p. 122) Through total classroom discussion, teachers and students can work at ways of resolving problems in the school and classroom. Children in these meetings learn to resolve their own issues and help others who are facing problems.

The Open-Ended Meetings are viewed as ". . . the cornerstone of relevant education . . . ." (Glasser, 1969, p. 134) In these meetings the students should be encouraged to discuss issues related to their lives, their class and their curriculum. Rather than seeking problem-resolution, the teacher helps students discuss their knowledge about specific subjects being discussed, thus promoting their educational development.

The meetings ". . . directly related to what the class is studying" (Glasser, 1969, p. 138) are Educational-Diagnostic Meetings. These can help the teacher ascertain how effectively one's teaching has been and provides information as to how one may improve upon the educational process. These meetings are highly subject-oreiented and can help teachers improve in their professional efforts.

Muro (1978) has indicated some guidelines for conducting class-room meetings and he emphasizes having students actively participate in planning the meetings. They can develop goals and take responsi-bility for different activities in the group. Muro stresses the need for the group to meet frequently and for the students to be encouraged to interact to develop a cohesive group. The leadership of the group needs to be examined, and Muro encourages leaders to examine what they are doing as they conduct group meetings. Audio or video tapes could be utilized to monitor performance in the group meetings.

The counselor's role in the use of classroom meetings can be twofold. The counselor can conduct the classroom meetings for teachers. This, however, places an excessive burden on the counselor who may not be able to meet with each class on a regular basis. A more suitable approach is for the counselor to educate the teachers to conduct the classroom meetings. This task is a function of the counselor's role as a consultant to the teachers in the school. Further description and analysis of the consultation role of the middle school counselor will be presented in Chapter Nine.

Ethical Guidelines

The Association for Specialists in Group Work, a division of the American Personnel and Guidance Association, has developed "Ethical

Guidelines for Group Leaders" (ASGW, 1980). The middle school counselor may also wish to consider some standards that were developed by Olsen (1971). Olsen's standards indicate that the counselor should be a highly competent, responsible professional, who does not misrepresent his or her qualifications. In addition, he/she respects the confidentiality of group members and stresses their responsibility to protect the confidentiality of others in the group. The group leader is to respect the integrity of those in the group and assure their physical and emotional welfare while in the group. Screening of students prior to entering the group and providing appropriate follow-up upon termination from the group are responsibilities of the competent professional. It is critical that the counselor disclose to potential members the types of group experiences they can anticipate, which can help in deciding whether or not to enter a group. The responsible professional must also consider the social, moral and legal codes of society which establish limits regarding individual interactions and behaviors in the group. Respecting the freedom of choice of group members is another expectation of the group counselor. Members have the right to choose to participate in specific group activities and should not be humiliated or ridiculed for deciding not to participate in certain activities. If the group counselor learns that a person is being helped by another professional, the group counselor is responsible for discussing with the other professional the feasibility of having the client remain in the group. Lastly, the group counselor is responsible for participating in and assisting others in conducting research regarding group approaches.

It is critical that counselors be knowledgeable about various group approaches that can be used in the middle school. Each professional must adapt and develop procedures that are most suitable to themselves and their clients.

REFERENCES

Association for Specialists in Group Work. *Ethical Guidelines For Group Leaders.* Falls Church, Virginia: Association for Specialists in Group Work, 1980.

Bassin, A. Reality therapy in the classroom. *The Journal for Specialists in Group Work,* 1978, *3*, 63-77.

Dinkmeyer, D. Group counseling theory and techniques. *School Counselor,* 1969, *17*, 148-152.

Glasser, W. *Reality Therapy.* New York: Harper and Row, Publishers, 1965.

Glasser, W. *Schools Without Failure.* New York: Harper and Row, Publishers, 1969.

Ivey, A.E. Counseling psychology, the psychoeducator model and the future. *The Counseling Psychologist,* 1976, *6,* 72-75.

Johnson, D.W. Reaching Out: *Interpersonal Effectiveness and Self-Actualization.* Englewood Cliffs, New Jersey: Prentice Hall, Incorporated, 1972.

Muro, J.J. The Glasserian classroom meeting: Some problems, remedies, and promises. *The Journal for Specialists in Group Work,* 1978, *3,* 86-96.

Ohlsen, M.M. *Group Counseling.* New York: Holt, Rinehart, and Winston, 1970.

Olsen, L.C. Ethical standards for group leaders. *Personnel and Guidance Journal.* 1971, *50,* 238.

Trotzer, J.P. *The Counselor and the Group: Integrating Theory, Training and Practice.* Monterey, California: Brooks/Cole Publishing Company, 1977.

Vriend, J. & Dyer, W.W. A case for a technology of group counseling and delineation of major group categories. In J. Vriend and W.W. Dyer (Eds.), *Counseling Effectively in Groups.* Englewood Cliffs, New Jersey: Educational Technology Publications.

Chapter Six

CRISIS INTERVENTION

MARY BALLOU

Introduction

This chapter will focus upon crisis. It will briefly review crisis theory and explain a model for intervening in crisis with specific topical issues — drugs and death. Additionally, resources for further reading will be given. The chapter is intended to speak to the counselor or counselor in training with an emphasis upon effective helping in the crisis situation. It is not intended as an extensive academic treatment of crisis theory and research. Rather, in keeping with the goals of the text, the emphasis here is upon providing the reader with an understanding and a conceptualization of specific behaviors which will provide assistance to people in crisis.

Crisis is not a strange, unique or infrequent event in peoples' lives or in society, as is, for example, a fugue state or a reactive psychosis. On the contrary, crisis is a much more common event and one that need not carry the mystique of psychiatric labels. Yet even though crisis is apt to be a part of peoples lives, discomfort and lack of knowing how to handle a crisis exist. Indeed many people actively seek to avoid a person who is in crisis; but a counselor does not have that luxury. A counselor must learn to face and help a person who is in crisis. In order to do so, a counselor must learn about crisis, its stages and those behaviors which will give assistance to a person in crisis.

Crisis is not a pleasant event. Strong emotions, helplessness and confusion are part of the experience. Being with a person in crisis is very different from sitting in a counseling office with a client; the emotions are strong, the need great, and intense involvement is demanded.

Crisis — What the Literature Says

The crisis literature is extensive and still growing. Many disciplines are involved; such as nursing, medicine, psychiatry, psychology and social work. Crisis is an interdisciplinary topic. There have been many attempts to define crisis, beginning perhaps with Linndeman's work (1944) with the Cocoanut Grove fire of 1943, but brought sharply into focus in the work of Caplan (1964). Caplan writes: "A crisis is provoked when a person faces an obstacle to important life goals that is, for a time, insurmountable through the utilization of customary methods of problem solving. A period of disorganization ensues, a period of upset, during which many different abortive attempts are made. Eventually some kind of adaptation is achieved which may or may not be in the best interest of the person or his fellows." (p. 367) Such a description rests upon the idea that the human organism attempts to maintain a state of equilibrium through adaptation and problem-solving.

Parad and Caplan (1965) see three related aspects with the potential for producing crises: "(1) a hazardous event which poses a threat; (2) a threat to instinctual need which is symbolically linked to earlier threats that resulted in vulnerability or conflict; and (3) an inability to respond with adequate coping mechanisms" (p. 25). Miller and Iscoe (1963) define crisis as "the experiencing of an acute situation where one's repertoire of coping responses is inadequate in effecting a resolution of stress" (p. 196). Similarly, Bloom (1963) writes of "a known precipitating event and slow resolution" (p. 499).

Naomi Golan (1969) integrates the work of Linndeman and Klien (1961), Caplan (1964) and Sifncos (1961) in working out four operational terms in the identification of crisis. They are: (1) the hazardous event; (2) the vulnerable state; (3) the precipitating factor; and (4) the state of active crisis (disequilibrium). Each of these terms has a distinctive part in crisis and for Golan are prerequisites for a crisis. The following case example will give you an understanding of Golan's four operational terms:

> Bill is entering middle school in the Midwest. He faces his first organized gym class. Football is scheduled for the fall physical education activity. Bill does not like rough contact sports and has successfully avoided them thus far. However, now he faces a situation of a new school and pressure from peers, parents, his male Midwest cultural norms and the demands of the school to participate in physical education — football. This is an anticipated *hazardous event* for Bill. He perceives football in gym class and the pressure from peers, parents and school as a threat to his physical safety and emotional integrity, as well as the potential loss of his current positive image with his peers. (He anticipates his clumsiness, his fears and others' put-downs) Bill is both anxious and depressed. This is Bill's *vulnerable state.* Additionally, in his past Bill has always been able to avoid football by suggesting other games to his friends but that strategy will not work here. So his past experiences do not enable him to cope with the current situation.

> For Bill the *precipitating factor* (the final link in the chain which changes the vulnerable state into a crisis) is the first day of gym class when the teacher is announcing that the fall activity will be football. All the other boys cheer, one turns to Bill and says, "Don't you like football, you sissy!" Bill turns red and tells the teacher he has a stomachache and heads for the nurse. The comment by the boy was the precipitating factor which turned Bill's vulnerable state into a crisis for him. Bill is in an active state of crisis, his tension has built to a point where he no longer has the ability to handle it. (p. 398)

Golan's writing is helpful because she offers the reader some clarity about the dynamics of crisis.

The literature also holds attempts to cast crisis into a different set. Rusk (1971), Blocher (1974) and Erikson (1968) see crisis as an opportunity, a cross-roads, a natural part of the cycle of growth and development in the process of life. These writers present crisis as not abnormal, terrible, sick, or atypical. Rather, crisis is presented as a natural occurence which, if solved positively, can be a growth enhancing event. The potential of significant change, insight, further integration, development of stronger and more coping skills can be a real outcome of crisis. Crisis is an opportunity – a chance to grow, remain the same, or regress. Both the opportunity and the natural occurence of crisis are the contributions of these theorists.

Jacobson, Stickler and Morley (1968) are representative of a group of crisis authors who have attempted to differentiate among kinds of crises. They write of generic and individual crisis. They see generic crises as those situational or maturational events which happen to large numbers of people and have specific and identifiable patterns of response. Events such as premature births, divorce, death, onset of puberty are, for them, generic crises. Individual crises on the other hand are seen by Jacobson et al. as those crises which call for the assessment of specific interpsychic and interpersonal processes of the individual in crisis. The conceptualizations of Jacobson et al. are limited, but they seem to have begun a trend to differentiate among kinds of crisis. For example, Aguilera and Messick (1978) divide crises into maturational and situational while Morrice (1976) sees crises as either developmental (involved with transitional stages) or accidental (caused by unexpected hazards of life).

Perhaps the most complex system for differentiating among crises has been set forth by Baldwin (1976). He describes a six class system ranging from Dispositional Crises to Psychiatric Emergencies.

Crisis – What is it?

There are those who write of specific kinds of crisis. For example, Linndeman (1965) on acute grief, Kubler-Ross (1970) on death and dying. Renshaw (1974) on suicide of children and Brown-Miller (1975) on rape. These are important works for they offer information about and insight into particular hazardous events. Also the reader can see a pattern among these works. Though the vocabularies differ, the process of the crisis and the helpful behaviors have a striking similarity.

For the purposes of this text, the following definition of crisis is adopted. Crisis is *"a perceived threat to an individual with which that individual cannot cope, resulting in a need for reorganization within the individual which has the potential for further growth and integration by that individual."* (Litwack, Litwack, Ballou, 1980) This definition has a number of important concepts embedded in it.

The first is that crisis is a normal and not uncommon event. Suicide attempts, rape, and drug overdoses are generally thought of as the type of events with which crisis is associated. While it is true that such events are often crises, it is also true that many other less sensational and less frightening events may prove to be crises for some individuals. The definition of crisis does not define crisis by the event but by the perception of the individual(s) involved.

Caplan (1970) and Golan's (1969) idea of crisis being perceived by an individual as a hazardous event whose nature may be a challenge or a threat and which is difficult to solve by familiar problem-solving methods, characterizes well the focus of our definition. For example, the beginning of menstruation may become a crisis for some young women. Helping professionals must set aside their personal beliefs as to what constitutes a crisis, and *attend to the situation as experienced by the person.* What may be stressful or a problem for one person, may be a crisis for another.

For example, in almost any classroom there are a number of children whose families have been disrupted as a result of desertion by one parent, divorce, remarriage of parents, and other circumstances. Yet these children will perceive and react very differently even though their family status is similar. Some will have crisis and some will not, yet all will have some reactions. There are, of course, many factors which determine whether a crisis will occur: the maturity of the child; the presence or absence of helpful and attentive people who are or become important to the child (parents, older friends, family members, teachers, counselors, ministers, etc.); how other people react, cultural messages; the strength of the child; earlier experiences; and existing coping abilities. Yet the bottom line is that some children will experience a crisis and some will not. Again, it is not the event which will determine crisis but a person's perception of that event and his/her ability to cope.

Spiegal (1957) points out that novel stressful situations are more apt to result in crisis responses than familiar stressful situations. If one has never encountered a particular situation, nor even a similar one, the chances are that one will not have developed the necessary coping skills and problem-solving abilities. A person's support system is important in such situations. If a person is alone, with no significant other person with whom to discuss feelings and problems, with no one to give support, love, concern, and a helping hand, stress is more likely to result in crisis. Also important are the evaluative norms — cultural messages and others' reactions about the event. Incest is considered worse and reacted to with more horror than divorce, for example. Such personal and social judgements influence the individual's perception of the event. Finally, if a person has not successfully resolved developmental tasks and is not well-adjusted to the general demands of life, then stressful situations may be more likely to produce a crisis. In fact, a current crisis frequently brings to the surface past unresolved conflicts, so that the current event is confounded by many other past events and feelings. People in crisis experience highly charged emotional states which may find expressions in anger, depression, agitation, aggression or suicidal impulses. These affective states and behaviors may result form the current crisis and/ or from past unresolved conflicts.

Caplan (1960) estimates that crisis states usually last from one to six weeks. At some point, most individuals find some solution to their problem and/or a reduction of the highly charged emotional state. The problem solution certainly can be adaptive and effective, eliminating the conflict, stress, and problem. It can also be maladaptive, whereby the intensity of the emotional state is decreased but the conflict and basic problem remain.

An example would be the early adolescent who has conflicts with his parents, and who acts out these conflicts at home and at school, resulting in parental restrictions and school discipline. His frustration leads him to break supportive ties with his parents and school. He attempts to resolve his situation (viewed as either a problem or crisis dependent on his perception) by turning to drugs and the support of peers. The boy has reduced his emotional tension but has likely not achieved an adaptive or effective resolution to his conflicts with his parents and the school. The chances are the conflicts and stress with his parents and school, as well as perhaps the law, will increase. In short, the boy's coping method was maladaptive, without any genuine resolution. Further difficulties, stress, and crises can be expected since his solution of drugs is inadequate, and his original problem of parental and school conflict remains unsolved.

When crises are genuinely positively resolved, not only is the situation precipitating the crisis met effectively and anxiety reduced, but frequently the individual becomes emotionally healthier, for the process of crisis resolution has the potential for increasing the behavioral repertoire, expanding problem-solving abilities, increasing self-knowledge, and resolving past conflicts. Frequently, people emerge from crises with a more integrated personality, an increased sense of self-worth and self-confidence, and a clearer understanding of who they are, what they want, and plans for attaining their goals. With effective crisis resolution, individuals frequently participate more fully in life, being less fearful, defensive, and restricted, and with happier, healthier lives.

Recognizing a crisis is important, but only the first task of the counselor. A counselor willl hopefully also be able to help an individual deal with his/her crisis. Being able to help another in crisis is critically important because:

(1) Many people ordinarily involved in the person's life will be unable to offer assistance.

(2) The need of the person in crisis is great, since by definition he/she is threatened and without satisfactory coping skills,

(3) The middle-school counselor is in an ideal situation with nearly immediate access to the students in the school, unlike many counselors in other settings. (In community mental health centers, for example, it is rare to see a client at the onset or even initial stages of a crisis.)

It is appropriate, then, to turn to those interventions which the counselor can perform to help the child in crisis. First it is necessary to understand that crisis is a process, within which there are different stages. Each stage of the crisis process calls for different interventions.

The Crisis Process: Stages and Interventions

Fink (1967) has proposed a generic model of crisis which has been selected for use in this chapter. His model views crisis as a process which has identifiable stages and implications for interventions. These interventions have been formalized by Ballou and Rebich (1977). Figure 1 shows Fink's model. The model attends to a variety of psychological dimensions in each stage of the crisis process. In a successfully-resolved crisis, a person passes through each stage, but not necessarily in order, or only once at each stage.

Crisis is defined as a perceived threat to an individual with which that individual cannot cope, resulting in a need for reorganization within the individual. This reorganization has the potential for further growth and integration by the individual.

Looking at this definition, several things become clear. Rape, drugs, death can produce crisis, but so can any other event, such as a "D" grade, losing a boyfriend, not being invited to a dance, or deciding between two equally good courses. The key is not the nature of the event, but the *perceptions* of the individual experiencing the event and their ability to cope with it.

The second thing that becomes clear is that crisis need not be avoided because it is scary. A person progresses thorugh the same process, regardless of crisis (e.g., death or no invitation to the dance). There is nothing magic about the assistance needed in the crisis situation, anyone who is genuinely caring, sensitive and knows about the process and its stages can help. Finally, the potential for growth (reorganization) and integration is great — the benefit of help received is perhaps more in crisis than at any other time. (Rapoport, 1972)

Recognizing crisis, as is stated earlier, is only the first half of crisis intervention. The counselor must intervene in a way that will be supportive to the person who may see no way out of the present temporary, but frightening, situation.

Using the Fink model, the counselor can more clearly identify and anticipate specific behaviors he/she is likely to encounter as a person goes through the stages of crisis. From a developmental point of view, it is essential that the early stages be experienced fully and sequentially, so that the final stage can occur and result in growth for the individual. First, by using the model, the counselor can acknowledge each stage — giving acceptance and support to the individual that these feelings are okay (i.e., they are understood and accepted).

The counselor working with the middle school child will need to adapt the mode of communicating acceptance and support (as well as the interventions which follow) to the communication pattern of the specific child. Some will be verbal and fit nicely into the descriptions presented here. Others, however, will act out, not talk out, their feelings and will receive non-verbal modes of communication better. The counselor then will need to develop different modes of communication suitable to the different communication patterns of the middle school children with whom she/he will work.

During the first stage of shock, support through empathic listening is essential. The counselor must reflect to the individual the feelings of fear, confusion, and disorientation the shocked person is experiencing.

Interventions during the shock stage fall into three main categories:

1. Providing medical treatment immediately, if it is needed.
2. Providing a safe, quiet atmosphere, where the client can have privacy.
3. Providing an opportunity for the client to talk about the problem — what's just happened.

Contact may be remaining close, holding a hand, or providing a shoulder to cry on.

Through listening, the counselor can begin to build a caring, supportive relationship — letting the client (student) know: "Here's someone I can trust." At the same time, the counselor can assess the dimensions and extent of the crisis. Often, gathering information from others may be neccessary to fill in missing, distorted, or hazy details.

Refraining from personal judgement is critical. Often, when the data are collected, the counselor may feel this is hardly a crisis; i.e., teenagers lose boyfriends daily, all of us have flunked an exam at some point. However, if that person sees the situation as a crisis, he/she does not want to be told, ". . . you're over-reacting." What he/she wants to hear is, ". . . I understand how you feel."

Thus, initially, good listening and supportive caring will be all the interventions needed during the shock stage. As the client moves into the second stage, defensive retreat, interventions become more difficult.

The confused, anxious client encountered in the shock stage may be transformed into an angry, hostile person with a totally unrealistic or dependent outlook. Or the frightened, hopeless victim may now be overly optimistic and see everything rosy.

Regardless of the transformation, the client is reverting to defensive behavior. While he/she still needs the support of the counselor, he/she does not need to have the unrealistic thinking or inappropriate behavior supported.

Confrontation of this unrealistic thinking can destroy these needed defenses and, while the client may see the inconsistency in thinking, he/she may also see the counselor as a threat to his/her safety and another force to be guarded against.

Thus, the counselor walks a shaky path between not supporting the unrealistic thinking, but not confronting the defenses. Add to this the counselor's role of supporting the client's right to feel, and this stage becomes difficult indeed.

The interventions that can be most effective at this stage are:

1. Reflecting the client's feelings.

2. Summarizing the content of messages.

3. Helping clarify feelings.

4. *Gently* asking the client to explain the consequences of his/her intended behavior.

5. *Not* personalizing angry or hopeless feelings the client might express, but acknowledging his/her right to feel.

6. Not avoiding the dependency that might be visible.

Hopefully, these interventions will tell the client the counselor is available, and will stick with him/her. Sticking with the client through defensive retreat is critical because not until the third stage, acknowledgement, does therapeutic counseling begin.

In the third stage, acknowledgement, the client begins to open the door to the world of reality — the door which has shut out pain, anxiety, and stress. Reopening the door and facing the reality can result in severe depression or guilt. Here is where suicidal thoughts may emerge. All the feelings of hopelessness and helplessness become rekindled when the event is seen clearly.

The event became a crisis because of its importance to the client, who did not have the necessary coping skills. Facing the situation again, but still without those needed skills, can be a very frightening and overwhelming encounter.

The counselor's goal is clear: To help the client develop new skills to cope with the situation, and cement the trust between counselor and client that has been developing. Clearly, communication to the client that one understands his/her feelings about the situation is critical. After communicating empathy, the counselor can concentrate on exploring these feelings and help the client be aware of what she/he is experiencing.

Interventions, then, must focus to clarify and define the event and its implications for the client in all dimensions, as the client indicates he/she is willing and ready to do. Then, the counselor can work with the client to increase problem-solving abilities, identify alternatives, explore tentative plans for problem solutions and supply necessary resources and data to aid in decision making. Throughout these problem-solving steps, the counselor must listen and empathize with feelings — not only remaining supportive, but realistic as well, in confronting unsound alternatives.

Once the client has progressed through shock, defensive retreat, and acknowledgement, he/she will reach adaptation and change, the final stage. Now, the client is ready to reorganize his/her life. The goals at this stage are multiple. Working together, the client and counselor decide upon the most workable solutions to the problem(s), and then integrate the new skills needed. They also integrate the meaning gained from this experience into the life and understanding of the client.

To be effective either in a crisis or preventive approach the counselor must have clear, accurate understanding of the issue and related concerns.

In many middle schools, the problem of substance abuse — both alcohol and drugs — is real. It is affecting growing numbers of students. While death has always occurred, the notion that children can be deeply affected by death is becoming accepted and acted upon. No longer is the death of a parent only talked about in the teachers' room. Within the educational system attempts should be made to assist the child with his or her reactions to death. Additionally, growing emphasis upon developmental theories are revealing middle school children have not as yet reached a developmental stage where ability to cope with this kind of hazardous event has evolved. It is proposed that the counselor with knowledge of the hazardous events, developmental stages and crisis theory should become proactive in the facilitation of the growth of students.

Crisis — Case Analysis

Cindy is an eighth grade student whose brother, Jack, has recently died in a school bus accident. Cindy is returning to school one day after the funeral. Most of the school personnel who have contact with Cindy are sympathetic and gentle with her but are avoiding her brother's death. The counselor sees Cindy in the hall, and observes she is not interacting with the other students around her, and is emotionally non-expressive. The counselor confirms these impressions with the teachers who have had contact with Cindy during the day. The next period Cindy is brought to the school nurse because in class she had begun to rock in her seat and repeat "no, no, no" to herself quietly. The counselor is called to the nurses' office. The nurse was preparing to send Cindy home but the counselor suggests the nurse wait until after she talks with Cindy and then decide if that course of action is still warranted. (The counselor suspects the parents are not able to assist Cindy because of their own grief.) The counselor believes Cindy is in defensive retreat. As the counselor begins to interact with Cindy this supposition is initially confirmed. During the interaction, Cindy moves to the acknowledgement stage with the associated pain, tears and grief. Cindy sobs that the counselor is the first person to talk with her about her brother's death. The counselor holds Cindy for a while until some of the sobbing lessens. Later the parents are called but only the mother comes. The counselor then begins to talk with both Cindy and the mother about what has happened and how they feel. It seems the father is denying the death of his son, refusing to allow the family to talk about it or express their grief. Indeed, he is forcing a "things as normal" approach upon the entire family. The mother is confused, torn between husband, daughter, and her own grief. The counselor discovers their minister, who is well trained in death and dying, is an important figure to the family, particularly to the father. Arrangements are made for the minister to visit the family that evening and for Cindy to see the counselor at school regularly. Both the minister with the family, and the counselor with Cindy, will enter into the process of crisis resolution.

This example illustrates a number of things. First, that in the usual course of events others avoid interacting around death (i.e., teachers, nurse, other students, even the minister until asked by the counselor). Second, the reactions of other family members can be counter-productive to the normal process of crisis. The family as a whole must be attended to. Third, various professionals, in and outside of the school, can work together (i.e., the teachers, the nurse, and the minister assist the counselor). And fourth, actively expressed concern and honest communication are critical in beginning the process of crisis resolution.

Crisis — Approaches to Intervention

In a middle school it comes to the attention of the counseling staff that problems with alcohol and drugs are increasing in the school. They bring their concerns to the principal, who responds by tightening the disciplinary policy and calling the police in an attempt to apprehend the people who are selling to the students. The counselors, however, doubt this will solve the problem. They know students often get the substances from the liquor and medicine cabinets of the parents. They also know that attempting to stop the supply and punish violators severely will not only be ineffective, but does not really address the problem. The principal is persuaded to allow in-school attempts to meet the problem by the counselors.

The counselors begin to map out an approach to identify and meet the problem. They arrange for an assembly where they talk to the student body honestly about the increased abuse, their concerns and the suspected underlying motivations for using abusive substances. Also at this assembly they invite staff of the local drug center to speak, believing their credibility might be stronger with the students. Over the next few days, the counselors meet with the students in classes to talk about the students reactions and gather thoughts about ways to deal with the problem. When all the information is gathered from the students, the teaching staff, the staff of the drug center and the counselors themselves, the problem is identified more accurately and specific aspects are clarified.

A number of possible ways to proceed to meet the problem are considered, selected and initiated. The idea of the fear-lecture approach is discarded. It is discovered the students simply do not believe adult presentation of medical and legal negative consequences of abuse. The idea of discussion groups focusing on what the youth need, and are concerned about, seems workable. The counselors know that developmentally some of the students are in the identity stage, involving them in issues of acceptance by others, their own values, and self-definition needs. Discussion groups are arranged with an attempt to get both students who do and who do not use alcohol and drugs in the same groups. The groups do not focus primarily upon the use of drugs and alcohol. Rather, they aim at discussing the issues in the lives of the students. Many of the adolescents face the same issues; however, while some do use drugs, others are dealing with similar personal issues in other ways. As the groups evolve, healthy discussions bring about understanding of the issues and personal insights, as well as some behavior change indicating a move from substance abuse.

Another procedure is to conduct teachers' in-service training seminars, the purpose of which is to help teachers understand and deal with substance use in better ways. Their former avoidance of the issues or use of standard moralizing arguments alienated the students. After in-service training, the teachers are encouraged to work together to develop sensitive and knowledgeable curricular materials for their classes. In English, the personal substance usage of the authors of the literature studied are presented and discussed. The students hear, from an English teacher, that Poe was an addict. They hear, too, in their social studies class, of the broad-ranging social implications of substance abuse to the society. In health, they hear not only of the physical implications, but begin to consider altered states of consciousness in more knowledgeable and accurate terms than their own personal experiences may have given them. And in history, they begin to study the moral additudes and behaviors of different cultures in different periods.

Finally, plans are laid for the student government, with the assistance of thir advisors, to study the substance abuse problem and the effectiveness of the preventive program. They will present their findings to the faculty and students at another assembly.

The above example illustrates a number of varying approaches to prevention. The basic ideas are important:

1. Include all the people involved in the problem both in the gathering of information and in the implementation of the plan.

2. Use a multi-leveled approach aimed at educating.

3. Look to the underlying influences and provide understanding and skills to enable alternative ways to more effective coping with the hazardous events.

4. Look at the problem as a lack of understanding, knowledge and skill, not as a wrong which should be punished.

The goal is to provide knowledge and alternative ways of meeting needs, with honest and accurate information about potential consequences of each alternative. If the preventive efforts are successful, the counselors will not have to perform crisis intervention as often, nor will the human loss and suffering be as great.

ADDITIONAL READING ON DEATH AND SUBSTANCE ABUSE

Cohen, S. *The Drug Dilemma,* McGraw-Hill, New York, 1976.

Corder, B., Smith, R. & Swisher, S. *Drug Abuse Prevention,* William C. Brown, Dubuque, Iowa, 1975.

Easson, W. *The Dying Child,* Charles Thomas, Springfield, Illinois, 1977.

Heikkinen, C. Counseling for Personal Loss, *The Personnel and Guidance Journal,* September, 1979.

Koepf, L, Lock, G., & Gammel, J., The Goal of Effective Drug Education, *Research Outlook,* Vol. 5, No. 1, 1974.

Ray, O. *Drugs, Society, and Human Behavior,* Mosby Company, Saint Louis, 1978.

Stanford, G., Perry, D. *Death Out of the Closet,* Bantam Books, New York, 1976.

Vicary, J. *The Affective Domain as Prevention,* Health Education, January/February, 1979.

Breecher, E. and Editors of Consumer Reports, *Licit and Illicit Drugs,* Little, Brown, Boston.

REFERENCES AND ADDITIONAL READING

Aguilera, D. & Messick, J. *Crisis Intervention Theory and Methodology.* Saint Louis: C.V. Mosby Company, 1978.

*Baldwin, B. Crisis Intervention: An Overview of Theory and Practice, *The Counseling Psychologist,* Vol. 8, No. 2, 1976.

Ballou, M., Rebich, C. Crisis Intervention: A Call for Involvement for the Health Professional, *Journal of School Health,* December, 1977.

Blocker, D. *Developmental Counseling.* 2nd ed. New York: The Ronald Press Company, 1974.

Bloom, B.S. Definitional Aspects of Crisis Concept, *Journal of Consulting Psychology,* 1963, 27, 498-502.

Borgman, R.D. *Social Conflict and Mental Health Services,* Springfield, Illinois: Charles C. Thomas, 1979.

Brown-Miller, S. *Against Our Will Men, Women, and Rape,* New York: Simon and Schuster, 1975.

Caplan, G. Patterns of Mental Disorders in Children, *Psychiatry,* 1960, *23,* 365-374.

Caplan, G. *The Theory and Practice of Mental Health Consultation,* New York: Basic Books, 1970.

Caplan, G. *Prevention of Mental Disorders in Children,* New York: Basic Books, 1961.

Caplan, G. *Principles of Preventive Psychiatry,* New York, Basic Books, 1964.

Erikson, E. *Identity, Youth, and Crisis,* New York: W.W. Norton Company, 1968.

Ewing, C. *Crisis Intervention as Psychotherapy,* New York: Oxford University Press, 1978.

Fink, S. Crisis and Motivation: A Theoretical Model, *Archives of Physical Medicine and Rehabilitation,* 1967, 48.

Golan, N. When is a Client in Crisis? *Social Casework,* July, 1969, *50,* 398-411.

Hipple, J.L. & Cimbodic, P. *The Counselor and the Suicidal Crisis: Diagnosis and Intervention,* Springfield, Illinois: Charles C. Thomas, 1979.

Insel, A. On Counseling the Bereaved, *The Personnel and Guidance Journal,* November, 1976, *55,* 127-129.

Jacobson, G., Sticker, J., Morley, W. Generic and Individual Approaches to Crisis Intervention, *American Journal of Public Health,* 58:2, February, 1968.

*Kubler-Ross, E. *On Death and Dying,* New York: Collier Books, 1970.

Lester, David & Brockopp, G. *Crisis Intervention and Counseling by Telephone,* Springfield, Illinois: Charles C. Thomas, 1976.

Linndeman, E. In H. Parad (Ed.) *Crisis Intervention: Selected Readings,* New York: Family Service Association of America, 1965.

Linndeman, E. Symptomatology and Management of Acute Grief, *American Journal of Psychiatry,* 101, 1944, 141-148.

Linndeman, E. & Klien, D.C. Preventive Intervention in Individual and Family Crisis Situations, in *Prevention of Mental Disorders in Children*, Caplan, G., Ed. New York; Basic Books, 1961.

Linndeman, E. Symptomatology and Management of Acute Grief, *American Journal of Psychiatry*, 101, 1944, 141-148.

Litwack, L., Litwack, J., Ballou, M. *Introduction to Health Counseling*, New York: Appleton-Century-Crofts, 1980.

Maslow, A. *Toward a Psychology of Being*, 2nd ed., New York: Van Nostrand Company, 1968.

Miller, K., & Iscoe, L. The Concept of Crisis: Current Status and Mental Health Implications, *Human Organizations*, Fall 1963, 22, 195-201.

Morrice, J.K.W. *Crisis Intervention: Studies in Community Care*, New York: Pergamon Press, 1976.

*Parad, H.J. (Ed.) *Crisis Intervention: Selected Readings*, New York: Family Service Association of America, 1965.

Parad, H.J. & Caplan, G. In H. Parad (Ed.) *Crisis Intervention: Selected Readings*, New York: Family Service Association of America, 1965.

Rapoport, L. Working with Families in Crisis: An Exploration in Preventive Intervention, *Social Work*, July 1972, 17 (4).

Rapoport, L. Crisis Oriented Short Term Casework, *Social Services Review*, 41: 38 (March 1967).

Renshaw, H. Suicide and Depression in Children, *The Journal of School Health*, 1974, 64 (9).

Rusk, T. Opportunity and Technique in Crisis Psychiatry, *Comprehensive Psychiatry*, (12) 1971.

Schantz, F.C. *Reactions to Crisis*. Paper presented at Speech and Hearing Workshop, Kansas University Medical Center, 1961.

Sifncos, P.E. A Concept of Emotional Crisis, in *Prevention of Mental Disorders in Children*, ed. Caplan, G., New York: Basic Books, 1961.

*Specter, G.A. & Claiborn, W.L. (eds.). *Crisis Intervention*. New York: Human Science Press, 1973.

Spiegal, J.P. The Resolution of Role Conflict Within the Family, *Psychiatry*, 1957, 20 (1), 9.

---

* Indicates especially good readings of crisis and crisis intervention.

Chapter Seven

THE HANDICAPPED CHILD

JOSEPH C. ROTTER

The Law

At last we have been granted the opportunity to fulfill a goal of guidance through the enactment and gradual implementation of P.L. 94-142, the Education for All Handicapped Children Act of 1975. By 1980, all handicapped persons between the ages of three and twenty-one must have available to them a free and appropriate public education.

There are approximately *eight million* (1977 Bureau of Education for the Handicapped) identified handicapped young people in this country with countless others who may never be served for lack of identification for many reasons. Many are considered embarrassments for their families and thus withheld from helpful services. Others go undetected because of absent or inadequate preventive evaluative measures.

The law defines "handicapped" children as those who are mentally retarded, hard of hearing, deaf, speech imparied, visually impaired, severely emotionally disturbed, orthopedically impaired, other health impaired, or hampered by specific learning disabilities.

Disability vs. Handicap

Although the law and much of the literature makes reference to persons with *handicaps*, in fact, the person has a disability. A handicap is something which is imposed upon someone who has a physical or emotional disability. Society is replete with handicapping conditions, such as architectural barriers, attitudinal barriers, cultural biases, and limited educational opportunities. It is the responsibility of that same society to "de-handicap" the environment to accommodate for the multiplicity of disabilities.

Since the term "handicapped" is used synonymously with disability in the literature and the law, it will likewise be used in this chapter. The commentary on handicapping conditions versus disabilities is offered as additional stimulation, if not complete justification, for, carrying the intent of the law to its limit, thus providing a free and appropriate public education for all handicapped children in the least restrictive environment and protecting the rights of the child and his/her parents as citizens and human beings.

These least restrictive environments include an array of alternative placements for the handicapped child. These alternatives are perhaps best described by the "cascade system of educational placement" (1977).*

LEAST RESTRICTIVE ALTERNATIVE

Level 1	Exceptional children in regular classes, with or without supportive services
Level 2	Regular class attendance plus supplementary instructional services
Level 3	Part-time Special class
Level 4	Full-time special class
Level 5	Special Stations
Level 6	————————Homebound—————————
Level 7	Instruction in hospital, residential, or local care settings

Assignment of pupils to settings governed primarily by the school system.

Assignment of individuals to the settings governed primarily by health, correctional welfare, or other agencies.

Special schools in public school system

As can be seen, any number of possible placements or combination of placements will apply in order for the law to be carried out to its full intent. The counselor must play a major role, as advocate for the child, in helping to secure the most appropriate placement.

---

*   The Cascade system of educational placement.
      From Bureau of Education for the Handicapped, 1977.

The Counselor's Role

The clearly definied counselor role in the middle school has been addressed elsewhere in this book and therefore need not be reiterated here. However, one reminder in support of the counselor's involvement in the education of the handicapped child is warranted. The counselor in the school should be an advocate for *all* children and thus provide comprehensive services to all. This *all* includes the handicapped child.

Indeed, counselors are serving the handicapped child as a recent study by Huber and Westling (1978) discovered. They found in their study of counselors in 67 counties in Florida that 93% of the middle school counselors surveyed worked in schools which had classes for the mildly retarded. One hundred percent of these counselors were providing counseling services for the retarded children in their schools.

Sproles, Panther and Lanier (1978) ably state: "The true success of PL 94-142 does not lie in fulfilling concrete tasks and conditions set forth by the law but rather in the attitudes of the persons involved" (p. 212). Disabled people themselves indicate that it is not so much the functional limitations but the attitudes of others that is so debilitating (Fix, 1977). Who else but counselors can provide the preventive, developmental, positive orientation to these children?

How and in what way should the counselor get involved?

Kameen and Huber (1979) in a survey of special educators in one state found the following priority rankings when educators were asked two questions:

What counselor activities should be emphasized most in working with disabled children? The data provided the following rankings –

1. Individual counseling

2. Parent consultation

3. Teacher consultation

4. Group counseling

5. Testing and evaluation

6. Referrals

7. Classroom group guidance

What topical areas should provide the focus for these activities? The rankings were –

1. Attitudinal

2. Behavioral

3. Interpersonal

4. Motivational

5. Personal Care

6. Informational

They concluded from the study that special educators felt that counselors should continue to serve in the capacity of counselor and not become quasi special educators. The authors of this book concur with these conclusions. The role the counselor assumes in mainstreaming the handicapped child should be directly related to the present functions of consulting, and coordinating. When there is an imbalance in any direction the counselor is being misused.

For example, some counselors have been responsible for coordinating placement meetings, securing parent permissions, and maintaining the child's file. When this happens, the counseling and consulting functions are necessarily neglected. If counselors are actually administering standardized instruments, they are being misused. Certainly counselors should be knowledgeable about measurement and evaluation to the extent that they should be able to interpret tests for children, parents and teachers as part of their counseling or consulting functions, but test administration should be someone else's job. The counselor's greatest contribution in implementing PL 94-142 is in the role of consultant to teachers and other school personnel, to parents, and to children to help them understand and accommodate this new person in the classroom (Rotter, 1979).

This does not imply that the counselor can afford to ignore the multi-dimensional complexities of integrating the handicapped child into the school setting. However, it should all be viewed from the counselor's uniquely established role in the school setting.

Specifically, the law states that,

> It is the purpose of this act to assure that all handicapped children have available to them . . . a free, appropriate public education which emphasizes special education and *related services* (italics added) designed to meet their needs. (Bureau, 1977)

It is this area of *related services* that involves the counselor most directly. The law goes on to delineate the following provisions:

1. The right to a free and appropriate education

2. Due process procedures for parents and children

3. Non-biased evaluation

4. Placement in the least restrictive environment

5. Individualized educational program (IEP)

More specifically, the counselor will find himself/herself involved in many if not all of the following activities as they relate to the handicapped child:

1. Personal adjustment
2. Attitudes toward persons who are handicapped
3. Self concept
4. Adjustment to disability
5. Sexuality and family life
6. Development of independent living skills
7. Interpersonal relationships
8. Group counseling
9. Group bibliotherapy
10. Educational placement
11. Course selection
12. Architectural accessibility
13. Career development
    Vocational Assessment
    Work adjustment
14. Protection of human subjects
15. Nondiscriminatory testing
16. Parent involvement
17. Communication skills

The counselor's ethical role regarding the protection of the dignity of the individual and due process is implicit throughout the process of implementing PL 94-142 in the schools. It behooves the counselor, therefore, to be familiar with the due process procedure when dealing with the handicapped and, for that matter, all the children in the school. A sample statement regarding due process used in one school district is included for your information in Appendix B.

The counselor must work with the following populations in an attempt to make the transition for the handicapped child least traumatic:

1. the handicapped child
2. other children in the school
3. teachers
4. parents of the handicapped child

5. other parents

6. the school administrators

7. the community

There is a very subtle form of discrimination directed toward the handicapped child in the regular classroom. Yet, a handicapped child's presence can be used as a positive learning experience for everyone. The counselor can observe the interactions among children and between teachers and children to discover what type of discrimination exists. The counselor can then consult with the teacher and assist in conducting classroom activities on topics such as likenesses and differences, acceptance of others, and group cooperation (Rotter, 1979).

The counselor should conduct teacher inservice and discussion groups to help teachers relate to the affective effects of differing handicapping conditions and learn how to relate to handicapped children in the regular classroom. Likewise, the counselor should conduct parent groups, including both parents of the handicapped and non-handicapped, which would focus on a sharing of concerns, problems, and anxieties. Such experiences can help parents realize the similarities in their children as well as reduce the anxieties of parents of non-handicapped children with regard to the presence of handicapped children in the regular classroom (Rotter, 1979).

To obtain a detailed description of the counselor's role regarding the handicapped, the reader is encouraged to pursue some of the readings listed in the references at the end of the chapter as well as to enroll in workshops and coursework on this topic, for as Humes (1978) states:

> Counselors will be increasingly involved in program planning, mainstreaming efforts, program monitoring, and counseling parents. Counselors are advised to understand the law and to prepare for it rather than have it thrust upon them. (p. 192)

Learning Disabilities Checklist

The following checklist can be most helpful to counselors, teachers and parents in identifying perhaps the most difficult to detect handicap, learning disabilities.

They cannot be seen as readily as other disabilities such as orthopedic, visual, or auditory problems. There are, however, certain warning signals that indicate that a child may be having some achievement or social problems. The New York Institute for Child Development (1977) offers the following learning disabilities checklist for grades one through eight:

1. Does your child have difficulty understanding what he/she reads?
2. Does your child avoid sports or activities that involve catching and throwing a ball?
3. Is your child very afraid of heights? (i.e., won't climb on the jungle jim; doesn't like to be picked up)
4. Is your child extremely daring?
5. Does your child's running seem uncoordinated or sloppy?
6. Does your child get lost frequently?
7. Is your child easily distractible?
8. Does your child confuse right from left?
9. Does your child use one hand for some things and the other hand for other things?
10. Is your child always up and down from the table during meals?
11. Is your child a discipline problem?
12. Does your child go up or down stairs one step at a time?
13. Does your child seem very bright and articulate when in conversation but cannot seem to understand what he/she reads?
14. Is your child the class clown?
15. Is your child not working up to his/her potential?
16. Does your child seem to "tune-out" at times?
17. Is your child unusually forgetful?
18. Does your child find it necessary to touch everything he/she sees?
19. Does your child frequently walk into things or trip?
20. Is there inconsistency in your child's performance? (One day performs a task well, the next day can't)
21. Does your child have a short attention span?
22. Does your child move his/her lips while reading or follow the line with his/her fingers?
23. Does your child get frequent headaches?
24. Is your child ever purposely destructive?
25. Does your child frustrate easily?
26. Is your child unusually sensitive to light, noise, touch, or certain clothing material?
27. Was your child a late walker?
28. Was your child a prolonged tip-toe walker?
29. Was your child's speech late or abnormal?
30. Is your child a bed-wetter?
31. Does your child have uncontrollable rage reactions?
32. Does your child complain of seeing things bigger or smaller than they are?
33. Is your child unable to keep up with the other children's activity levels?
34. Does your child have a poor appetite?
35. Does your child have a history of allergies?
36. Is your child irritable before and/or shortly after meals?
37. Does your child crave sweets?
38. Has your child experienced excessive weight loss or gain?

39. Does your child frequently go out of the lines when coloring?
40. Did your child have trouble learning how to tie and/or button and/ or lace?
41. Was your child colicky?
42. Was your child an unusually cranky baby?
43. Was your child an unusually passive baby?
44. Is your child a bully?
45. Is your child always picked on by his peers?
46. Is your child a loner?
47. Does your child seek out older or younger playmates?
48. Does your child's walking or running seem clumsy or disjointed?
49. When your child reads out loud, does he/she get mixed up or lose his/ her place?
50. Does your child not complete his/her homework assignments?

If the child displays at least 10 of these signals there should be concern that the behaviors may be interfering with academic achievement or positive social relationships. Counselors, parents, and teachers must work together to help identify these characteristics so that preventive measures may be taken.

Any external evaluative tool, however, should be used only as a part of a comprehensive screening process which includes input from the child himself/herself. In addition, counselors, like teachers, must be aware of the learning style, be it auditory, visual, or tactile, that best enhances learning for each child.

Conclusion

PL 94-142 has increased the counselor's role in the elementary school. A caution that must be observed is that in trying to serve a larger population counselors could begin to focus on putting out fires and thus lose their preventive emphasis (Rotter, 1979).

The law has brought affect in education to the forefront. The affect created in a classroom, school, and community by the inclusion of handicapped children in the mainstream of society is tremendous. All of us will grow from this forward step in education.

REFERENCES and ADDITIONAL READING

Bureau of Education for the Handicapped, 1977.

Buscaglia, L. (Ed.) *The disabled and their parents: a counseling challenge.* Thorofare, New Jersey: Charles B. Slack, 1975.

Chiba, C., & Semmel, M. Due process and least restrictive alternative: new emphasis on parental participation. *Viewpoint,* 1977, 53, 17-29.

Cochrane, P.V., & Manini, B. Mainstreaming exceptional children: the counselor's role. *School Counselor,* 1977, 25, 17-22.

Cohen, S. Improving attitudes toward the handicapped. *Educational Forum,* 1977, 42, 9-20.

Deblassie, R.R., & Cowan, M.A. Counseling with the mentally handicapped child. *Elementary School Guidance and Counseling,* 1976, 10, 246-253.

Dwokey, D. Mainstreaming: Moving special education out of the basement. *Compact,* 1977, 10, 2-5.

Education of handicapped children, Part II. *Federal Register,* 1977, 42, (163).

Fairchild, T.N. *Counseling exceptional children.* Austin, Texas: Learning Concepts, 1977.

Fix, C., & Rohrbacker, J.A. What is a handicap? The impact of attitudes. *Personnel and Guidance Journal,* 1977, 56, 176-178.

Gearheart, W.R., & Weisham *The handicapped child in the regular classroom.* St. Louis, Calif.: C.V. Mosby, Co., 1976.

Gickling, E., & Theobald, J. Mainstreaming: Affect or effect. *Journal of Special Education,* 1975, 9, 317-328.

Hammill, D.D., & Bartel, N.R. *Teaching children with learning and behavior problems.* Boston: Allyn and Bacon, 1978.

Huber, C., & Westling, D. The school guidance counselor and the mildly retarded: roles and preparation. *Mental Retardation,* 1978, 15, 174-177.

Humes, C.W. School counselors and PL 94-142. *School Counselor,* 1978, 25, 192-195.

Kameen, M.C. (Ed.) Special issue on creating least restrictive environments for handicapped children. *Elementary School Guidance and Counseling,* 1979, 13, 150-228.

Kameen, M.C., & Huber, C.H. Counselors and disabled children: the special educators viewpoint. *School Counselor,* 1979, 27, 24-27.

Lasker, J. *He's my brother.* Chicago: Whitman, 1974.

Learning disabilities checklist. The New York Institute for Child Development, Inc., 1976.

McDowell, R. Parent counseling: the state of the art. *Journal of Learning Disabilities,* 1976, 9, 614-619.

Morse, D. Counseling the young adolescent with learning disabilities. *School Counselor,* 1977, 25, 8-16.

Parks, L.A., & Rousseau, M.K. *The Public Law supporting mainstreaming.* Austin, Texas: Learning Concepts, 1977.

Rotter, J.C. in McIntosh, D., Minifie, E., Rotter, J., Selmond, T. & Turner, K. PL 94-142 and the elementary school counselor: an interview. *Elementary School Guidance and Counseling,* 1979, 13, 152-163.

Semmel, S.S. (project director) *A Manual on Individualized Education Programs: The Classroom Teachers Perspective.* Bloomington, Indiana: Center for Innovation in Teaching the Handicapped, 1979.

Shank, F.A. Developing positive attitudes toward exceptional children: A tested technique. *Guidance Clinic,* 1979, May, 15-16.

Shotel, J., Iano, R., & McGettigan, J. Teacher attitudes associated with the integration of handicapped children. *Exceptional Children,* 1972, 38, 677-683.

Sproles, J.A., Panther, E.E., & Lanier, J.E. PL 94-142 and its impact on the counselor's role. *Personnel and Guidance Journal,* 1978, 210-212.

Chapter Eight

The COUNSELOR'S WORK WITH SPECIAL POPULATIONS:

EDUCATION FOR CHOICE

NANCY H. WILSON

> You risked your life, but what else have you ever
> risked? Have you ever risked disapproval? Have you
> ever risked economic security? Have you ever risked a
> belief? I see nothing particularly courageous in risking
> one's life. So you lose it, you go to your heroes heaven
> and everything is milk and honey til the end of time.
> Right? You get your reward and suffer no earthly
> consequences. That's not courage. Real courage is
> risking something you have to keep on living with,
> real courage is risking something that might force you
> to rethink your thoughts and suffer change and stretch
> consciousness. Real courage is risking one's cliches.
>
> Tom Robbins

Special populations, such as the culturally different, minorities and women, present a unique challenge to the profession of counseling. Our nation has been called the "melting pot" of the world with its diverse blend of ethnic, racial and religious groups. We espouse equality for all but our educational system is one of many societal institutions which has so far failed to adequately live up to our own ideals. Equal opportunity in adult life can be a reality only when equal preparation and foundations have been laid in childhood years.

This chapter addresses the problem of stereotyping and the middle school counselor's role in working with special populations. Counselors of school-age children are in a particularly opportune position to positively affect the course of male and female development of both minority and majority groups. The full development of human potential requires an optimal education. An optimal education as here defined is one that provides an environment and experiences which prepare any individual to make and implement meaningful choices about the pattern of his/her life with horizons being determined solely by personality, ability and individual choice. School counselors can be a vital force in effecting this reality.

104

Generalizations vs. Stereotypes

All individuals operate from a frame of reference which enables them to structure, understand and interact with the world. Included in such a framework are assumptions concerning the nature of people. Consequently, it is highly unlikely that any person can enter a situation or encounter without forming first impressions which are influenced by personal experiences and values. Our past and present lend subtle to bold hues to the way we color the "objective" reality of present interactions. Such impressions and generalizations about human behavior are necessities, but should be merely guidelines which are tentatively employed and remain constantly open to alteration, amendment, and challenge.

Generalizations, however, can either continue as generalizations or become stereotypes. Sue (1977) defines stereotypes as —

> rigid preconceptions we hold about *all* people who are members of a particular group, whether it be defined along racial, religious, sexual or other lines. Belief in a perceived characteristic of the group is applied to all members without regard for individual variations. (p. 5)

The inherent and obvious danger of such oversimplified generalizations is that they blind the holder to logic or reason. Input is slanted to fit with prior misconceived beliefs and attitudes.

The history of the evolution of civilization contains many instances of intense feelings and unbending views between members of diverse cultures. Consider the stereotypical views between the Romans and Barbarians, the English and Irish, the Americans and Indians, the Nazis and Jews, to name but a few examples. Rigidly held, culture-specific beliefs were tenaciously held even in the face of contradictory logic and evidence, and most often they were in some way harmful to the individuals so classified.

Sexism and racism are not new problems. They have a history spanning centuries. Although the specific stereotypic beliefs have varied, depending upon the time, place and groups involved, it is fair to say that these views were unflattering at the least and most often were derisive, contemptuous and degrading. Some infamous, overt stereotypes still encountered today are of Blacks as happy-go-lucky, watermelon-eating Sambos with fat, eye-rolling mammies; of Chicanos as sombrero-clad peons or fiesta-loving macho banditos; of Puerto Ricans as switchblade-carrying teenage gang members; and of Poles as stupid, senseless morons. In religious doctrines women have been said to be responsible for the evil of the world (Genesis 2:4-3:24); a curse according to an orthodox Jewish prayer blessing God for not making the reciter a heathen, slave or a woman; and patently inferior to man according to the Islamic Koran.

Minorities throughout history have taken the brunt of stereotypic thinking and prejudicial actions. Socialization practices have
tended to train minorities and women "to know their place" and unfortunately, such practices are still encountered today despite their
sometimes more subtle demeanors. The one fact that continues to be
unrecognized is that men and women, majorities and minorities are
all detrimentally affected by assumptions of superiority/inferiority
in that each is unable to benefit from the potential contributions of
the other toward the end of mutual gain. It is a no-win game.

Our schools must accept partial responsibility for perpetuation
of antiquated patterns and beliefs. Education must take a thorough
look at where we have been, where we are, and where we need to go.
Just as we have been a major factor in perpetuating outmoded myths,
so likewise can we be instigators of new patterns of thoughts and behaviors.

The School as an Agent of Change

It shall be unlawful for any person to discriminate
on the basis of age, race, sex or national origin.

Legal and judicial precedent have construed the "equal protection" clause of the Fourteenth Amendment of the United States
Constitution to protect all citizens against discrimination, yet it
occurs in varying degrees each day all around us. It is apparent that
legal reform has failed to cure these ills. Although our culture has, to
some degree, undergone social reform in the last twenty years, it too
has failed to wipe out discimination because its underlying belief and
attitude bases have yet to be discarded. Stereotypes and prejudices
are learned behaviors and, as such, can be unlearned if directed effort
is applied.

Even if wholesale societal reform were accomplished, however,
would these individuals be able to take advantage of the opportunity
to make meaningful personal choices? The answer is a decided "no",
unless developmental work is done to equip these individuals to
recognize and respond to the opportunities afforded by the environment. The limits minorities and women often put on themselves are
as significant as the effects of overt discrimination.

It is apparent that remediation alone is not the key. Education
as a major societal institution must address itself to both remedial
and developmental aspects of this issue in an effort to provide both
the atmosphere and requisite responding abilities which will enable
individuals to fulfill their potentials.

Educational Goals

Minuchin (1972) outlined four goals or tasks relevant to the education of a liberating society and development of decision-making abilities in its individual members. The goals are:

(1) *Minimization of stereotypes.* The school should stress the development of an atmosphere which expects and values variety, acknowledges changing patterns and encourages investigation, and minimizes the probabilty of a "self-fulfilling prophecy" with regard to sexually or racially linked behavior wherein the growing child increasingly can come to exemplify the attitudes, roles and adjustments that society predicts for him/her rather than freely choosing personal life patterns.

(2) *Provision of broad exposure to experiences, ideas and models.* Instead of presenting limited alternatives, the school must provide the most effective, broad, and involving exposures to ideas, media and people so that knowledge can be integrated and is available to the child over the years, thereby putting children at the center of their learning process.

(3) *Education in skills for choice, problem-solving, and evaluation.* Children must be exposed to and experience the process of skillful problem-solving and decision-making during the schooling process so that the ability is cultivated to be able to think about and direct one's own life; to tolerate confusion and uncertainty; to develop alternatives; and to experiment, make decisions and evaluate the end product.

(4) *Enhancement of self-differentiation and self-knowledge.* An optimal educational atmosphere requires not only that the child come to know his/her adequacy in formal comparative terms, as is done in traditional evaluative procedures, but that she/he also come to know and value self as a unique individual, with a personal pattern of interests, skills, feelings and relationships.

All schools have formal goals in the physical, social, emotional and intellectual domains. As effective agents of change, the school must deal with the concerns of racism and sexism within all four areas. The middle school counselor will most likely concentrate on the social and emotional realms at both remedial and developmental levels, but she/he must be aware of integrating the guidance program with other existing programs in the school and/or be a factor in instituting such other programs where they do not exist.

The Middle School Counselor

THE COUNSELOR'S WORK WITH SPECIAL POPULATIONS
Working with Females: Special Considerations

U.S. Department of Labor statistics report that nine out of ten females will work some time during their life. Further, half the women in the United States between ages 18 and 65 are in the labor force, the percentage continually rising. It is predicted that 11,000,000 additional females will join the work force in the next decade and by 1990, the full-time homemaker will be a distinct minority. It is true that our culture is undergoing radical economic and social changes which show no signs of rapid deceleration or reversal.

A pertinent question for schools today is whether young girls are being prepared to meet the challenges that lie ahead. With respect to the school counselor, what role can she/he play in helping young girls gain that foundation which will enable them to plan realistically and reach out for personal success and happiness in whatever form that might take?

Many girls still grow up with an unrealistically romantic image of life — school, marriage, family and live happily ever after. But the reality of our culture tells us that this is the atypical rather than typical pattern. A more typical life pattern of today's female includes school, work and/or marriage, rearing a family (sometimes combined with work by choice or necessity) and return to work after the youngest child begins school. The odds for any given female being employed outside the home during some period in her life are high indeed. This quiet revolution in our culture presents a special challenge to those responsible for counseling young females.

Counseling as a profession is first and foremost concerned with the development and utilization of all human resources. "Education for choice" is a key phrase, yet subtle factors operating in our whole socialization process do not afford this right to all members of our culture, including females. Whether a female follows the traditional roles or explores new options is not the issue, for either route is totally honorable. Having the right to make such choices for oneself after free exploration of the alternatives is the challenging issue.

Female Socialization and Conflict

As Carmichael (1977) observed, each child is color-coded at birth. The baby's name is typed on a pink-for-girl, blue-for-boy card and put on the bassinet in which is placed the child, wrapped in a pink or blue blanket lest a bystander lose sight of its intrinsic girlness or boyness and mistake it for a baby.

Babies are all born the same color — a blue-gray translucence. Only with the first moments of life and the baby's initial breath does the child begin to change from blue-gray to black, white, brown or yellow. Indeed all children are born equal, but immediately race is noted and sex is checked. From that moment on, the world begins imprinting on that individual what it wants from a white boy, black girl, yellow female, or brown male. Such expectations are varied, contingent on race, sex and social class.

From early years, the child learns what is approved and what is disapproved. Little boys are thrown up into the air and caught with glee, but few dare to do the same with little girls because they are supposedly too "fragile". The language of non-verbal communication sometimes overrides that which is voiced aloud.

The work of Maccoby and Jacklin (1974) cites studies documenting different treatment of girls and boys, and though no conclusive proof was found that children consistently are treated differently because of sex, they do find that children are reinforced for engaging in sex-typed behaviors. So, as the old saying goes, boys will be boys and girls will be girls. Or perhaps more accurately, boys will be as they are told boys will be and likewise for girls. Children in elementary school often evidence behavioral and achievement patterns consistent with sex-role expectations. Thus, if the school expects little boys to be aggressive and little girls to act helpless and stay out of aggressive activity, chances are great the expectations will be fulfilled. Similarly, if males are expected to excel in math, while females bumble through, that is usually the outcome.

A significant concern in working with females is the enhancement of sound, strong self-images from early ages. Tradition has shown this to be a primary problem area. Much research, including that of Broverman, Broverman, Clarkson, Rosenkrantz & Vogel (1970) has shown that the masculine stereotype is more positively viewed by both males and females.

According to our culture, boys are clever, independent, brave, rational, confident, creative, assertive, stoic, objective, resourceful, competent, noisy, active, analytical, courageous, unsentimental, autonomous, aggressive, competitive, and initiative. Girls, by contrast, are docile, kind, subjective, intuitive, dependent, helpful, neat yielding, receptive, innocent, conforming, passive, nurturant, empathic, and sensitive (Bardwick & Douvan, 1972; Lerner, 1974; Williams, 1977). Such differences carry over to vocational aspirations, with the majority of males choosing varied and active careers and females choosing traditional and nurturing options (Looft, 1971).

Despite this more positive male image, both sexes are limited, however. Males are told to repress emotions, be successful, competitive and physically agile, while females receive the message that physical attractiveness and sexuality is their most valuable asset and marriage the road to personal fulfillment (Guidette, Glitzer & Greenwood, 1976).

Females are caught in a double bind. Competence is viewed as a masculine trait, and our culture values achievement and competence. So if a girl chooses competence, she is dubbed "masculine"; and if she rejects it, she learns to degrade herself. Baruch (1973) and Connell & Johnson (1970) found that the higher a girl's score on a femininity standard test scale, the lower her self-esteem. It seems a clear case of being doomed if she does and doomed if she does not. Fear of social rejection seems to be a crucial factor in perpetuation of sex-typed behavior, a view consistent with the research of Horner (1974) which found a general fear of success pattern in females.

Psychological theories contend that adequate sex-role development is a critical hurdle. Included in this concept is the need to be like most members of the same sex, yet research supports this as advantageous only for the male. By contrast, healthy self-concepts and adequate adjustment are negatively related to being feminine and to identification with the mother (Connell & Johnson, 1970; Gray, 1959; Heilbrun, 1968).

Another area of conflict in female acculturation is optimal cognitive development. Longitudinal research has repeatedly revealed a disturbing pattern. Kangas & Bradway (1971) reported results of a study in which pre-schoolers were administered intelligence tests in 1931 and these same individuals were again tested some forty years later. They found that the more intelligent the boys were, the more they gained in intelligence with age. Conversely with girls, the brighter they were, the less they gained. Almost a decade before that, Kagan & Moss (1962) found that children of both sexes least likely to gain in intelligence were those highest in femininity traits and those most likely to gain were to a higher degree emotionally independent, a trait common in boys but often neither approved of nor encouraged in young girls.

Lack of encouragement from family and friends seemed to be a critical factor in the decision of fewer women than men in one study to go on to graduate school, despite the superiority of the women's grades (Baird, 1973). A critical message to those responsible for fostering healthy development in all children of all ages should be the clear need for encouragement of intellectual pursuits without the hidden message attached to be successful only so far.

Moving against the system is hard work and without an adequate base of self-sufficiency, self-confidence and support from significant influence persons, it would be the rare individual who would be successful. The path is always filled with conflicts and dilemmas, but to the person with a lack of self-confidence, they often seem insurmountable. Perhaps a more sensible approach is to alter the system to impart the message that it is O.K. to succeed and to feel good about oneself. It is a basic human right.

To be optimally effective, therefore, the school counselor should be knowledgeable about the total cycle of female development, including the various psychological mechanisms hypothesized to account for female attitudes toward self and achievement. Among these cited by Wolleat (1979) are:

(1)   the motive to avoid success (Horner, 1974);

(2)   direct vs. vicarious achievement (Lipman-Blumen & Leavitt, 1976);

(3)   the home/career conflict (Farmer & Gohn, 1970); Matthews & Tiedeman, 1964);

(4)   delayed crystalization of occupational choice (Campbell, 1974; Harmon, 1975);

(5)   reduced academic self-confidence (Tomlinson-Keasey, 1974);

(6)   low risk-taking (Maccoby & Jacklin, 1974);

(7)   sex-role orientation (Alper, 1974; Entwisle & Greenberger, 1972);

(8)   stereotyping of activities as male domains, e.g., mathematics (Fennema & Sherman, 1977); and

(9)   the attribution of success to external factors and of failure to internal factors (Deaux, 1976). (p. 23)

The androgynous person is that individual who incorporates the most desirable and healthy characteristics by tradition attributed to either males or females. A desirable goal is to implement programs at *all* levels of the school which promote female development along androgynous lines.

Working with Minorities and the Culturally Different: Special Considerations

Just as females encounter culturally determined obstacles and roadblocks, so also do persons of different racial and ethnic origin. Schools are a major societal institution which serve to perpetuate the best of our culture. Unfortunately, they have helped to perpetuate some of the less desirable characteristics. A case in point is the preservation of unfair prejudice and bias toward those who are different from the dominant white, middle-class majority that our schools represent.

Wittingly or unwittingly, the school often imparts the message that "different" must be viewed in a framework where one entity by definition is better than another. But "different" does not imply superiority; it simply means there are variances among or between. In some issues, different can include variances in quality, but in the issues of race, ethnicity or sex, different is synonomous with neither inferiority nor superiority.

Consider the minorities and ethnic groups one can find in our culture. The United States has within its population representatives of most countries and nations of the world. We have persons of all races, all religions, and all political persuasions. We have subgroups who have been here for generations and those like the Vietnamese who have only in recent years been introduced to our country on any large scale.

We have a diverse, multicultural society, yet we in school conduct our programs at times as if our audience were made up entirely of children from the stereotypical white, middle class family composed of mother, father, and two children. In fact, however, in most schools children from such families are a distinct minority — perhaps the most privileged minority in terms of educational treatment.

Denying a child's culture is synonomous with denial of the child since all individuals are products of their culture. The child spends approximately seven hours a day in school, or less than one-fourth of his/her total week. The majority of the remaining time is spent within the child's native group. We sometimes wonder why the minority child might be having trouble relating or adjusting to the school environment. We must look at our system and ask if the culturally different child is being given a fair chance, or is she/he the proverbial stranger in a strange land.

Most children have the same basic needs — autonomy, self-dignity, personal integrity, acceptance and recognition as a person of worth. The school, and the counselor in particular, must strive to work within the framework of the children's culture and environment, helping them express feelings; define, understand and accept themselves; and recognize both their unique strengths and weaknesses.

Minorities face concerns similar to those described for women. The issues of tracking, lack of self-confidence and self esteem, inadequate development of life-planning skills, insufficient encouragement of cognitive development and lack of adequately informed educators to recognize the developmental hurdles critical to minorities as a result of being culturally different — are core concerns.

Counselor Attributes

Who can work with minority children most effectively? How helpful are the helpers? There is some research to indicate that the helpers are often more harmful than helpful. Let's look at some characteristics that seem to be common to the most effective counselors.

Self-awareness. First and foremost, a counselor should be aware of his/her own values and attitudes. When interacting with another person, you are not only learning about that other person, but are at the same time communicating information about yourself on both verbal and non-verbal levels. The counselor must strive to communicate congruent messages on all levels to the counselee that she/he is accepted and valued as a person of worth. The counselor must be able to convey the qualities of empathy, warmth, positive regard, congruence and authenticity. We must examine our own values about those who are culturally different and in turn recognize and deal with those attitudes which might overtly or covertly send unhelpful messages.

Cultural awareness. Outside of their parallel struggle for equality, there seem to be relatively few common elements among culturally different groups (Moore, 1974). For example, the counselor must not assume across the board that the lower class Puerto Rican child is like the lower class black child. They can be as different from one another as they are from the traditional white, middle-class child. Affective understanding is not enough when working with the culturally different.

The counselor should first identify those diverse groups represented in the school and make a concentrated effort to study their cultural heritage. For example, consider some differences between the white, middle-class child and his/her Puerto Rican counterpart. The Puerto Rican child is taught not to answer back or look up while being disciplined. Looking down is a measure of respect. Older brothers and sisters often serve as surrogate parents whom younger children are taught to heed. Such older siblings may attend conferences regarding the younger child. The parents may not speak English at all and are not used to receiving notes from service professionals concerning their children. Cultural tradition calls for home visits as opposed to visits to the school (Wilson, 1972). Such knowledge would be of obvious importance to a counselor working with a Puerto Rican child.

In addition to reading, it is perhaps most beneficial to learn by first-hand experience with these peoples. In order to better understand the values, goals and behaviors of the child from such cultures, experience and understanding of the group's religions, history, art, music, dance, and literature is needed. Experiencing and understanding cultural scripts are equally important to life scripts in the counseling process.

Language awareness. Often the language patterns of minority groups are different from those of standard English. Verbal communication is of obvious value in working with these children. Acceptance of a child's verbal and non-verbal language means acceptance of him/her. Likewise, rejection of the same means rejection of the child. Counselors can learn much about these children's personalities by being observant of communication patterns. For example, the verbal language of blacks is quite rich, the vernacular containing specific words which signify subtle differences in meaning rather than the use of modifiers such as adjectives or adverbs to communicate meaning (Smith, Barnes & Scales, 1974).

The counselor must be bilingual in such instances to the extent that she/he can recognize and understand such idioms well enough to establish communication with the child. In some areas, however, it is highly desirable if not necessary to speak another language. Parent contacts are sometimes impossible without it or a translator, not to mention its benefit in personal communication with the child.

Counseling repertoire. The counselor needs a flexible repertoire of counseling skills. The traditional individual and group counseling skills are necessary, but sometimes not sufficient in working with minority students. Language is of obvious value but is not always the most effective vehicle for change. In addition to the verbal approaches, the counselor should be familiar with those approaches which influence the environment of the child so that the child faces the consequences of his/her own behavior. This in many groups would extend to the family to affect optimal results.

The counselor must serve as a consultant to teachers and principals to help create a more sensitive and responsive educational environment. The counselor's skills in coordinating school and community resources to help the child are likewise a vital ingredient for success.

The counselor must also recognize the limitations of many standardized tests for these children. Whether it be the child whose ethnic group values accuracy over speed with inaccuracy, or the child who is having difficulty with the highly verbal nature of most tests, the counselor must be aware of the possible delimitations and consequences of misinterpretations.

The position of the counselor is indeed delicate. While assisting the culturally different child to partake fully of the social and economic resources of the larger culture, she/he must not sacrifice those qualities of uniqueness and value to the culture of the child. The danger of loss of personal identity by denying one's heritage is realized by the astute counselor. Flexibility and sensitivity are key ingredients.

Myers, Moore and Callao (1974) present a composite of the effective individual working with minority and culturally different children.

> Those who work with children as teachers or counselors need to be aware of their own value structures and prejudices. Children need to

experience both empathy and respect for their customs, patterns of behavior, and environmental conditions. Differences should be valued over homogeneity; within group differences should be looked at so that stereotypes and generalizations are avoided. The counselor and teacher must assume responsibility for their part in school-wide programs designed to foster understanding among students and staff. Culturally different children should be encouraged to feel that they are an integral part of the total school population, and all children should be helped to develop self-confidence, a positive self-image, and an appreciation of others. (p. 308)

IMPLEMENTATION
Activities and Resources

We have discussed many issues and concerns in the counselor's work with special populations. The goals seem clear, but the means toward achieving these goals are often somewhat less apparent. It is not intended that the reader construe the issues presented as either easily or quickly remedied. Overnight miracles are highly improbable, for these concerns and patterns have developed over an extended period of time. It is rather the intent of this chapter to clarify some of the issues and to present sample areas of concentration and activities to help counselors design their own strategies for their unique settings.

Counselors are encouraged to use all ideas with a generous blend of personal creativity. The majority of the suggestions listed below are adaptable to working with females and/or the culturally different with only slight variations.

Counselors, too, are encouraged to develop their own materials. Such materials should not only equalize the work and family roles of men and women, but should also reflect the multi-racial and ethnic makeup of our culture, the variety of sizes and shapes of people alone with contemporary hairstyles and dress. A large budget for these programs is not necessary. The counselor is limited only by his/her own imagination.

The following are areas of focus and resources which the middle school counselor can find helpful in the planning and implementation of a program to work with special populations.

(1) *Values clarification activities* are an excellent tool in helping individuals develop clear values by examining their own life experience. The emphasis is upon increasing the child's clarity of thinking and basis for thoughtful choosing. Such exercises allow children to examine critically their own attitudes and beliefs. Many activities are available in the following references, among others:

Simon, S.B.; Howe, L.W.; & Kirschenbaum, H. *Values Clarification: A Handbook of Practical Strategies for Teachers and Students.* New York: Hart Publishing Co., 1972.

Simon, S.B. *Meeting Yourself Halfway: Thirty-One Values Clarification Strategies for Daily Living.* Niles, Ill.: Argus Communications, 1974.

Rotter, J.C., & McFadden, J. *Values Orientations in School.* Charlotte, N.C.: Psychoeducational Press, 1978.

(2) *Self-awareness and self-concept enhancement* are areas of real concern in working with special populations. The counselor should include in his/her program a supportive environment through activities and opportunities for children to discover themselves, their strengths and weaknesses and be given an opportunity to develop a sense of adequacy and worth. Examples of the many sources for such activities are:

Canfield, J. & Wells, H. *100 Ways to Enhance Self-Concept in the Classroom.* New Jersey: Prentice-Hall, Inc., 1976.

Curwin, R. & Curwin, G. *Developing Individual Values in the Classroom.* California: Learning Handbooks, 1974.

Palomares, U.H., & Ball, G. *Magic Circle – Human Development Program.* La Mesa, California: Human Development Training Institutes, Inc., 1974.

(3) *Assertiveness training* is an effective tool to help children who have difficulty expressing what they need or want in an appropriate manner. Rasbaum-Selig (1976) describe a ten-session training model which was used with fifth and sixth graders. This approach has potential in working with females and the culturally different who have trouble with constructive assertion of individual needs and rights. Such a program would help students to discriminate between nonassertive, aggressive and assertive behavior; to become aware of their rights in various interpersonal situations; to be able to identify emotional blocks preventing them from acting assertively; to learn skills to reduce such blocks; and to develop assertive behaviors through behavior rehearsal.

Rasbaum-Selig, M. Assertive training for young people. *School Counselor,* 1976, *24,* 115-121.

Jakubowski-Spector, P. *An introduction to assertive training for women.* Washington, D.C.: APGA Press, 1973.

Lange, A., & Jakubowski, P. *Responsible assertive behavior: Cognitive-behavioral procedures for trainers.* Champaign, Ill.: Research Press, 1976.

(4) *Decision-making and problem-solving skills* allow an individual to assume a systematic problem-solving approach to making effective and wise decisions. Good decisions come from a sequence of steps beginning with identifying the problem, personal values and goals, and possible alternative solutions. Alternatives are critically examined, a decision is then made, tried out, and evaluated. This is an important life skill for all children, but most especially for special population students. Activities in this area are often found in sources on values clarification and self-concept enhancement since effective decision-making is a vital ingredient in both. Several additional resources:

Dupont, H., Gardner, O.S. & Brody, D.S., *Toward Affective Development.* Circle Pines, Minnesota: American Guidance Service, 1974.

Landon-Dahm, M. *An Affective Learning System for Group Facilitators.* Centerville, Ohio: Learning Development Systems, 1975.

(5) *Career education* is a most important area for working with special populations. An optimal education involves extensive and on-going career awareness activities for all children, but it is especially vital for these individuals if they are to be included in the mainstream of American life. Extensive materials have been developed for comprehensive career education programs. including the middle school level. Most state departments of education have these available to counselors.

(6) *Group guidance with a focus on stereotyping* is an excellent way to examine the issues involved. A large variety of media and approaches are available for use. A combination of discussion, personal recollection, role-playing, examination of media (TV, radio, books, etc.), interviewing and independent research are often helpful.

One consciousness-raising independent research activity, for example, is to have each child present the following riddle to five other people outside of class.

A father and son are in a car accident. The father is killed and the son is taken to the hospital. Because of the seriousness of his injury, a brain surgeon is called. The doctor arrives, looks at the boy and says, "I cannot operate on this patient. He is my son." How can this be?

Afterwards a group discussion should be conducted on the responses. The brain surgeon, of course, was the child's mother, but oftentimes the riddle is a stumper. The issues behind the stereotypical thinking are sometimes more apparent when combined with first-hand involvement.

In discussing minority groups, group discussion could be held on the concepts of majority and minority. Have the students recognize and discuss characteristics unique to minority groups. Have students identify feelings of majority and minority group members and discuss these feelings in relation to improving communication between the groups. Role-playing could be used.

The Emma Willard Task Force on Education prepared a collection of twenty-five consciousness raising activities directed toward issues of females. Most are adaptable with only slight variation to focus on issues of minorities and the culturally different. This list is available in *Sexism in Education,* 3rd ed., 1972 (Box 14229, University Station, Minneapolis, Minnesota, 55414). Also reprinted in Gersoni-Stavin, D. *Sexism and Youth.* New York: R.R. Bowker Company, 1974.

Commercially prepared materials are also available. Among these is the kit *Focus on Self-Development,* Stage Two, Responding (Science Research Associates), which has a unit on cultural differences. Eight children from various ethnic groups talk about their cultural backgrounds on one cassette recording. Points for discussion are included.

Free to Be You and Me is available in book, record, and film and can be used in whole or in part with middle school students. Its theme, that children must be free to choose for themselves from life's multitude of options, unhampered by stereotyping, is presented in a colorful and entertaining way which is stimulating to this age group.

> Book: Lagsbrun, F. (ed.) *Free to Be You and Me.* New York: McGraw-Hill, 1974.

> Record: Bell Records, Division of Columbia Picture Industries, Inc., 1776 Broadway, N.Y., N.Y. 10019. Also available at many record outlets.

> Film: McGraw-Hill Text Films, Dept. SF, 1221 Avenue of the Americas, N.Y., N.Y. 10020. Available in one 40-minute or three 15-minute reels.

(7) *Bibliocounseling* encourages children to focus on selected topics through reading materials. An excellent reference guide for appropriate reading materials for children is *The Bookfinder* (Guidance Associates). This volume is indexed by subject and author and provides a comprehensive listing of books on topics related to multicultural education and the problems of sexism and racism. Each entry has an abstract of the book and is referenced by age level. Other sources of listings are available through libraries and many bookstores.

In addition, it is helpful to teach children to monitor their own reading and the media for prejudice, discrimination and stereotyping since these media are powerful opinion shapers. The Council for Interracial Books suggests several guidelines for use in their pamphlet "10 Quick Ways to Analyze Children's Books for Racism and Sexism". In brief, they are:

1. Check the illustrations.
   Look for stereotypes.
   Look at roles portrayed. Who's doing what?

2. Check the story line.
   What are the standards for success?
   How are problems presented and resolved?
   What role do women/minorities play?

3. Look at the lifestyles.

4. Weigh the relationships between people.

5. Note the heroes and heroines.

6. Consider the effects on a child's self-image.
   Are norms established which limit the child's aspirations and self-concept?

7. Consider the author's or illustrator's background.

8. Check out the author's perspective.

9. Watch for loaded words.

10. Look at the copyright date.

The pamphlet with extended discussion of the guidelines is available from the Council at 1841 Broadway, New York, N.Y. 10023.

CONCLUSIONS

Standing at the interface of childhood and adolescence, the middle school child is in a delicate period of transition and change. The middle school counselor is in an apporture position to be a friend who helps ease the inevitable growing pains of confusion and uncertainty. It is in this setting that the counselor has the opportunity to facilitate responsible self-awareness, self-confidence, and self-reliance within these children.

The counselor has a unique challenge in working with special populations. Enhancement of an educational environment which encourages individuals to reach out and discover the possibilities is a multifaceted program which can include individual and group counseling, group guidance activities, consultation with parents, teachers and administrators and coordination of school and community resources to most adequately meet the needs of the individual child. Counselors must strive to be a model of culture-free, sex-fair practices and tactfully to encourage critical self-study by teachers and administrators whose programs and procedures significantly affect and guide the child's school experience.

The optimal multi-cultural education has yet to be realized. However, the disparity between real and ideal is a gap that can be bridged through care, sensitivity and much hard work on the part of concerned educators. Middle school counselors cannot fully achieve these goals alone, but neither should they fear to take the first step. Success breeds success. Through the efforts of the sensitive, caring counselor, it is possible to affect positively the quality of life for females, minorities and the culturally different. It is a goal worth the undertaking.

REFERENCES

Alper, T. Achievement motivation in women: now-you-see-it-now-you-don't. *American Psychologist*, 1974, *28*, 194-203.

Baird, L. *The graduates*. Princeton, N.J.: Educational Testing Service, 1973.

Bardwick, J., & Douvan, E. Ambivalence: the socialization of women. In J.M. Bardwick (Ed.), *Readings on the psychology of women*. New York: Harper & Row, 1972.

Baruch, G. The motive to avoid success and career aspirations of 5th and 10th grade girls. Paper presented at the meeting of the American Psychological Association, Montreal, August, 1973.

Baruch, G.K. The traditional feminine role: some negative effects. *School Counselor*, 1974, *21*, 285-289.

Broverman, I.K.; Broverman, D.M.; Clarkson, F.E.; Rosenkrantz, P.S.; & Vogel, S.R. Sex-role stereotypes and clinical judgments of mental health. *Journal of Consulting and Clinical Psychology*, 1970, *34*, 1-7.

Campbell, D. *SVIB-SCII manual*. Stanford, Calif.: Stanford University Press, 1974.

Carmichael, C. *Non-sexist childraising*. Boston: Beacon Press, 1977.

Connell, D.M., & Johnson, H.E. Relationship between sex-role identification and self-esteem in early adolescence. *Developmental Psychology*, 1970, *3*, 268.

Deaux, K. *The behavior of women and men*. Monterey, Calif.: Brooks/Cole, 1976.

Entwisle, D., & Greenberger, E. Adolescents' views of woman's work role. *American Journal of Orthopsychiatry*, 1972, *42*, 648-656.

Farmer, H., & Gohn, M. Home-career conflict reduction and the level of career interest in women. *Journal of Counseling Psychology*, 1970, *17*, 228-232.

Fennema, E., & Sherman, J. The study of mathematics by high school girls and boys: related variables. *American Educational Research Journal*, 1977, *14*, 159-168.

Gray, S. Perceived similarity to parents and adjustment. *Child Development,* 1959, *30,* 91-102.

Guidette, M.J.; Glitzer, B.; & Greenwood, J. Altering sex-role stereotypes: the soft sell. *School Counselor,* 1976, *24,* 128-131.

Harmon, L. Career counseling for women. In D. Carter & E. Rawlings (Eds.) *Psychotherapy for women: treatment toward equality.* Springfield, Ill: Charles C. Thomas, 1975.

Heilbrun, A. Sex-role identity in adolescent females: A theoretical paradox. *Adolescence,* 1968, *3,* 79-88.

Horner, M. The measurement and behavioral implication of fear of success in women. In M. Mednick, S. Tangri, & L. Hoffman (Eds.) *Women and achievement.* New York: Wiley, 1975.

Kagan, J., & Moss, H. *Birth to maturity.* New York: Wiley, 1962.

Kangas, J., & Bradway, K. Intelligence at middle age: A thirty-eight year follow-up. *Developmental Psychology,* 1971, *5,* 333-337.

Lerner, H.E. Early origins of envy and devaluation of women: implications for sex role stereotypes. *Bulletin of the Menninger Clinic,* 1974, *38,* 538-553.

Lipman-Blumen, J. & Leavitt, H. Vicarious and direct achievement patterns in adulthood. *The Counseling Psychologist,* 1976, *6*(1), 26-32.

Looft, W.R. Sex differences in the expression of vocational aspirations by elementary school children. *Developmental Psychology,* 1971, *5,* 366.

Maccoby, E.E., & Jacklin, C.N. *The Psychology of Sex Differences.* Stanford, Calif.: Stanford University Press, 1974.

Matthews, E., & Tiedeman, D. Attitudes toward marriage and career and the development of life style in young women. *Journal of Counseling Psychology,* 1964, *11,* 375-384.

Minuchin, P. The schooling of tomorrow's women. *School Review,* 1972, *80,* 199-208.

Moore, N.F. in Myers, D.D.; Moore, N.F.; & Callao, M.J. Issues and dialogue: counselors speak out. *Elementary School Guidance and Counseling,* 1974, *8,* 304-309.

Myers, D.D.; Moore, N.F.; & Callao, M.J. Issues and dialogue: counselors speak out. *Elementary School Guidance and Counseling,* 1974, *8,* 304-309.

Smith, G.S.; Barnes, E.; & Scales, A. Counseling: the black experience. *Elementary School Guidance and Counseling,* 1974, *8,* 245-253.

Sue, D.W. Generalizations, Yes — stereotypes, no! *Personnel and Guidance Journal,* 1977, *56,* 5.

Tomlinson-Keasey, C. Role variables: Their influence on female motivational constructs. *Journal of Counseling Psychology,* 1974, *21,* 232-237.

Williams, J.H. *Psychology of women: behavior in a biosocial context.* New York: Norton, 1977.

Wilson, C.E. An introduction to the Puerto Rican child. *Human Needs,* 1972, *1,* 10-14.

Wolleat, P.L. School-age girls. *The Counseling Psychologist,* 1979, *8,* 22-23.

Chapter Nine

CONSULTING

JOSEPH C. ROTTER

Give a man a fish and you feed him for a day. Teach
him to fish and you feed him for life.

Proverb

The middle school counselor has the role of consultant to teachers, parents, school administrators, and other significant persons in the life of a child. As middle school children begin to develop unique interests and strive for more autonomy, the adults in their world can enhance or thwart that developmental process. The counselor, through consultation with these other adults, can provide the mechanism which allows both children and adults to realize their goals. Generally, parents want their children to succeed. Success, however, often derives from parental ideals rather than a collaborative effort which considers the desires of the child. Parents and teachers often misunderstand the developmental needs of the middle school child. The counselor can be the agent to bridge the distance between what is and what can be.

This chapter will address the counselor's role as helper to these adults who are striving to better understand the middle school age child.

Systems of Consultation

Consultation is a process involving at least three parties: (1) the consultant whose services are sought; (2) the consultee; and (3) a third person or organization (the subject of the consultation).

The consultant may be viewed as having *expert knowledge* within the area of concern expressed by the consultee or may be seen as someone who can facilitate *problem solving* processes although not possessing an expertise in the subject matter. The traditional medical model and social work model as well as some mental health models assume the posture of the consultant as a content expert.

For example, a physician (consultee) may call a specialist (consultant) for advice on a given patient. The specialist, having expert knowledge regarding a certain illness, can advise the physician as to how to treat the case or the specialist may treat the patient directly. In most cases, however, the specialist will work directly with the patient and the referring physician does not apply the needed treatment known solely by the specialist. Furthermore, most patients would prefer to have the expert perform the necessary diagnosis and treatment especially when life or limb are involved. The following diagrams graphically demonstrate this process.

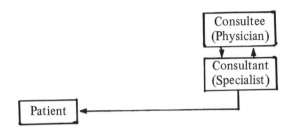

This system of consultation assumes an expert knowledge based on the part of the consultant, an expert is giving advice to a lesser expert (McClung and Stunden, 1970). For example, one definition of consultation has been offered by Caplan (1970) as ". . . a process of interaction between two professional persons – the consultant, who is a specialist, and the consultee, who involves the consultant's help in regard to a current work problem with which he is having some difficulty and which he has decided is within the other's area of specialized competence."

The problem solving approach to consultation may be described as follows: the consultee calls on the consultant with a problem regarding a client. The consultant assists the consultee in generating alternative means of resolving the problem. Through the consultation *process* the consultant helps the consultee arrive at solutions residing within the consultee or at his/her disposal. The consultant in this situation is not required to be an expert in the contact area but must possess certain facilitative problem solving skills. In this situation, the consultant would not likely work directly with the client. This model may be diagrammed as follows:

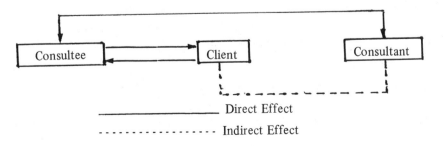

_____ Direct Effect

- - - - - - - - - - - - - - - - - Indirect Effect

This system assumes a collaborative relationship between consultant and consultee as defined by Lippitt (1959), Dinkmeyer and Carlson (1973), and Nelson (1973).

Dworkin and Dworkin (1975) use a table to identify and describe four models of consultation. (See Table 9:1.)

The four models (consultee centered, group process, social action, and ecological) represent the thinking respectively of Gerald Caplan (1959, 1970), Ronald Lippitt (1959, 1966, 1971); Lippitt, Watson and Westly (1958); Saul Alinsky (1969, 1970a, 1970b, 1972); and James Kelly (1966, 1968, 1969, 1970a, 1970b); Trickett, Kelly and Todd (1971).

The table shows the level and degree of involvement each model shares. As one reads from left to right the role of the consultant changes from expert to facilitator, to strategist, and lastly to that of a team member.

In addition, consultation may be viewed with regard to the inherent target populations. Mental health consultation (Caplan, 1970) is oriented to a clinical setting whereas social work consultation seems to be socially oriented (Kadushin, 1977). The former assumes more of a therapeutic role whereas the latter is educational in nature. There are other models of consultation reflecting a specialized field such as medical consultation or nursing patient consultation. However, the middle school counselor should derive his/her model of consultation through a synthesis of the clinically oriented mental health approach and the social work model. The counselor in the school setting is not limited to the confines of the school building but instead relates to many publics. The school building may be considered the clinic where controlled conditions, however eratic, exist. The community reflects the larger social milieu affecting his/her work as a consultant.

Consultation in the School Setting

Research regarding the effects of consultation has been encouraging. The consultant has been shown to be effective in working with consultees. However, little conclusive evidence exists to indicate that the consultant has had significant impact on the third party, e.g., the child in the classroom. Perhaps this is the fault of the research design. Much of the research to date has been limited in its consideration of the following variables: (a) impact variables, i.e., characteristics of the parties and problems; (b) process variables, i.e., techniques used; and (c) output variable, i.e., the changes resulting from consultation (Meyers, Parson & Martin, 1979). Continued and

Table 9:1: The Consultation Process — Four Models

Dimensions	Consultee-centered	Group process	Social action	Ecological
Definition of consultation	Process of interaction between two professionals; consultant and consultee	Voluntary relationship between a helper and a help-needing system	Relationship between a community and indigenous community leaders	Relationship between a professional team and an ecosystem
Self-perception of the consultant	Professional Expert Model Resource	Resource Model Facilitator Participant-observer	Community organizer Strategist	Planner Team member Researcher
Target Population	Professional care-givers	Social system or sub-system	Indigenous community leaders	Ecosystem (inter-related systems and sub-systems)
Motivation of client system	Anxiety Conflict Crisis	Organizational problem: Internal/external pressure "Images of potentiality"	Unmet basic human needs	Crisis initiated by maladaptation or malfunction of a social system
Entry	Sanctioned, invited short or long term	Invited or self-initiated short or long term	Invited or uninvited long term	Invited long term
Goals	Increased skills, understanding, knowledge, objectivity, mastery of feelings, crisis resolution	Organizational change Mobilization of creative resources Internal consultants	Transfer of power base Fulfillment of basic human needs	Awareness of system functioning Increased coping and adaptive mechanisms

Dworkin, American Journal of Community Psychology — June 1975.

more sophisticated research needs to be conducted to substantiate the effectiveness of the ever expanding consultant role of the middle school counselor.

Schowengerdt, Fine & Poggio (1976) discovered that consultants who displayed warmth, understanding, and empathy were significantly more likely to have teachers who were satisfied with consultation. He found that the quality of the interaction between the consultant and teachers was more important than the amount of time spent.

Consultation by school counselors has been defined by several writers in the field. Brown, Wyne, Blackburn & Powell (1979) state that ". . . consultation involves *indirect* service to . . . students by assisting others, such as teachers, to provide the needed intervention" (p. 4). They go on to say that —

> . . . consultation is usually a process based upon an equal relationship characterized by mutual trust and open communication, joint approaches to problem identification, the pooling of personal resources to identify and select strategies that will have some probability of solving the problem that has been identified, and shared responsibility in the implementation and evaluation of the program or strategy that has been initiated. A secondary outcome of consultation should be that both the consultant's and the consultee's repertoire of knowledge and skills will be enhanced to the end that both persons will function more effectively in similar situations in the future. (p. 8)

Nelson (1973) says that, "consultation is an exchange between equals involving listening and discussing in the interest of a child. It has the potential for releasing the creativity of the parent or teacher and counselor for the benefit of that child. Each person's ideas have a sounding board, and the outcome tends to occur" (p. 249).

Van Hoose (1968) offers four basic tenets in the consulting process:

1. Consultation is a collaborative effort at problem solving or prevention.

2. The purpose of the specific consulting relationship should be clarified.

3. Understanding of the individual roles and perceptions is a major goal.

4. Consultation should be a learning process for everyone involved.

There is a need for collaboration between consultant and consultee. The results of consultation reflect the mutual respect each party has for the other, not unlike the counseling relationship.

Speaking of counseling, Faust (1968) offers a distinction between consultation and counseling. He states that, "the primary difference can be found in (a) focus and (b) the kinds of relationships that are developed . . . (as consultant) the counselor focuses on some unit external to the consultee." p. 32-33.

Carlson (1975), in writing about the future of school counseling states, "counselors persist in dealing with the microcosm rather than the macrocosm in which the individual lives." What he is saying is that counseling has limitations. The counselor and child, if not cautious, can lose sight of the influences external to the counselor's cozy office.

This importance of consultation may be capsulized as follows:

1) It permits large segments of the population to be reached by relatively few significant people,

2) it provides a means for teaching guidance skills and principles to other significant persons in the child's life,

3) it can serve to develop, in school and at home, an awareness of the unique developmental concerns of the child and the resources to work with them,

4) it may be one solution to the problem of shortages of skilled counselors in the schools (Werner, 1978),

5) it may serve as a basis of information to those who need to keep abreast of developmental concerns.

Having carefully defined consultation and specifically school counselor consultation, let us turn now to the uniqueness of consultation in the middle school. As discussed in earlier chapters, the middle school child has qualities of children at other levels but certainly is unique. The counselor in the middle school is indeed in the middle — often functioning at an elementary school level and at times like that of the secondary school counselor — yet clearly unique. Children at this level display vast differences yet are much alike. They are often annoying to parents and uncooperative at school. They need as much guidance, patience and understanding as any age group to help them move to higher developmental levels. They are beginning to take that big step from parental dependence to self-sustaining initiative. This in itself can be as difficult for the adults in the child's life to accept as for the child himself/herself.

The consultant in the middle school can be viewed in relation to consultants at other levels by degree of emphasis devoted to this function. Perhaps the following diagram will help to distinguish consultation practice at the various levels.

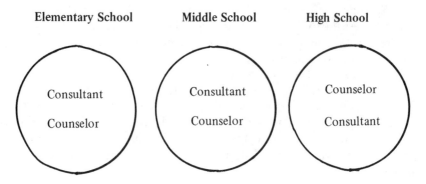

In simple terms, the child's development moves from a dependent social milieu to more independent personal phases as he/she moves through the school years. For example, the adults in a child's life are more overtly involved during the early school years. As the child moves through middle school the adults begin to lose their importance as the peer group becomes a greater influence. The amount of time devoted to consultation will generally capture less of the counselor's time as the child moves through the school years. This by no means implies that the skills necessary for consultation diminish but only perhaps the time needed or devoted to consultation changes. The intent of the diagram is not to suggest a standard for devotion of counselor time to these two functions but only to illustrate that the emphasis changes and to point out the uniqueness of the counselor's role at the middle school level.

Target Populations

The middle school counselor's role as consultant reaches many populations including parents, teachers, school administrators, children and community resources. The target consultee may not always be a person but could be a system. Examples of such systems would include the mass media, e.g., TV, radio, newspapers; community organizations, e.g., NAACP, YMCA, Girl Scouts, Rotary, churches, mental health; and governmental concerns, e.g., legislative bodies, family court, legal services, child advocacy groups. This section will develop the consultant's role as he/she works with these various consultees.

The two groups most likely to serve as consultees in the middle school are parents and teachers, as they relate to the pre-adolescent, who, at times, behaves like the child he or she was in earlier times and, at times, as an adolescent. The once close physical relationship begins to give way to distancing. Those once supportive adults are beginning to be viewed as inept, bungling idiots. This autonomous behavior often leads to strain between adults and the emerging adolescent.

Unlike the elementary school where parents often accompany their children to school the first day, the middle school child is beginning to reject the idea. If they don't ride the bus or walk they exit from the car as quickly as possible out of fear that they might be seen with these adults called parents. Parents and teachers have a difficult time predicting how this child will act. Thus, the desperate need for someone with whom they may consult.

When a parent or teacher brings a concern to the counselor, the following stages of the consulting process can be followed to facilitate movement and prevent defensive reactions.

Initial Stages of Consulting Process

1. Person comes with a problem.
2. Respond to expressed feelings.
3. Identify specific problem (be specific about behavior).
4. Look at antecedent behavior.
5. What happened after problem behavior?
6. What did you do (consultee)?
7. *"Open end"* – "Then what happened?"
8. How did you feel when child misbehaved?
9. Look at some positive aspects of the problem child.
10. How did you respond to him/her then?
11. How did you feel about him/her then?
12. Identify the goal or desired outcomes.
13. Observe and record relevant behavior.
14. Develop a plan.
15. Initiate the plan.
16. Follow-up.
17. Always remain calm, give hope, and buy time when necessary.

The following sample dialogue between a parent and counselor may clarify these stages:

    Co: I appreciate you letting me come over today. You mentioned that you have been having a problem with D.

    Cl: Yes, it is impossible to get D. ready for school in the morning without a big fight.

The Middle School Counselor

Co: Sounds like you're really frustrated.

Cl: Yes! By the time she's finally leaving for school I'm ready to wring her neck.

Co: Could you describe a typical morning for me — what happens, what time she gets up, what your routine is, things like that?

Cl: Well, we wake D. up at 7:00. By 7:15, if we're lucky, she might be out of bed and in the kitchen for breakfast. She . . .

Co: You've called her more than once to get her out of bed?

Cl: Usually several times. But if we don't, she just lies there.

Co: Does she answer? Is she awake?

Cl: Oh yeah, she's awake. She just doesn't want to get up. She complains she doesn't feel good or she's cold.

Co: What makes her finally get out of bed?

Cl: I do — or C. (father) does.

Co: How do you do that?

Cl: We yell a lot.

Co: How are you and C. feeling by this time?

Cl: Disgusted, and mad, and rushed.

Co: What happens next?

Cl: Well, she eats breakfast. Or I should say she plays with breakfast! (laughs) I guess you've really caught me on a good day. We had a horrible time with her this morning. I told C. before he left that you were coming over and that you couldn't have picked a better morning. I could really unload on you. D. really isn't a bad kid. This is the only thing she's really a problem about and we've tried everything we can think of, but nothing works.

Co: Let's go back to breakfast. You said she played at breakfast.

Cl: Well, it's not really playing. It's more that she fusses with her brother, or daydreams, or other things that waste time. She can stretch a five minute meal into twenty minutes.

Co: What time is it by now?

Cl: You mean when she starts or when she finishes.

Co: Well, both.

Cl: She usually starts by 7:15 or 7:20 and finishes by about 7:30 to 7:40.

Co: What are you doing while she's eating?

Cl: Usually fixing her lunch and trying to make her hurry and eat.

Co: How do you make her hurry?

Cl: (laughs) I hate to admit it but I nag a lot — keep reminding her it's getting late.

Co: After breakfast what happens?

Cl: Well, she brushes her teeth and gets dressed. That's when the real fun begins. She dawdles at the sink until one of us finally stands at the bathroom door and glares while she brushes her teeth. Then she takes forever getting dressed.

Co: What are you doing while she's getting dressed?

Cl: Usually I'm starting to get ready myself or straightening up and yelling at D. to hurry up.

Co: What time does D. leave?

Cl: At 8:00.

Co: How does she get to school?

Cl: We have a neighborhood carpool.

Co: Is she usually ready when the carpool gets here?

Cl: Yes, but I'm ready to kill her and sometimes she's almost in tears. I really want her to leave in the mornings with a good feeling. I just hate sending her to school with us both upset. Well, that's my problem — solve it (laughs).

Co: (laughs) I wish it were that easy. I can see that this is really bothering you. There are a couple of things you mentioned that I'd like to go back to and talk about. You said that D. often complained about not feeling good when she first woke up. Does she ask to stay home because she doesn't feel good?

Cl: No — it usually isn't mentioned again.

Co: I guess what I'm getting at is this. Could it be that there is something about school that D. doesn't like? Some reason she doesn't want to go? Maybe she puts off getting up and all the rest because she doesn't like school or her teacher.

Cl: No, I don't think that's it at all. She likes school and her teachers and she is doing very well. I've never heard her complain about anything at school. I guess I should have mentioned that this problem didn't start when school started this year. We had it last year during fifth grade. On Sunday mornings it's a horror show at our house, and even this summer and on Saturdays, if we have somewhere to go, she usually doesn't want to get ready.

Co: That's interesting. I guess we should be glad it's not a school problem. There was something else you said I wanted you to clarify. Let me think. Oh yes, you said that you and C. had tried everything you could think of. What are some things you've tried?

Cl: Gee, I don't know. Oh we tried punishing her, and I really can't remember what else. I guess mostly we've just tried different ways of keeping after her — being nice, yelling . . .

Co: Let me ask you something.. Whose responsibility is it to see that D. gets ready in time?

Cl: Most mornings it's mine. Sometimes C. helps.

Co: Have you ever tried letting it be D.'s?

Cl: What do you mean?

Co: I mean, have you ever let D. be completely responsible for getting herself ready? What do you think would happen if you stayed out of it completely and didn't help her keep track of the time or anything?

Cl: I don't think she'd ever get ready.

Co: Have you ever wondered why D. is so slow about getting ready?

Cl: Probably she depends on us to keep after her.

Co: Could it be she enjoys the attention, even though it's negative attention? She's certainly keeping you busy with her.

Cl: That could be. But a lot of mornings she ends up as upset as I am. How can she enjoy going off to school mad and teary?

Co: Probably she doesn't. Let's go back to responsibility again. You said you thought that if you stayed out of it she would never get ready on time. But am I right that you would like for D. to get up, eat breakfast, and get dressed without any, or maybe I should say with very little help or reminders from you? Is this right?

Cl: Yes.

Co: Then you would like for D. to assume responsibility for getting herself ready?

Cl: I've never thought of it in terms of responsibility before but yes, that's what I'd like. That's definietely what I'd like.

Co: Well, would you be willing to give D. total responsiblity and see what happens?

Cl: I'm willing, I'm just afraid it won't work. She's too used to our keeping after her.

Co: I think she's going to need some help at first. Not help getting ready, but help realizing that you're not going to help, if that makes sense. I think it's important that you talk to D. about what's going to happen. Perhaps explain it to her in terms of, "I don't like having you leave for school all upset and with me mad at you and I'd like for us to try a new way of getting ready in the mornings. OK?" I think she'll probably go for the idea. Does she have an alarm clock or could you get one for her?

Cl: Yes, we have an extra one we don't use.

Co: Give her the clock. It will help start the morning off as her responsibility. Then if it's really going to be her responsibility, you'll stay out of it. Just do the things you would normally do for her — like fix breakfast and lunch. I guess that's about all the jobs that are your responsibility.

Cl: But what if she's not ready at 8:00?

Co: What happens if she's not ready at 8:00? I mean what are the natural consequences that happen to D. if she's not ready on time?

Cl: She misses her ride. But then we'd have to take her to school.

Co: Can she walk if she misses her ride?

Cl: No, it's too far.

Co: What happens if she's late for school?

Cl: Nothing much. I'm supposed to write an excuse and tell why.

Co: Are you usually dressed and ready so that you could take her as soon as she's ready if she misses her ride?

Cl: No, but I guess I could be.

Co: No, don't be. I mean let's say that D. misses her ride because she's not ready on time. The natural consequence is that you take her when you get ready, not rushing or changing your schedule, and she is late for school.

Cl: But it seems like that is only adding to the problem. I don't understand.

Co: Would it embarass D. to walk into school late?

Cl: It might. But the school requires a written excuse from me. What would I say? That D. is late because she wasn't ready and missed her ride?

Co: That sounds good. Do you think the natural consequences of not being ready—going in late and the teacher knowing why—will be undesirable enough to D. that she'll want to avoid them?

Cl: I think so. It's worth a try.

Co: Let me see if I can summarize what we've said. You'll talk to D. and explain that getting up and ready in the morning is to be her responsibility from now on. Then you and C. will stay out of it. Try to ignore her if she starts dilly-dallying and let her suffer the natural consequences. If she's not ready at 8:00, don't hurry to take her. Let her wait while you get ready and then be late for school. Hopefully, that will only happen once. If it happens more than once, you might want to reevaluate the consequences — maybe they don't bother D. — or the plan itself. Think this will work?

Cl: I hope so. It sounds good. D. is very independent about most things so I think the idea of her taking over will appeal to her. We'll give it a try!

Co: Let me know what happens. Maybe we could talk about it again in a week or so.

In working with other adults avoid using roadblocks to communication but instead focus upon attending, listening, and responding skills. Thomas Gordon (1970) lists the communication roadblocks:

1. DIRECTING, ORDERING, COMMANDING (You must ... You have to ... You will ...)

2. WARNING, THREATENING, ADMONISHING (You had better . ... If you don't, then ...)

3. MORALIZING, PREACHING, OBLIGING (You should ... You ought ... It is your duty ... It is your responsibility ... You are required ...)

4. PERSUADING WITH LOGIC, ARGUING, INSTRUCTING, LECTURING (Do you realize ... Here is why you are wrong ... That is not right ... The facts are ... Yes, but ...)

5. ADVISING, RECOMMENDING, PROVIDING ANSWERS OR SOLUTIONS (What I would do is ... Why don't you ... Let me suggest ... It would be best for you ...)

6. EVALUATING, JUDGING NEGATIVELY, DISAPPROVING, BLAMING (You are bad. You are lazy. You are not thinking straight. You are acting foolishly. Your hair is too long.)

7. PRAISING, JUDGING OR EVALUATING POSITIVELY, APPROVING (You're a good boy. You've done a good job. That's a very good drawing. I approve of . . . That's a nice thing to do.)

8. SUPPORTING REASSURING, EXCUSING, SYMPATHIZING, (It's not so bad . . . Don't worry. You'll feel better. That's too bad.)

9. DIAGNOSING, PSYCHOANALYZING, INTERPRETING, READING-IN, OFFERING INSIGHTS (What you need is . . . What's wrong with you . . . You're just trying to get attention . . . You don't really mean that. I know what you need. Your problem is . . .)

10. QUESTIONING, PROBING, CROSS-EXAMINING, PRYING, INTERROGATING (Why . . ? Who . . ? Where . . ? What . . ? When . . ? How . . ?)

11. DIVERTING, AVOIDING, BY-PASSING, DIGRESSING, SHIFTING (Let's not talk about it now. Not at the dinner table. Forget it. That reminds me. We can discuss it later.)

12. KIDDING, TEASING, MAKING LIGHT OF, JOKING, USING SARCASM (Why don't you burn down the school? When did you read a newspaper last? Get up on the wrong side of the bed? When did they make you principal of the school?)

There is nothing more frustrating to counselors than having a client who will not communicate. There is nothing more frustrating to parents or teachers than someone who tries to tell them what to do. The consultee must understand that he/she is being heard. Active listening skills are extremely useful in initiating discussion with parents or teachers.

Consultation in Action

As the growing child is confronted by continuous personal, physiological, social, and ecological changes he/she may question the direction he/she is headed. In a society moving so rapidly that even adults find it difficult to keep up, the problems of the emerging adolescent are only compounded. Counseling and guidance functions of the counselor can directly help the child face the changes. Consultation with the adults in the child's life can bring relief to the adults and indirectly affect the child.

Most consultation will take place with individuals. A teacher may bring a concern to you about a child in her/his classroom or a parent may call you about her/his child's behavior at home. These concerns may be crisis in nature such as loss of interest in school, reluctance to share in responsibilities at home or more serious drug or suicidal problems. Or, they may be developmental concerns, such as wanting information regarding further stages of child development. A rule of thumb that can be most helpful is to assume that the problem belongs to the person presenting it until you are convinced otherwise. Assume that the presented problem is owned by the person presenting it, whether a teacher, parent, school administrator, or child. Many problems will take care of themselves without contact with the person referred to by the consultee as the problem source. Often the consultee is the source or can benefit enough from collaboration with the consultant to resolve the problem himself/herself. Madsen and Madsen (1974) claim that one third of the problems go away just by talking about them. A teacher who presents a concern to a consultant may discover that his/her relief through this discussion or catharsis affects his/her attitude toward the child in question, thus increasing his/her ability to understand and interact positively with the child.

Teacher Study Groups

In addition to individual consultation with parents and teachers, small discussion groups may be formed for the purpose of clarifying the relationships between adults and the middle school child. With teachers, the "C" group outlined by Dinkmeyer & Carlson (1973) can be very useful.

THE "C" GROUP

Purpose:

1. To develop an understanding of the practical applications of the dynamics of human behavior. To enable participants to develop hypotheses regarding behavior and specific recommendations.

2. To become aware of the interrelationship between patterns of child behavior and one's own life style. To experience the benefits of group learning.

3. To help teachers to see patterns of behavior in children and to develop procedures for improving relationships and behavior.

4. To provide a channel for open communication so members can share experiences and insights.

Practical Value for Teachers:

1. Sharing of similar concerns about children and the learning process.

2. Learning how to deal more effectively with children's misbehavior.

3. Becoming acquainted with skills in leading classroom discussions concerned with pupil attitudes, behavior beliefs, and perceptions.

4. Becoming aware of our methods of relating to others and receiving feedback on how we come over to others.

Rationale:

Most problems are interpersonal and social. Problems with children originate in group interactions and can be best solved by the teachers participating in a teacher group. The "C" group developed because of the mounting evidence that lectures, discussion, and telling would not help change the basic attitudes of teachers, parents, and students.

Schools have not devised effective ways for teachers to share with each other effective procedures. The "C" group is a channel for communication. The group provides support, a chance to express personal feelings and to share common problems and solutions for those problems, and a chance to gain feedback for oneself.

What Does "C" Stand For:

The group has been titled "C" group because the dynamic forces which operate in the group all begin with the letter "C": collaboration, consultation, clarification, confrontation, communication, concern and caring, confidentiality, commitment, change, and cohesion.

Possible Organizational Format:

1. Meet once a week for one hour.

2. Meet at least six to eight times.

3. Meet at a time convenient for the four to six teachers involved. (p. 215)

Parent/Child Study Groups

Getting parents into schools can be difficult. Experience has shown, however, that one way to get parents to school is to offer them some hope for better relationships with their children. One such method is called the parent or child study group. These groups of parents meet with the counselor once a week for several weeks (usually eight to ten weeks) to discuss child rearing concerns. A letter such as the following may be sent to parents.

Dear Parents,

Do you sometimes have trouble getting your child to bed? Do you wish that your child would be on time for meals? Have you ever wished your child would pick up his or her room without a family war? Have you ever been exhausted after breakfast because it took all your energy to get everyone out of bed, dressed and off to school?

If you have ever had one or more of these experiences, YOU ARE A NORMAL PARENT. Many parents have these experiences each day but rarely have the chance to share them with other parents. When parents with like concerns get together and share their problems and successes almost every parent benefits from the exchange of ideas.

Such a discussion group is now being formed for the parents of the Our Town Middle School.

The group will begin on Tuesday, October 12, at 6:00 PM in the school cafeteria. The group will continue for approximately eight weeks, meeting from 6:00 to 7:30 PM each Tuesday evening. There will be no charge.

If you would like more information about the discussion group, please contact me at _____.

We look forward to sharing many ideas with you in the upcoming weeks.

Sincerely

John Doe, Counselor
Our Town Middle School

Times, of course, may vary. You may wish to have one group scheduled during the school day and another in the evening to accommodate work schedules. Any number of aids are available to help you begin your groups such as *Parent Effectivencss Training* (Gordon, 1970), *Systematic Training for Effective Parenting* (Dinkmeyer and McKay, 1976) and *Living with Children* (Patterson and Gullion, 1976). A review of these and other approaches to parent training is offered by Henry (1981). Through these formal programs you may demonstrate your effectiveness and thus win lasting allies. In addition, parents discover that this person called "Counselor" is not such a mysterious creature after all.

Good group skills are imperative in working with groups of parents or teachers. The following is offered as a brief summary of some of the skills useful in working with groups:

1. Structuring − purpose, procedures

2. Linking − differences and similarities

3. Feedback − beliefs, feelings and behaviors affecting others − modeling

4. Redirecting − maximizing group involvement

5. Questioning − open and closed

6. Encouragement — improvement

7. Brainstorming — withhold comment until all suggestions are made

8. Obtaining commitments — what to do between sessions

9. Summarizing — what have we learned?

The exercises on pages 138-141 have been used with parents and teachers very effectively in helping them understand the influence they have on children and have triggered some helpful ideas for problem resolution. A process outlining systems of encouragement and discipline (Rotter, McFadden & Kannenberg, 1981) follows the exercises.

Exercise 1

WHO INFLUENCES THE BEHAVIORS OF CHILDREN
Identification of Significant Influence People

Substantial scientific evidence suggests that the behavior of children is influenced by the people with whom they come in contact. The *extent* to which children learn from other people is partially determined by the amount of time spent with the various people with whom they have contact. In consideration of the substantial amounts of time which children spend in the home and in the school, parents and teachers can represent significant learning or behavioral influences in the lives of children.

Listed below are some people who may have influenced *your* learnings and behaviors. Consider those who have significantly influenced you and then consider the amount of time which was spent with those people.

Influence Person	Time Spent with Person
Close friend	_____
Scout leader	_____
Grandparents	_____
Teachers	_____
City Mayor	_____
Grocery Check-out Person	_____
Counselor	_____
Acquaintances	_____

Parents	_____
Uncle/Aunt	_____
Dentist	_____
Insurance Person	_____
Zoo Keeper	_____
Employer or Employment Situation	_____
Neighbor	_____

Exercise 2

IDENTIFYING YOUR CURRENT SIGNIFICANT INFLUENCE PEOPLE AND THE EFFECTS THEY HAVE ON YOUR BEHAVIOR

As a parent or teacher your behavior influences your children or students by increasing, decreasing, or maintaining many of their behaviors; however, people who are of significant influence also affect your behavior on a day-to-day basis. This exercise will help you identify your "significant influence people," specific behaviors which you exhibit in their presence, and the effects the significant influence person has on these specific behaviors. First, fill in the appropriate amount of time spent with each of these people per week. Now choose a behavior which you frequently exhibit in the presence of each of these people. Finally, record how the responses of these significant influence people tend to affect your specific behavior (increase, decrease, or remain the same).

PERSON	*HOURS PER WEEK*	*SPECIFIC BEHAVIOR*	*EFFECT*
Spouse	*65*	*Remove Trash*	*increase*
Husband/Wife	_____	_____	_____
Neighbor	_____	_____	_____
Acquaintance	_____	_____	_____

Employer   _____   _____   _____

Pastor   _____   _____   _____

Close Friend   _____   _____   _____

Parent   _____   _____   _____

Sister/Brother _____   _____   _____

Storekeeper   _____   _____   _____

Law Officer   _____   _____   _____

Exercise 3

WHAT ENCOURAGEMENT AND DISCOURAGEMENT RESPONSES DO YOU USE WHEN INFLUENCING THE BEHAVIOR OF CHILDREN?

In the spaces below, write approval and disapproval responses *you* have used (in response to a child's behavior) in your attempts to influence the behavior of children.

ENCOURAGEMENT RESPONSES			*DISCOURAGEMENT RESPONSES*	
Verbal or Written	Nonverbal	Material	Verbal or Written	Nonverbal
_____	_____	_____	_____	_____
_____	_____	_____	_____	_____
_____	_____	_____	_____	_____
_____	_____	_____	_____	_____
_____	_____	_____	_____	_____
_____	_____	_____	_____	_____
_____	_____	_____	_____	_____
_____	_____	_____	_____	_____

Exercise 4

HOW DO YOU PROCESS A PROBLEM FROM BEGINNING TO END?

     First, think of some child behaviors (either acceptable or problem behaviors) which you or a colleague have recently influenced. Then write down the influential person who was involved with the child. Now write down the response typically made by the influential person after the performance of the behavior exhibited by the child. Identify the type of response made by the teacher or parent (encouragement, discouragement, extinction or ignoring response, etc.). Finally, relate the effect which the teacher or parent response had on the child's behavior (increase, decrease, not changed). Use either real or hypothetical child behavior examples.

John is sitting quietly and studying during study hour.   *teacher*   *Good work John! (type: encouragement)*   *increase in quiet study behavior during study hour.*

_____   _____   _____   _____

Other Target Groups

The mass media's effect on the lives of young people has been heavily documented in the literature. It behooves the counselor to acknowledge these facts. The impressionable middle school child draws from TV, radio, commercial advertising, recordings and others. Parents, as well as teachers, exclaim their disbelief at the values professed by the children around them. Many such values are extracted not from the home but from external sources such as the mass media. The counselor can be effective in capitalizing on this means of communication to assist parents and children in identifying and establishing life goals. So often we criticize the technology out of fear. Make the technology work for you.

One counselor arranged to face the public as often as possible through TV, radio, and the newspaper. Spot public service announcements are often free and can be most effective. Examples of 15-20 second announcements promoting guidance services in the middle school are presented here.

Remember the song "My Time Is Your Time"? Parents often feel that they may be imposing on teachers when they talk with them. Teachers, however, feel they need the support of parents, and they certainly encourage them to visit the school. Middle school counselors work to bring the home and school together so that the song "My Time Is Your Time" is changed to "Our Time Is the Child's Time." Please visit your child's school, and support the counselor's efforts to facilitate your child's growth.

Often children face times when they feel unloved, unwanted, unaccepted, and unsuccessful. These feelings can be identified early in children before they become permanent emotional characteristics. Middle school counselors ask you to be sensitive to those difficult times faced by the growing child. The school and home need to work together to give children feelings of being loved, wanted, accepted, and successful.

It's important for a child to have proper nutrition. It's also important for a child to have supportive help with emotional and social development. Through a teamwork approach of parents, administrators, teachers, and counselors, we can provide needed guidance for these early years. Middle school counselors invite you to join this team for your child's sake.

One day there was a student who suddenly became afraid of school. She felt sick whenever she entered her classroom. Through consultation, the teacher and the counselor helped the parents and the child understand the problem, and they used an approach to help her return to the classroom. Middle school counselors work to bring parents and teachers together in helping children meet difficulties encountered as they grow.

Have you ever wished that you had tried some other kind of occupation? Did you receive help in school in choosing an occupation? Middle school counselors emphasize the need for starting to think about careers during the early years of school and continuing throughout the school experience. Your schools are working to assist children to better understand their place in the world of work.

Have you ever felt lonely, experienced failure, lost something you love? Children experience these same feelings. One of the ways to help children cope is through small-group counseling. In these groups, middle school counselors and children share ideas and feelings to grow in self-understanding and plan ways to handle tasks they face in growing up.

There is a person in your school known as the middle school counselor. This counselor tries to support the teacher's and the principal's efforts to help children develop in positive ways. Teachers know there are times when a child needs to be alone with someone to talk out concerns. At times like these the teacher can depend on a counselor to work with these children through individual counseling sessions.

Middle school counselors conduct consultation with parents in trying to help them develop effective relationships with their children. They do not pretend to have all the answers for children's many needs. But parents find that it helps to discuss ideas they might consider trying. The middle school counselor provides one avenue to help children.

(adapted from Barnette and Turner, 1976)

A SIP OF DISCIPLINE AND ENCOURAGEMENT

The Behaviors of Children

The values of the home, teachers, administrators, counselors, etc., will, to a great extent, determine which behaviors exhibited by children will be viewed as being acceptable (good or positive) or problem behaviors (negative behaviors).

Positive or acceptable behaviors exhibited by children

Increasing positive or acceptable behaviors using A SIP of Encouragement

S   Specify the acceptable behavior and count the number of times it is exhibited during a week.

I   Identify the positive, negative, and neutral influences which currently affect the momentum of the specific acceptable behavior.

Negative Influences

| Neutral Influences | acceptable or positive behaviors | neutral Influences |

Positive Influences

Positive Influences: Responses by "Significant Influence People" (parents, teachers, counselors, etc.) that strengthen or increase the positive behavior. These positive influences almost always involve encouragement responses or positive behavior modeling.

Negative Influences: Responses by "Significant Influence People" that weaken the acceptable behavior. Negative influences that weaken an acceptable behavior are usually discouragements, extinction procedures, or ignoring behaviors.

Negative or problem behaviors exhibited by children

Decreasing negative or problem behaviors using A SIP of Discipline

S   Specify the problem behavior and count the number of times it is exhibited during a week.

I   Identify the positive, negative, and neutral influences which currently affect the momentum of the specific problem behavior.

Negative Influences

| Neutral Influences | problem or negative behaviors | Neutral Influences |

Positive Influences

Positive Influences: Responses by "Significant Influence People" (parents, teachers, counselors, etc) that weaken or reduce the problem behavior or strengthen more positive, alternative behaviors. Positive influences that weaken a problem behavior include: discouragements, extinction procedures, or ignoring responses. Positive influences which strengthen more positive, alternative behaviors are encouragements or positive behavior modeling.

A Sip of Discipline and Encouragement – *continued*

Neutral Influences: Responses by "Significant Influence People" that do not increase or decrease the frequency of an acceptable behavior.

P Plan a change strategy. This plan will maximize positive influences (encouraging acceptable behavior) and minimize negative influences. Implement your plan of action and, after a two-week period, recount the number of times the acceptable behavior occurs more frequently, you plan is working. If there is no change or the acceptable behavior is occurring less frequently, plan a new strategy, implement, and evaluate.

Negative Influences: Responses by "Significant Influence People" that strengthen or maintain the problem behavior. Usually encouragement responses.

Neutral Influences: Responses by "Significant Influence People" that do not increase or decrease the frequency of the problem behavior.

P Plan a change strategy. This plan will maximize positive influences (discouraging, ignoring, or using extinction procedures on problem behaviors *or* encouraging more acceptable, alternative behaviors) and minimize negative influences. Implement your plan of action and, after a two-week period, recount the number of times the problem behavior occurs each week. If the problem behavior occurs less frequently, your plan is working. If there is no change or if the problem behavior occurs more frequently, plan a new strategy, implement, and evaluate.

Reproduced from:

Rotter, J., McFadden, J., & Kannenberg, G. *Significant influence people: A SIP of discipline and encouragement*, Saratoga, CA: R & E Research Associates, 1981.

Some Cautions

The counselor as consultant is often placed in the position of change agent. This position of change agent can be most threatening to those around him/her. It, therefore, is imperative that the consultant understand that change is very often met with resistance by those most affected by it. Eicholz and Rogers (1964) present a framework for identifying rejection to change that can be most helpful to the consultant (see Table 9:2). Most of the rejection responses in the last column suggest some fear, guilt, or other underlying reason for resistance to change. It is important that the consultant understand these resistances and provide the necessary forum to assist in overcoming these negative feelings.

Table 9:2. A Framework for the Identification of Forms of Rejection

Form of Rejection	Cause of Rejection	State of Subject	Anticipated Rejection Response
1. Ignorance	Lack of dissemination	Uninformed	"The information is not easily available."
2. Suspended judgement	Data not logically compelling	Doubtful	"I want to wait and see how good it is, before I try."
3. Situational judgement	Data not materially compelling	1. Comparing	"Other things are equally good."
		2. Defensive	"The school regulations will not permit it."
		3. Deprived	"It costs too much to use in time and money."
4. Personal	Data not psychologically compelling	1. Anxious	"I don't know if I can operate equipment."
		2. Guilty	"I know I should use them but I don't have time."
		3. Alienated (or estranged)	"These gadgets will never replace a teacher." ("If we use these gadgets they might replace us.")
5. Experimental	Present of past trials	Convinced	"I tried them once and they aren't any good."

Source: Eichholz and Rogers, 1964

Lippitt (1973) offers an example of how facilitating and hindering forces worked for or against change (Table 9:3). The consultant must understand the operant forces within the school and individuals and promote those kinds of facilitating activities that will prevent undue resistance to necessary change.

Facilitating

Table 9:3. Forces Relevant to the Facilitation and Hindrance of Innovation and Diffusion of Teaching Practices

Facilitating Forces	*Hindering Forces*
1. Peer and Authority Relations	
A. Sharing sessions or staff bulletins become a matter of school routine.	A. Little communication among teachers.
B. Public recognition given to innovators and adopters; innovation-diffusion seen as a cooperative task.	B. Competition for prestige teachers.
C. Sharing ideas is expected and rewarded; norms support asking for and giving help; regular talent search for new ideas.	C. Norms enforce privatism.
D. Area team liaison supports new ideas.	D. Colleagues reject ideas.
E. Principal or superintendent supports innovation-diffusion activity.	E. Principal not interested in new ideas.
F. Principal helps create a staff atmosphere of sharing and experimentation.	F. School climate does not support experimentation.
G. Staff meetings used as two-way informing and educating sessions.	G. Principal does not know what is going on.
H. Teachers influence the sharing process.	H. Teacher ideas do not matter.
I. In-service training program gives skills needed to innovate and adapt.	I. No continuing education program for staff.
2. Personal Attitudes	
A. Seeking new ways.	A. Resistance to change.
B. Seeking peer and consultant help.	B. Fear of evaluation and rejection or failure.
C. Always open to adapting and modifying practices.	C. Dogmatism about already knowing about new practices.
D. Public rewards for professional growth.	D. Professional growth not important.
E. See groups as endemic and relevant for academic learning.	E. Negative feelings about group work.
F. Understand connection between mental health and academic learning.	F. Mental health is "extra."
G. Optimism.	G. Pessimism.
H. Test ideas slowly.	H. Afraid to experiment.
I. Suiting and changing practice to fit one's own style and class.	I. Resistance to imitating others.

3. Characteristics of the Practice

A. Relevant to universal student problems.

A. Does not meet the needs of a class.

B. Can be done a little at a time.

B. Requires a lot of energy.

C. Consultant and peer help available; needed skills are clearly outlined.

C. Requires new skills.

D. Clearly aids student growth.

D. Requires change in teacher values.

E. A behavioral change with no new gimmicks.

E. Requires new facilities.

F. Built-in evaluation to see progress.

F. Will not work.

G. Innovation has tried a new twist.

G. Not new.

H. Student, not subject, oriented.

H. Not for my grade level or subject.

I. No social practice can be duplicated exactly.

I. Effectiveness reduced if practice gains general use.

4. Physical and Temporal Arrangements

A. Staff meetings used for professional growth; substitues hired to free teacher(s) to visit other classrooms; lunchtime used for discussions; students sent home for an afternoon so teachers can all meet together.

A. No time to get together.

B. Extra clerical help provided.

B. Too many clerical duties to have time to share ideas.

C. Staff meetings for everyone to get together occasionally; grade level or departmental meetings.

C. Classrooms are isolated.

D. Meetings held in classrooms.

D. No rooms to meet in.

Source: Lippit et al. in Havelock, 1973.

People tend to be more receptive to change if the change agent is within the organization (Zaltman & Duncan, 1977). The counselor who serves in residence within the school has an advantage, therefore, over someone from central administration or outside the school system. To function as a successful agent, the counselor must establish credibility through effective service to the school.

Summary

There are many approaches to the consultation process reported in the literature and practiced by counselors. A few have been presented in this chapter. The reader is encouraged to refer to the bibliography for further study.

Regardless of the approach or approaches you adopt for your setting, keep in mind that the consulting function is a major part of your job as a middle school counselor. In order to serve the children in your care it is essential that you consult with the various populations affecting them. Your role as consultant can be very time consuming but also extremely exciting and rewarding. Your effectiveness as a consultant can be the best selling point of your guidance program.

REFERENCES

Alinsky, S. *Reveille for radicals.* New York: Vintage Books, 1969.

Alinsky, S. Citizen participation and community organization in planning and urban renewal. In F. Fox et al. (Eds.), *Strategies of community organization.* Itasca, Illinois: F.E. Peacock Publishers, 1970. (a)

Alinsky, S. Of means and ends. In F. Fox et al. (Eds.), *Strategies of community organization.* Itasca, Illinois: F.E. Peacock Publishers, 1970. (b)

Alinsky, S. *Rules for radicals.* New York: Random House, 1972.

Barnette, E.L., & Turner, D. And now a word from . . .*Elementary School Guidance and Counseling,* 1976, *10,* 177-183.

Brown, D.E., Wyne, M.D., Blackburn, J.E. & Powell, W.C. *Consultation: A strategy for improving education.* Boston: Allyn & Bacon, Inc., 1979.

Caplan, G. *Concepts of mental health and consultation: Their application in public health social work.* Washington, D.C.: U.S. Department of Health, Education, and Welfare, Children's Bureau, 1959.

Caplan, G. *The theory and practice of mental health consultation.* New York: Basic Books, 1970.

Carlson, J., Splete, H., and Kern, R. (Eds.) *The consulting process.* Washington, D.C.: American Personnel and Guidance Association, 1975.

Dinkmeyer, D., & Carlson, J. *Consulting: Facilitating human potential and change processes.* Columbus, Ohio: Charles E. Merrill, 1973.

Dinkmeyer, D., & McKay, G. *Systematic training for effective parenting.* Circle Pines, Minn.: American Guidance Services, 1976.

Dworkin, A.L., & Dworkin, E.P. A conceptual overview of selected consultation models. *American Journal of Community Psychology,* 1975, *3,* 151-159.

Eichholz, G.C., & Rogers, E.M. Resistance to the adoption to audio-visual aids by elementary school teachers: Contrast and similarities to agricultural innovation, in Matthew Miles (Ed.), *Innovation in Education,* New York: Teachers College Press, 1964, 299-316.

Faust, V. *The counselor-consultant in the elementary school.* Boston: Houghton Mifflin, 1968.

Gordon, T. *Parent effectiveness training.* New York: Peter Wyden, 1970.

Havelock, R.G., & Havelock, M.C. *Training for change agents.* Ann Arbor: Institute for Social Research, University of Michigan, 1973.

Henry, S.A. Current dimensions of parent training. *School Psychology Review,* 1981, 10, 4-14.

Kadushin, A. *Consultation in social work.* New York: Columbia University Press, 1977.

Kelly, J. Ecological constraints on mental health services. *American Psychologist,* 1966, *21,* 535-539.

Kelly, J. Towards an ecological conception of preventive interventions. In J. Carter, Jr. (Ed.) *Research contributions from psychology to community mental health.* New York: Behavioral Publications, 1968.

Kelly, J. Naturalistic observations in contrasting social environments. In E. Williams & H. Raush (Eds.), *Naturalistic viewpoints in psychological research.* New York: Holt, Rinehart & Winston, 1969.

Kelly, J. Antidotes for arrogance: Training for community psychology. *American Psychologist,* 1970, *25,* 524-531. (a)

Kelly, J. The quest for valid preventive interventions. In C.D. Spielberger (Ed.), *Current topics in clinical and community psychology,* Vol. 2. New York: Academic Press, 1970. (b)

Lippitt, G. *Visualizing change: Model building and the change process.* Fairfax, Va.: NTL Learning Resources Corporation, 1973.

Lippitt, R. Dimensions of the consultant's job. *Journal of Social Issues,* 1959, *15,* 5-12.

Lippitt, R. On finding, using, and being a consultant. *Social Science Education Consortium Newsletter,* 1971, *11,* 1-2.

Lippitt, R., & Jung, C. The study of change as a concept in research utilization. *Theory into Practice,* 1966, *5,* 25-29.

Lippitt, R., Watson, J. & Westly, B. *The dynamics of planned change.* New York: Harcourt, Brace & World, 1958.

Madsen, C.H., & Madsen, C K. *Teaching/discipline: A positive approach to educational development.* Boston: Allyn & Bacon, Inc., 1974.

McClung, F. Stunden, A. *Mental health consultation to programs for children.* Chevy Chase, Maryland: National Institute for Mental Health, 1970.

Meyers, J., Parson, R., and Martin, R. *Mental health consultation in the schools.* Washington, D.C.: Josey-Bass Publishers, 1979.

Nelson, R.C. *Guidance and counseling in the elementary school.* New York: Holt, Rinehart, and Winston, 1973.

Patterson, G.R. & Gullion, M.E. *Living with children: New methods for parents and teachers.* Rev. Ed.; Champaign, Illinois: Research Press, 1976.

Rotter, J.C., McFadden, J., & Kannenberg, G. *Significant influence people: A SIP of discipline and encouragement.* Saratoga, Ca.: Rand E. Associates, Inc., 1981.

Schowengerdt, R.V., Fine, M.J., & Poggio, J.P. An examination of some bases of teacher satisfaction with school psychological services. *Psychology in the Schools,* 1976, 13, 269-275.

Trickett, E., Kelly, J., & Todd, D. The social environment of the high school: Guidelines for individual change and organizational redevelopment. In S. Golann & C. Eisdorfer (Eds.), *Handbook of community psychology*. New York: Appleton-Century-Crofts, 1971.

Van Hoose, W.H. *Counseling in the elementary school.* Itasca, Illinois: F.E. Peacock Publishers, 1968.

Werner, J.L. Community mental health consultation with agencies. *Personnel and Guidance Journal*, 1978, *56*, 364-368.

Zaltman, G., & Duncan, R. *Strategies for planned change.* New York: John Wiley and Sons, 1977.

Chapter Ten

PSYCHOLOGICAL ASSESSMENT

GARY M. MILLER

Introduction

The purpose of this chapter is to examine the place and purpose of psychological assessment in the middle school. A brief historical overview of psychological testing and its evolution into psychological assessment will be discussed in the opening section of the chapter. The development of an appropriate middle school assessment program will be included along with guidelines for the preparation of the assessment procedure. Using data that have been collected, a model for interpretation of results and the rights of children regarding psychological assessment will also be presented.

Historical Trends

Using tests and test data for decision making is not a new venture. As early as 2200 B.C., the Chinese emperor administered tests at three year intervals to ascertain the fitness of public officials to stay in office. From these early efforts, a "civil service" examination system evolved in China and operated until 1905 when it was abolished. (Dubois, 1970).

Through contact with the Chinese, both Great Britain and France instituted civil service examinations. Eventually testing for civil service purposes was adopted by the United States Civil Service Commission. This resulted in an acceptance of testing efforts as a systematic process in employee selection, retention and promotion.

The actual thrust toward testing for educational purposes can be traced to the efforts of Esquirol. In 1838, Esquirol noted varying degrees of mental retardation. The use of language by the individual tested was considered the most critical factor of intellectual performance.

At the same time that Esquirol was conducting his work, Seguin was working on training the mentally retarded. In 1837, he established the first school for the mentally retarded. Seguin came to the United States in 1848 and many of his ideas for helping the mentally retarded were well received (Anastasi, 1968).

Sir Francis Galton is seen by many as the developer of the testing movement. This English biologist conducted numerous studies in heredity. His efforts led to the keeping of systematic anthropometric records on students enrolled in schools. Galton believed tests of sensory discrimination could help gauge a person's intelligence. In addition, he developed rating scales, questionnaires, free-association techniques and statistical tests to examine individual differences.

In the late 1800's, James McKeen Cattell derived the concept of the "mental test." Cattell developed tests to assess the intellectual abilities of college students. Through these efforts, he incorporated sensory descrimination and reaction time in the testing process. Numerous other test developers followed Cattell, but perhaps the most influential development was occurring in France.

French educators were concerned about providing educational experiences for subnormal children enrolled in schools in Paris. A commission was established in 1904 to study this issue and, through the joint efforts of Binet and Simon, the first Binet-Simon Scale emerged. Their scale attempted to examine the subject's judgment, comprehension and reasoning. Two revisions were made in France in 1908 and 1911. The adaptation of these scales to American culture occurred in 1916 through the efforts of L.M. Terman at Stanford University. This version, the Stanford-Binet Scales, was revised in 1937 and 1960. In 1972 the norms were updated.

The early testing efforts utilized individually-administered tests. However, the need for group testing eventually emerged. In 1917 Robert M. Yerkes headed a committee whose responsibility was to develop an instrument to classify military recruits quickly, based on their intellectual functioning. The principal decisions the military needed to make focused on the rejection of inductees, the selection of candidates for officer training and the discharge of personnel. The person credited with developing the first group intelligence tests for the military is Arthur S. Otis. His test was submitted to the United States Army and later revised into the Army Alpha and Army Beta tests (Anastasi, 1968).

From these initial developments, the testing movement in the United States has experienced significant growth in many diverse areas. There have been arguments for and against testing, yet it appears that this multi-million dollar enterprise, serving wide and diverse populations, will remain on the scene for some time to come. It is critical that we be aware of the intent of the testing in which we engage. Although the instruments are well developed and researched, in the final analysis, it is the test consumer who must benefit from such efforts. Consequently, the counselor must be fully aware of the implications of the testing efforts in the school and its impact on the entire school community.

Rationales for Psychological Assessment

The central purpose of any school's testing program is to help the students in the school. Tests can help identify the individual differences in students. This understanding can help school personnel design teaching efforts to better meet the specific needs of each student. The counselor can use such information to assist the individual in setting and achieving goals.

Promoting the self-understanding of students represents the second rationale for having a testing program. Through sharing the results of tests and examining their implication for the student, the counselor can be a catalyst to assist the student in gaining greater understanding.

A third justification of a testing program relates to the decision-making which students engage in throughout their school years. Data about abilities, aptitudes and interests can be used as the student explores educational and career issues requiring sound decisions.

The diagnostic role of tests for middle school youth is critical. Counselors, teachers, and students can use various diagnostic instruments to determine areas of deficiency and plan appropriate strategies to assist the student in dealing with some of these weaknesses. These instruments can also assist in the processes of identifying exceptional children. These children can then participate in the educational activities specifically designed and developed to meet their needs.

To provide for the needs of the school, the counselors need to be able to evaluate the guidance program. Tests can assist the counselor in assessing the effectiveness of guidance programs and in making the necessary adjustments to maintain a viable program of activities and services (Shertzer and Stone, 1981).

Research efforts of the counselor can also benefit from the use of specific testing procedures. The counselor can develop and test various hypotheses or examine the impact of the educational program of the school on students. These findings can then be used as a component in planning the entire educational program of the schools.

The concept of psychological assessment has been explored by Loesch and Miller (1975) and Loesch, (1978). According to Loesch and Miller psychological assessment is ". . . the process of assessing human attributes through the use of both objective and subjective techniques." (Loesch and Miller, 1975, p. 38). They note "From a procedural viewpoint, psychological assessment requires that the person making the assessment utilize the counseling skills of observation and communication in addition to test administration and scoring skills." (Loesch and Miller, 1975, p. 38). This concept seems quite compatible with Van Riper (1974), who stresses the need to involve the client in the appraisal process as a full partner, not just as a student or client. The counselor must be concerned about the contributions which testing can add to the counseling process.

Establishing the Testing Program

Middle school youth are viewed as unique and their educational program is seen as promoting their uniqueness. Therefore, the psychological appraisal program must be compatible and useful for this group of students and school personnel. Prior to developing an appraisal program, it is helpful to consider the standards presented by Hill (1969) for test users:

1. The tests should be used with the interest of the client in mind.

2. The counselor needs to understand the client and how the information collected can be helpful to the client after testing.

3. The testing program should be headed by a highly competent person.

4. To maintain a viable testing program there must be a continual upgrading of the skills of the test users.

5. Parents and community members need to understand the tests and their use.

6. The use and interpretation of test results should be part of a comprehensive effort to help the child.

7. The results that are shared need to be accurate, current, complete, and of a developmental nature.

8. Counselors should strive to reduce the anxiety and competitiveness that accompanies the testing effort.

9. Ways need to be developed to assist children in understanding and using the data appropriately.

10. A viable school testing program needs to undergo periodic, systtematic evaluation.

11. The ethical standards of the American Personnel and Guidance Association and the American Psychological Association must be upheld when using tests.

Counselors need to consider how well the established appraisal program in their schools are meeting these suggested standards. Clarifying the nature and purpose of tests, reporting results, and using test data appropriately are critical concerns for the counselor. In addition, being able to examine the testing program objectively and systematically is a consideration to be addressed by the counselor and other educators in the school.

To review tests prior to their administration, the counselors need to consult several sources for information on the tests. One can examine the test itself and determine its usefulness for one's school. Also, examining critical reviews in Buros' *Mental Measurements Yearbook* and *Tests in Print* can also provide helpful information. Lastly, reviews of tests in professional journals can assist in the decision making about the testing program. After completing various reviews, the counselor can develop a card file using a model developed by Miller (1975):

Figure 10:1. Test Review Card Front

Front

```
Test Review Card

Test —


Publisher —
Purpose —
Levels —
Comments:


Reviewers —



Source — _____ Mental Measurements Yearbook
```

Figure 10:2. Test Review Card Back

Back

```
┌─────────────────────────────────────────────────────────────────────┐
│                                                                       │
│   Total Administration Time _____            │
│                                                                       │
│   Subtests or Subareas                                                │
│                                                                       │
│   1.                        6.                                        │
│   2.                        7.                                        │
│   3.                        8.                                        │
│   4.                        9.                                        │
│   5.                       10.                                        │
│                                                                       │
│   Validity                      Reliability                           │
│                                                                       │
│   ____ Content                  ____ Kuder-Richardson                 │
│   ____Concurrent                ____ Split-Half                       │
│   ____Construct                 ____ Alternate Form                   │
│   ____Criterion Related:        ____ Test-Retest                      │
│       Predictive                                                      │
│   ____Criterion Related:                                              │
│       Diagnostic                                                      │
│                                                                       │
└─────────────────────────────────────────────────────────────────────┘
```

Helpful information recorded on such cards can facilitate the selection of tests for the school's program.

One must also decide how extensive the assessment processes will be. A common strategy is to test all students in the school with the specific tests selected by the counseling staff. This mass or "saturation" testing reaches everyone, yet one might question the ultimate help tendered to each pupil tested under such circumstances. There may be much time and money invested which may not fully meet the needs of the students. A more conservative approach discourages mass testing and encourages assessment as the needs of the individual emerge. As Goldman (1969) has stated: "No more tests should be administered than are needed and the results of which can be used" (p. 54). To demonstrate how such an approach may be utilized, Loesch (1977) has developed a comprehensive flowchart for the use of tests. He believes such a systematic approach can insure the proper integration of tests in the counseling process.

Figure 10:3

A FLOWCHART MODEL FOR USING TESTS IN COUNSELING

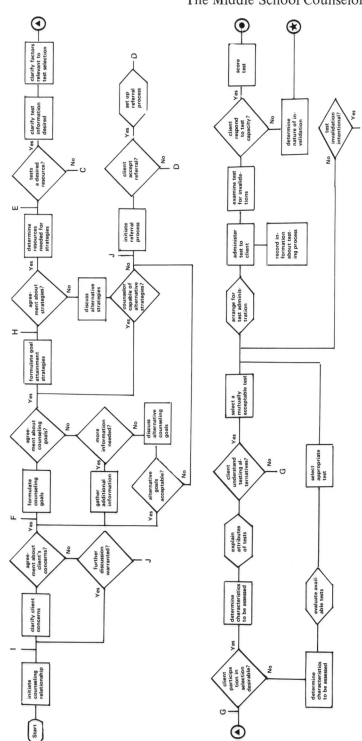

Figure 10:3 – Continued

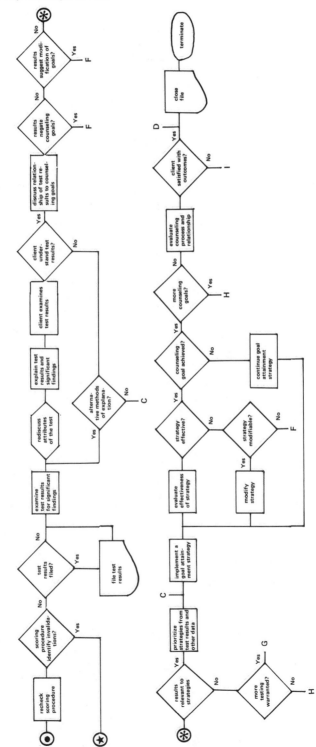

As can be seen, this procedure follows a critical path with decisions made throughout influencing the progress of the counseling-appraisal relationship.

Given that many schools do utilize the mass testing approach, there are various ways to develop programs suitable to the school's needs. The Michigan School Testing Service has developed three specific types of programs to be used in the Michigan schools. Program I is a basic initial program while Programs II and III represent the more comprehensive testing programs. Below are listed some of the suggested types of tests appropriate for middle school students whose schools may be using one of the three programs suggested by the Michigan School Testing Service (1978-79). For the middle school, grades 6-8, the following programs are suggested (Michigan School Testing Service, 1978-79, p. 2-3) in Figure 10:4.

Figure 10:4. Suggested Testing Programs

		Grade 6	Grade 7	Grade 8
Program		Scholastic Aptitude	_____	Scholastic Atitude
I		Achievement Battery	_____	
Program		Achievement Battery	Scholastic Aptitude	Achievement Battery
II				
Program		Achievement Battery	Scholastic Aptitude	Achievement Battery
III			Achievement Battery	

As can be seen, even in Program III, the testing recommended is not excessive. The data gathered from such efforts can contribute to the over-all psychological assessment program in the middle school.

The Tests

In establishing the testing program the middle school counselor can select from a wide variety of tests, which have forms on levels suitable to middle school aged youth. Some suggested achievement tests include:

1. California Achievement Tests, 1970 or 1977 Edition.

2. Comprehensive Tests of Basic Skills.

3. Comprehensive Tests of Basic Skills Expanded Edition.

4. Iowa Tests of Basic Skills, Forms 5 and 6.

5. Metropolitan Achievements Tests, 1970 or 1978 Edition.

6. Sequential Test of Educational Progress, Third Edition.

7. Stanford Achievement Test, 1973 Edition.

Some scholastic aptitude or intelligence tests which might be included in a testing program include:

1. Californa Short-Form Test of Mental Maturity.

2. Cognitive Abilities Test, Form 3.

3. Cognitive Abilities Test.

4. Henmon-Nelson Tests of Mental Ability.

5. Lorge-Thorndike Intelligence Test.

6. Otis-Lennon Mental Ability Test.

7. School and College Ability Tests, Third Edition.

Two specific aptitude tests a counselor might wish to incorporate in a testing effort are:

1. Differential Aptitude Tests.

2. Iowa Algebra Aptitude Test, 1967.

Since the youth in middle schools are in the exploratory stage (Super, et al., 1957) of their career development, some interest inventories that may help in their explorations would include:

1. Hall Occupational Orientation Inventory.

2. Kuder General Interest Survey, Form E.

3. Ohio Vocational Interest Survey.

4. Vocational Interest, Experience, and Skills Assessment.

In addition, specific career development instruments could be incorporated in the testing program. Some of these are:

1. Assessment of Career Development.

2. Career Awareness Inventory.

3. Career Maturity Inventory.

4. Career Planning Program.

5. Planning Career Goals.

Interpretation of Test Results

Once the counselor has selected and administered specific appraisal instruments, he or she must prepare to interpret the results to the students. A model presented by Miller (1977) provides a five-step procedure which can be used on an individual or group basis with children. The first step involves exploring the feelings of the child at the time of testing. This helps the counselor to understand both the physical and emotional feelings of the child, which may influence performance at the time of testing. This process helps to establish a counseling relationship which permits the child to express feelings in an empathic environment.

Since there may be some lag time between the actual testing sessions and the interpretation of the results, the counselor is advised to re-explain the purpose of the assessment to the child. During this time the purpose of the effort can be further clarified and the various measurement concepts that will be incorporated in the interpretation process can be discussed. Concepts such as norm groups, percentiles, and stanines can be included.

The third step in the process involves presenting the results in a slow, concise manner that facilitates questioning by the child. Encouraging the individual to discuss the personal meaning the scores have is critical at this time. If the child does not seem to fully grasp some specific aspects of the results the counselor can help clarify and reclarify them as needed. At this time the skills of empathic listening and appropriate responding by the counselor are crucial.

The integration of the assessment results with information and knowledge the child already possesses represents the fourth step in the model. Information the person already knows can be related to the assessment findings and a discussion of the personal meanings these have for the child can ensue. Any discrepancies that might exist as well as confirmations of personal knowledge can be discussed at this time.

The final step attempts to provide for the interpretation of the child's learnings from the previous four steps. At this time the child is assisted in examining and exploring how the findings apply. Specific plans may need to be made which include the child, the parents, teachers and the counselor, as effective strategies are developed to assist the child.

This model is one the trained counselor can use with numerous types of assessment instruments. The counselor needs to be fully aware of the various technical aspects of the instruments and follow through the interpretation process incorporating the procedures in the model.

Final Considerations

As counselors work with middle school aged youth, especially in the area of psychological assessment, they must be cautious to protect the dignity and the rights of the child. In 1975 Loesch clearly articulated the rights of youth regarding psychological assessment:

1. Children have the right to properly conducted assessment procedures. (p. 290).

2. Children have the right to be assessed through the use of the most appropriate instruments and techniques available. (p. 291).

3. Children have a right to complete comprehensive and honest feedback on their assessed characteristics and performance. (p. 292).

4. Children have the right to an explicit explanation of their results including as extensive an analysis of the assessment data as is possible. (p. 292).

5. Children have the right to know how the results of the assessment procedures will be used and to whom they will be made available. (p. 293).

6. Children have the right to discuss the assessment process and results with an individual qualified to provide accurate information. (p. 293).

7. Children have the right to further or other varieties of assessment as merited or desired. (p. 295).

8. Children have the right to feedback that explains how the assessment data applies to them as unique individuals. (p. 296).

These statements clearly define the rights of the student who participates in any assessment effort. The counselor, as the helping professional, can do much to promote these and insure that the dignity of the person is upheld.

SUMMARY

This chapter has traced some historical aspects of the testing movement and clarified the concept of psychological assessment. The testing program was discussed and specific instruments were noted. A review process for examining tests was presented along with a model for interpreting results. Specific statistical data about tests was deleted, as there are numerous texts which address these in great depth. Lastly, the rights of children regarding psychological assessment efforts were presented.

REFERENCES

Anastasi, A. *Psychological Testing,* 3rd ed. New York: The Macmillan Company, 1968.

Dubois, P.H. *A History of Psychological Testing,* Boston: Allyn & Bacon, 1970.

Goldman, L. Tests should make a difference. *Measurement and Evaluation in Guidance,* 1969, 2: 53-59.

Hill, G.R. Standards for tests users. *Measurement and Evaluation in Guidance,* 1969, 2: 191-148.

Loesch, L.C. & Miller, G. M. Psychological assessment as a functional resource in elementary school counseling. *Michigan Personnel and Guidance Journal,* 197 5ª, 6(2): 37-44.

Loesch, L.C. A child's guide to educational and psychological assessment. *Elementary School Guidance and Counseling.* 1975, 9: 289-297.

Loesch, L.C. Flow Chart Models for using tests. *Measurement and Evaluation in Guidance.* 1977, 10: 18-23.

Miller, G.M. A Test Card File. *The School Counselor,* 1975, 22: 372-374.

Miller, G.M. After the testing is over. *Elementary School Guidance and Counseling,* 1977, 12: 139-143.

Shertzer, B. & Stone, S.C. *Fundamentals of Guidance.* 4th ed. Boston: Houghton Mifflin Company, 1981.

The University of Michigan Bureau of School Services. *Michigan School Testing Service,* Ann Arbor, Michigan: The University of Michigan Bureau of School Services, 1978-79.

Van Riper, B.W. From clinical to a counseling process: Reversing the test appraisal process. *Measurement and Evaluation in Guidance,* 1974, 7: 24-30.

Chapter Eleven

CAREER DEVELOPMENT

GARY M. MILLER

Introduction

This chapter explores the career development of middle school youth. Strategies for the development of a career guidance program are presented as well as ways to review materials to incorporate in a career guidance program.

Career Guidance Background

Career guidance has been the backbone of the guidance and counseling movement in public schools. According to Miller (1973), the three principal factors that have contributed to vocational guidance are the interest which developed in personality dynamics, the expansion of studies in psychotherapy, and the re-examination of the concept of work and its meaning to individuals. In addition to these factors, Havighurst (1964) has noted that one's vocational development is a lifelong process.

Let us examine some of the ideas of Borow (1970) to gain a fuller perspective of career guidance. He has supported the inclusion of career experiences early in the educational lives of children and has suggested that education and counseling be provided to expand the options for students. Education and counseling can also prevent premature educational and vocational decisions.

Career Development Concepts

During the middle school years, students engage in two vocational development stages, as described by Havighurst (1964). From the age of five, the kindergarten age for many students, through the age of ten, which encompasses the fifth grade, students begin to identify with various workers. This identification helps to develop the career aspect of one's ego ideal (Havighurst, 1964). From ages ten to fifteen students begin to acquire the basic traits and habits of industry. They begin to organize their work and energy in order to complete a given task. In some cases, they begin to put work-oriented activities ahead of play-oriented ones (Havighurst, 1964).

165

Another view of career development which seems compatible with the development of middle school youths is that of Donald Super (1953) and Super, Crites, Hummel, Moser, Overstreet, and Warnath (1957). According to Super, the self-concept of the person influences vocational development.

> . . . the self concept is a product of the interaction of inherited attitudes, neural and endocrine make-up, opportunity to play various roles, and evaluations of the extent to which the results of role playing meet with the approval of superiors and fellows (Super, 1953, p. 190).

Super (1953), contends that one's work satisfactions and life satisfactions are directly related to finding suitable expressions of one's abilities, interests, personality factors and values.

Throughout the elementary and middle school years, students are involved in the growth stage, the first of five stages of their vocational development (Super, et al., 1957). It is during this stage, from birth to age fourteen, that self-concept develops. Key family and school personnel influence this development. Super, et al. (1957) have noted that the first substage within the growth stage is fantasy, experienced by children ages four to ten. During this time needs and fantasies play a central part of development. In the second substage, the interest substage, involving youngsters ages eleven to twelve, likes are the principal motivators of aspirations and activities. As children reach the third substage, capacity and abilities are given more emphasis and the young person begins to look at job requirements and training for specific occupations.

In addition to the developmental aspects influencing the career development of students, the counselor must also consider the numerous social factors that affect students. Lipsett (1962) has itemized six specific social factors which include:

1.   Social class membership
2.   Home influences
3.   School
4.   Community
5.   Pressure groups
6.   Role perception (Lipsett, 1962, pp. 436-437)

Knowledge of Super's (1957) stages and substages, and Lipsett's (1962) social factors can help the counselor examine the interaction between the student's career development and social factors. Figure 11:1 represents this matrix.

**Figure 11:1. Vocational Development Stages and Social Factors
of Middle School Students**

Vocational Development Stages   *Social Factors*

Growth Stage (Birth 14)	Social Class	Home	School	Community	Pressure Groups	Role Perception
Fantasy Substage (4 - 10)						
Interest Substage (11 - 12)						
Capacity Substage (13 - 14)						

Figure 11:1 shows that, as the student progresses through the various substages developed by Super, et al. (1957), he or she is also influenced throughout each substage by numerous social factors (Lipsett, 1962). As the student makes the various progressions he/she may require the assistance of the counselor.

Starting A Career Development Program

A career development program in the middle school must be developed in an orderly, systematic fashion. By carefully developing a reasonable plan for the program, the counselor can maintain a positive, credible image as a professional who is knowledgeable and concerned for the students, the school system and the entire community.

To develop an effective career guidance program, one must first ascertain the need for a program. Research can support the need and studies such as Wehrly's (1973) investigation of the occupational knowledge of students in grades four, six, and eight or Brough's (1969) research on counseling in a junior high school setting can accentuate the need for an organized program. An even better approach would be to conduct a local study to reflect community needs. Goldman's (1978) work on research for counselors can be beneficial in doing a preliminary investigation.

As one begins to clarify the need for a program, the pupils to be served and their specific needs can be identified, data which can be secured in the initial research effort.

Once needs and constituents are identified, goals and objectives suitable to the school can be developed in various ways. One approach would be to contact a state guidance consultant and discover what specific goals and objectives the state has for middle school career guidance programs. Contacting other states' guidance consultants can also help.

The counselor may wish to develop some specific goals and objectives for his or her own specific situation. A school-wide guidance committee can be formed to develop these goals and objectives. One helpful approach may include brainstorming ideas and consolidating them into workable goals, then rank-ordering these to develop a final list.

Appropriate goals and objectives, should be organized into a workable sequence. By such sequencing the guidance committee can plan its program for the school year and build in accountability checks along the way to assess how well plans are being met. Such an ongoing effort can add credibility to the program, alert the staff to changes that may need to be made, and result in a flexible, workable program.

An example of some specific goals and objectives that have been developed in the state of New York (1977) for students in grades four to six and seven to nine are presented in Figure 11:2. Note that general goals and specific objectives along with useful activities are presented throughout this model. Schools using these need to develop assessment procedures to determine how effectively their goals and objectives are being met.

Career Development Strategies

There are numerous strategies for providing for a comprehensive career development program in the middle school. Some of these are quite simple to organize and implement, while others are involved and complex.

Hansen (1972) has identified some of the considerations. She suggests that the counselor consider the strengths of the students, their changing values and their goals. The counselor needs also to consider the potentialities of the students and the necessity to help students develop these potentialities in order to reach their goals in life. Regarding Lipsett's (1962) factors, we also must realize the impact that family, friends and significant others may have on the students' goals. Since during the middle school years the students are in a state of rapid developmental change, the counselor must consider

Figure 11-2. New York State Career Guidance Model

Develop Ability to Gather, Analyze, and Use Career Information.

	Acquire Knowledge	Organize Information	Analyze Information	Apply Skills	Demonstrate Knowledge
4-6	Learn about jobs in school and neighborhood	Collect information about self and family	Analyze information presented in media to define problems (T.V., books, advertisements)	Make transportation plans and personal budget	Describe steps in a problem solving process
7-9	Use occupational information sources about jobs	Collect information about high school, college and occupational requirements	Consider information as it affects changes and barriers to personal plans	Read want ads and write resumes	Make notes from reference materials

Develop Awareness of Own Abilities, Aptitudes, and Interests and an Understanding of Others With the Capacity to Act Upon This Knowledge.

	Develop Awareness of Self and Others	Develop Positive Self Concept	Achieve Success by Applying Knowledge
4-6	Develop positive relationship with peers and adults	Identify interests, roles and personal contributions	Identify likes and dislikes in school subjects
7-9	Work with peers and adults to resolve problems	Construct definition of self concept	Establish positive relationships with teachers and peers

Figure 11:2 – *continued*

Identify Valued Life Situations, Priorities, and Preferences Which Form Basis for Career Decisions and Understand How These Affect Decisions.

	Identify Values	Clarify Values	Manage Values	Identify Feelings	Demonstrate Social Maturity	Apply Values
4-6	Identify values and satisfactions of others	List in rank order personal interests, abilities and satisfactions	Choose alternative ways to manage conflicts in use of time	Reflect feelings of others		
7-9	Identify how others use the valuing process	Recognize situations that require choices	Develop high school plans related to values of self and others		Demonstrate patience and openness	Clarify what will be of value in future work

Develop Ability to Choose Among Various Options, to Obtain Useful Career Information, to Select from Possible Occupational Choices, and to Translate Choices Into Reality.

	Understand Decision Making and Problem Solving	Practice Decision Making and Problem Solving	Apply Decision Making and Problem Solving
4-6	Relate to independence	Use in respect to self-responsibility	Use in group participation
7-9	Use to resolve conflicts	Use to solve general problems	Use in self-management

Figure 11:2 – *continued*

Develop Ability to Set Goals, Identify Steps to Accomplish Goals, Identify Resources to Achieve Goals, and Understand Factors that Cause Alternative Plans to be Selected.

	Explore Individual Activities And Attitudes	Explore Environment	Understand Planning Process	Apply Planning Process
4-6	Define "interests," "abilities," "aptitudes," "values," and "achievements"	Identify ways that classmates and workers can help peers	Understand family expectations	Make plan to achieve personal goals
7-9	Analyze interests and achievements	Analyze work environments	Understand use of alternatives in planning	Make an educational and training plan

Develop Knowledge and Skills Needed to Apply for and Obtain Jobs, Remain Employed, and Advance in Job Situations.

	Acquire Knowledge and Skills	Collect and Organize Information	Analyze and Use Information	Develop and Exhibit Positive Work Relationships	Apply Decision Making and Problem Solving Skills
4-6	Learn about jobs in school and neighborhood	List in rank order personal interests, abilities and satisfactions	Analyze information presented in media (T.V., books, advertisements)	Develop positive relationships with peers and adults	Collect and organize information about jobs and self
7-9	Explore environment with respect to interests and opportunities	Collect information about high school, college and occupational requirements	Consider information as it affects changes and barriers to personal plans	Work with peers and adults to resolve conflicts	Apply decision making and problem solving in self-management

Reprinted with permission of New York State Department of Education.

the developing personal styles of each student as they engage in various career development strategies. Lastly, Hansen (1972) notes the need to develop strategies that are activity-oriented as the students explore the multifaceted aspects of education, work and occupations. Keeping these suggestions in mind one can begin to explore specific strategies.

One approach is to develop a career resource center where students can browse and explore numerous kinds of information about careers and career development. Minor (1975) has developed some goals for such a center that are useful for the counselor to consider. Minor's (1975) first goal is to provide current information for the students. This updated information should provide a clear and realistic view of various careers and employment projections for the future. Information about local career options also needs to be accurate and easily accessible to the students.

Teachers and counselors cannot be forgotten when a career resource center is developed. Minor (1975) suggests that exploratory material about careers be available for teachers to incorporate in their classes. Resource guides often accompany such information for use by teachers. Counselors can also use such information for individual and group counseling.

Materials in the career resource center need to promote exploration of local community resources. Such locally-based information can also help to stimulate career exploration and motivate students to examine locally-based options (Minor, 1975).

A final consideration in the development of a career resource center is making sure that the materials are representative for minorities. With changing career expectations, students need to be exposed to information which realistically reflects the emerging needs of minority groups (Minor, 1975).

Another strategy one can adapt is the use of bulletin boards in the school. Students can help the counselor maintain bulletin boards which are current and appealing. The counselor can also secure assistance from teachers in developing bulletin boards related to each teacher's subject-area speciality. Whether the bulletin boards are developed by students, counselors or teachers, keep them current and change them about every three weeks during the school year.

Some schools have developed field-based experiences for students. Students visit actual work sites and speak with individuals employed in some of the occupations. This provides a realistic picture of the occupation for the students. Students could record the visits with video or audio equipment to use when they discuss the occupations after their field experiences.

Another approach involving the media requires that students listen for or observe various occupations depicted on radio or television. Students could conduct such a survey and then discuss these occupations in group guidance sessions.

In a group guidance setting the counselor can have students engage in role plays, depicting various occupations. Such role plays can incorporate the tools and materials used in some occupations to provide a "hands on" effect for the participants. In addition, students can present occupational information focusing on such topics as the preparation needed, the daily occupational requirements, possibilities for advancement, and salary or hourly pay.

A helpful strategy that may be used is an adaptation of the Career Awareness Program developed by Miller and Waidley (1974). This four-step program was designed to help students systematically explore and prepare for occupations. The part of the program the middle school counselor can use focuses on the incorporation of standardized assessment results and occupational information. The counselor can provide for assessment of students' interests, and then examine these results along with other appraisal information and school data as an avenue for discussing and exploring occupations. Coupled with the occupational information provided from the career resource center, the counselor can conduct an in-depth exploration of occupations with students. This approach can be done on an individual basis or in a group setting.

Three other approaches for providing career information have been highlighted by Herr and Cramer (1979). They note the use of curriculum infusion as an appropriate guidance information strategy. Such an approach encourages teachers to include guidance information within the classroom setting. This approach promotes an awareness of the relationship of specific occupations to subjects students are studying in their classes. By providing such an infusion, the teacher can promote a better understanding of how courses and occupations can eventually mesh for the students. The infusion concept makes career guidance a school-wide endeavor and not an ancillary service in the school.

Another strategy presented by Herr and Cramer (1979) relates to decision-making and gaining career information. They suggest having students examine life decisions and develop three alternatives for each of these, which they will eventually discuss. This approach incorporates the use of the 15 United States Office of Education career clusters for exploring occupational options.

Herr and Cramer (1979) have also suggested promoting community involvement as their third possible strategy. This format includes having community personnel visit the school as well as having students involved in field experiences, similar to those presented earlier.

Strategies for promoting career development are varied. Each counselor needs to know what the students need, what resources are available and, from this, develop an approach suitable for the school.

Evaluating Career Materials

Whenever the counselor develops a career development program, it is critical that the information meet specific standards. In 1972 and in 1977 the National Vocational Guidance Association developed a detailed set of guidelines for evaluating career guidance information. Weinrach (1974) has itemized nine criteria that the content of career guidance information should meet. The literature should clearly and simply present the common traits of the work involved in a career. The work setting should be clearly depicted (1) as should the personal, psychological and monetary rewards one may possibly gain from such a career. Weinrach (1974) has also stressed the need for the information to describe the possibilities for advancement, the entry requirements and occupational forecast. The three final considerations include clarification of alternative careers related to the career one is examining as well as the licensing and/or membership requirements and the personal aspects needed for the person to gain success in a given career. Using Weinrach's (1974) Career Literature Evaluation Checklist presented in Figure 11:5, the counselor can systematically review career literature and evaluate its applicability to the setting.

Weinrach (1974) has also stipulated criteria and developed a checklist for the use of films and filmstrips. According to Weinrach, the preparation and revision dates of the material should be indicated prior to the presentation. In addition, the information should be free of sexual religious, racial, ethnic or social bias. Also, appropriate credits for the information need to be included and additional references for supplemental materials may be most helpful to the user of the materials. Lastly, the materials need to correspond to the grade level and vocabulary level of the group for which it is intended. Weinrach has developed a checklist for evaluating films and filmstrips used in career guidance.

Figure 11:3. REVIEWER'S RATING SHEET

Name of reviewer: _____ Date: _____

This is a review of: _____

Publisher: _____ Price:_____

Our intended audience is: _____

	Appropriateness for intended audience		
	low	average	high

A. Content:
1. Explicit statement of purpose
2. Integrity of title
3. Realistic objectives
4. Accurate, adequate and realistic presentation of ideas, concepts or information
5. Eliciting of user response

B. Technical considerations:
1. Packaging
2. Credits
3. Technical qualities
4. Length

C. User's Guide:
1. Credits
2. Purpose, objectives and intended audience
3. Description
4. Results of field testing
5. Follow-up activities

D. Social Orientation:
1. Sex/age/occupational role bias   xxx*
2. Ethnic/race and religious bias   xxx
3. Value orientation, social status and self-serving purposes   xxx
   * Media are either bias-free or they are not.

E. Summary:
1. The major strengths of this product for our population are:

2. The major weaknesses of this product for our population are:

3. Unusual or unique characteristics of the product:

4. On the basis of the result of this review, I recommend that:

Figure 11:4. CAREER FILM and FILMSTRIP EVALUATION CHECKLIST

Title: _____ ( ) BW   ( ) color

Producer/Distributor: _____

Cost: Purchase $_____   Rental $_____   Length _____ min.

Intended audience: _____

	Unsatis-factory	Satis-factory	Excellent
1. A description of the nature of the occupation, field, or industry.	_____	_____	_____
2. A realistic portrayal of the work setting.	_____	_____	_____
3. The benefits and satisfactions of the occupations.	_____	_____	_____
4. The entry requirements.	_____	_____	_____
5. The possibilities of advancement.	_____	_____	_____
6. The employment outlook.	_____	_____	_____
7. Related occupations to which a person might transfer.	_____	_____	_____
8. Whether or not licensing or union membership is required.	_____	_____	_____
9. Personal qualifications.	_____	_____	_____
10. Relevancy for the intended audience.	_____	_____	_____
11. The proper length.	_____	_____	_____
12. Freedom from bias.	_____	_____	_____
13. Credits.	_____	_____	_____
14. The purpose.	_____	_____	_____
15. A complete user's guide.	_____	_____	_____

Evaluated by: _____   Date: _____

The professional middle school counselor needs to consider numerous factors in using career information. The two checklists presented in Figures 11:4 and 11:5 will be helpful. Another helpful approach to providing for career exploration is the use of simulated guidance materials.

Simulated Materials

Over the past several years a number of simulated career information programs have emerged. Weinrach (1978) defines these as:

> Simulated refers to any experience or activity that is designed to provide clients with an opportunity to practice, initiate or model specified behaviors or to increase clients's awareness or knowledge about specified guidance-related topics. The materials may include any kind of media, such as kits, filmstrips, cassettes, and games or activity, such as role playing, structured group experiences and psychodrama. The use of such materials is designed to elicit the active involvement of the user (p. 288).

Simulated career guidance materials should: (1) stimulate discussion of the career; (2) provide specific knowledge, which, under other circumstances would require much time to secure; (3) be non-threatening and (4) help clients learn new skills in a controlled environment (Weinrach, 1978).

To provide a genuine learning experience for the student, Herr and Cramer (1979) have suggested that simulations be characterized by:

1. A supportive climate
2. Exposure of the individual's normal behavior
3. Feedback
4. Experimentation
5. A cognitive map
6. Practice
7. Planning application

Herr and Cramer (1979) have described some of the popular career guidance simulations currently in use. These simulations include the Life Career Game (Boocock, 1967), Making of Life Decisions (Johnson and Myrick, 1972), the Computerized Vocational Information System (Harris, 1968), DISCOVER: A Computerized Career Guidance Program (Rayman and Harris-Bowsbey, 1977), and the Educational and Career Exploration System (Thompson, Lindeman, Clack, and Bohn, 1970).

Again, Weinrach (1978) has developed a procedure to evaluate the simulated guidance activities. He examines four specific areas: (1) content; (2) technical considerations; (3) the user's guide and (4) the social orientation of the simulation. In addition a summary area that examines the strengths, weaknesses, unique traits and recommendations by the reviewer is included. A sample of the rating sheet developed by Weinrach (1978) for simulated materials is presented in Figure 11:3.

Retrieval Programs

The ability to secure career guidance information rapidly has been enhanced by various information retrieval programs. One popular program, Vocational Information for Education and Work (VIEW) (Smith, 1968) was developed in San Diego County, California, and adaptations of it have been incorporated by other states under various names. Decks of IBM cards containing information regarding career opportunities in one's own city, county and state represent the backbone of this system. This system allows for update of data so that more current information can be made available to the students and their counselors.

In South Carolina, The South Carolina Occupational Information Coordinating Committee (SCOICC), composed of representatives from eight state agencies, has developed a program for providing cur-

Figure 11:5. CAREER LITERATURE EVALUATION CHECKLIST

Title: _____

Publisher/Distributor: _____

Cost $_____ each   Number of pages: _____

Intended audience: _____

	Unsatis-factory	Satis-factory	Excellent
1. A description of the nature of the occupation, field, or industry.	————	————	————
2. A realistic portrayal of the work setting.	————	————	————
3. The benefits and satisfactions of the occupations.	————	————	————
4. The entry requirements.	————	————	————
5. The possibilities of advancement.	————	————	————
6. The employment outlook.	————	————	————
7. Related occupations to which a person might transfer.	————	————	————
8. Whether or not licensing or union membership is required.	————	————	————
9. Written on the level of the intended audience.	————	————	————
10. Interesting format.	————	————	————
11. Enhancing photographs and graphs.	————	————	————
12. Recent date of publication.	————	————	————
13. Freedom from bias.	————	————	————
14. Credits.	————	————	————
15. Bibliography.	————	————	————
16. Training information.	————	————	————
17. Sources of financial aid and training employment.	————	————	————

Evaluated by: _____   Date: _____

rent career, occupational and educational information to people throughout the state. Although it is currently designed for grades nine through twelve, there are plans to develop a program for the middle schools throughout the state. This program provides local and national career information. There are six specific files in the system which include: the occupational file, the college file, the college major file, the school subjects file, the apprenticeship file and the military file. Information from these files can be delivered through computer terminals or on microfiche. Currently, 43 sites are being served with the computer terminal access system and 43 are being served using the microfiche format. Eventually, the South Carolina Occupational Information System (SCOIS) will be linked to the Job Bank and Job Match systems currently in use by the Employment Security Commission. Such a system, with adaptations for middle school students, will rapidly facilitate the sharing of career information and data that will be useful for the students as they consider various careers.

In 1979 a Computerama program was held in Florida. At this program, seven computer-based guidance and occupational information systems were presented. Ms. Delores McCord, a career counselor, developed a criterion check list for each of these programs. Three of the systems appropriate for upper-level middle school students are presented on the criterion checklist in Appendix C.

As can be seen, the career development of middle school students can be complex. It involves many aspects of each student's life and can be promoted using both basic and highly technical strategies. Obviously each counselor needs to consider how fully to implement a suitable program.

REFERENCES

Boocock, S.S. The life career game. *Personnel and Guidance Journal,* 1967, *45,* 328-334.

Borow, H. Career development: A future for counseling. In W. H. Van Hoose & J.J. Pietrofesa (Eds.), *Counseling and Guidance in the Twentieth Century.* Boston: Houghton Mifflin Company, 1970.

Brough, J.R. A profile of junior high school counseling. *The School Counselor,* 1969, *17,* 67-72.

Goldman, L. (Ed.) *Research Methods for Counselors.* New York: John Wiley and Sons, 1978.

Hansen, L.S. A model for career development through curriculum. *Personnel and Guidance Journal,* 1972, *51,* 243-250.

Harris, J.A. The computerization of vocational information. *Vocational Guidance Quarterly,* 1968, *17,* 12-20.

Havighurst, R.J. Youth in exploration and man emergent. In H. Borow (Ed.) *Man in a World at Work.* Boston: Houghton Mifflin Company, 1964.

Herr, E. L. & Cramer, S.L. *Career Guidance Through the Life Span.* Boston: Little, Brown and Company, 1979.

Johnson, R.H. & Myrick, R.D. MOLD: A new approach to career decision-making. *Vocational Guidance Quarterly,* 1972, *21,* 48-52.

Lipsett, L. Social factors in vocational development. *Personnel and Guidance Journal.* 1962, *40,* 432-437.

Miller, C.H. Historical and recent perspective on work and vocational guidance. In H. Borow (Ed.) *Career Guidance for a New Age.* Boston: Houghton Mifflin Company, 1973.

Miller, G.M. & Waidley, .W. Looking toward the future: The career awareness program. *Journal of College Student Personnel,* 1975, *16.*

Minor, C.W. Developing a career resource center. In R.C. Reardon and H.D. Burck (Eds.) *Facilitating Career Development Strategies for Counselors.* Springfield, Illinois: Charles C. Thomas, Publisher, 1975.

National Vocational Guidance Association. Guidelines for the preparation and evaluation of career guidance media. Washington, D.C.: *American Personnel and Guidance Association Press* (Mimeograph). 1971.

National Vocational Guidance Association. NVGA guidelines for preparation and evaluation of non-print career media. *Vocational Guidance Quarterly*, 1977, *26*, 99-107.

New York State Education Department. *Career Guidance Model*. Albany, New York: The State Education Department, Bureau of Guidance, 1977.

Rayman, J.R. & Bowsbey-Harris, J.A. DISCOVER: A model for a systematic career guidance program. *Vocatonal Guidance Quarterly*, 1977, *26*, 3-12.

Smith, E.D. Innovative ideas in vocational guidance. *American Vocational Journal*, 1968, *43*, 19-21.

Super, D.E. A theory of vocational development. *American Psychologist*. 1953, *8*, 185-190.

Super, D.E., Crites, J.O., Hummel, R.C., Moser, H.P., Overstreet, P.L., and Warnath, C.F. *Vocational Development: A Framework for Research*. New York: Teachers College Press, Columbia University, 1957.

The South Carolina Occupational Information Coordinating Committee. *South Carolina Occupational Information System*. Columbia, S.C.: The South Carolina Occupational Information Coordinating Committee, 1979.

Thompson, A.S., Lindeman, R.H., Clark, S. & Bohn, M.J., Jr. *The educational and career-exploration system: Final trial and evaluation in Montclair High School*. New York: Teachers College, Columbia University, 1970.

Wehrly, B.L. Children's occupational knowledge. *Vocational Guidance Quarterly*, 1973, *22*, 124-129.

Weinrach, S.G. The busy counselor's guide to the evaluation of career information materials. *The School Counselor*, 1974, *22*, 53-57.

Weinrach, S.G. Guidelines of the systematic selection, evaluation and use of simulated guidance materials. *Personnel and Guidance Journal*, 1978, *56*, 288-292.

Chapter Twelve

RESEARCH and TRENDS

GARY M. MILLER

Introduction

As was noted in Chapter One the middle school movement in the United States has been a recent educational innovation. Since 1965 when Alexander and Williams proposed the rationale for the development of middle schools there have been numerous efforts to establish middle schools.

This chapter will examine some of the research focusing on the development of middle schools and the certification of middle school teachers, counselor certification and research on principals' and counselors' views of counselors' functions. Problems facing middle school guidance counselors and ways to promote positive counselor-principal interactions will be discussed. Also included will be some ideas about organizing a viable middle school guidance program.

The Growth of Middle Schools

Two years after the original proposal for the development of middle schools by Alexander and Williams (1965), Cuff (1967) reported that 29 of the 50 states had already developed middle schools. By 1969 some 1,101 middle schools were in operation (Alexander and Kealy, 1969). Pumerantz (1969) disclosed that only Connecticut had legislation defining the middle school and that many of the 50 states did not recognize the middle school concept.

A study reported in 1976 by Compton analyzed the growth of middle schools during the period from 1968 to 1974. He noted that in 1968 Alexander found 1,101 middle schools in operation and that by 1970 Kealy reported 2,298 middle schools. Compton found 3,723 middle schools in operation in 1974. In this study, the North Central and Southern regions of the country contained 64 percent of the middle schools.

The most recent research reporting on the growth of middle schools was reported by Brooks (1968a, 1978b.). This study, conducted in 1977, identified 4060 middle schools in the United States. Nebraska and the District of Columbia were the only two areas not having middle schools (Brooks, 1978a).

As one can see, middle schools have shown a steady growth. Almost 90 percent of the middle schools surveyed by Brooks (1978a) included grades five or six through eight: These schools obviously were designed to meet the needs of the pre-adolescents.

Teacher Certification

A study of the certification of middle school teachers was reported by George, McMillan, Malinka and Pumerantz (1975). In 1975, eight states had actually developed separate certification for middle school teachers. This shows an increase from the two states that had middle school teacher certification in 1968 (Pumerantz, 1968).

Regarding future plans for developing specific middle school teacher certification, George et al. (1975) discovered that 27 states planned such efforts. This represents a drop from the 39 states that planned such efforts reported in the Pumerantz (1968) study. However, it is only a net loss of six states, for there was an increase of six states actually developing middle school teacher certification between the time of the Pumerantz (1968) and George, et al. (1975) studies.

Middle School Counselor Certification

According to the findings by George, et al.(1975), certification for special school personnel employed in middle schools was almost nonexistent. In 1975, only Montana issued special certificates for middle school counselors. In 1979, Miller and Ammons surveyed the 50 state departments of education throughout the United States. They attempted to ascertain the types of certification required for counselors in states having middle schools. In addition they investigates which states were currently in the process of developing specific guidelines for certifying middle school counselors. The types of certification for middle school counselors and the number of states requiring that specific certification are presented in Table 12:1.

It is apparent that the most common certification is of the K-12 type. According to this data, no states had certification criteria exclusively for middle school counselors. This seems to support the findings of George et al.(1975) that most states do not have certification criteria for middle school counselors. However, George et al.(1975) noted that one state did have specific certification for guidance personnel, whereas according to Miller and Ammons (1980), no states had separate middle school counselor certification.

Miller and Ammons (1980) also found that Virginia and West Virginia were the only two states planning to develop certification criteria for middle school counselors. Also, Boston, Massachusetts, schools indicated some effort to establish criteria for certification.

Table 12:1. Nature of Counselor Certification for Middle School Counselors

Type of Certification	Number of States
K - 12	22
Either Secondary or Elementary	18
No Certification Required	3
Elementary Certification	2
Secondary Certification	1
Comprehensive Certification *	4

* Comprehensive certification is used as some states will accept several combinations of certification standards.

Obviously, the movement for certification of middle school counselors, separate from those requirements for elementary and secondary school counselors, is a slow one. As Miller and Ammons stated:

> Perhaps the time has come for state guidance to unite practicing middle school counselors and counselor education personnel to institute efforts designed to prepare professionals who have specialized training for working with middle school youth (1980, p. 27).

The Counselors' Functions

Counselors in middle schools are faced with a unique role. The fact that the children with whom they work have very specific needs, combined with expectations from numerous publics, can present dilemmas for the professional counselor.

The American School Counselor Association's statement on the role of the middle school counselor was noted in Chapter One. Considering this role statement and combining it with a statement regarding entry level counselor skills (Geisler, 1974), Pappas and Miller (1976) Miller and Pappas (1978a), Miller and Pappas (1978b) have conducted research on the functions of middle school counselors as seen by both middle school principals and counselors.

Pappas and Miller (1976) reported on a survey mailed to 120 middle school principals in Michigan. Total data were received from 68 schools and of these, 56 reported having organized guidance programs. Of the 42 entry level counselor skills gleaned from Geisler (1974), those which were considered the top ten counselor functions as seen by their principals are presented in Table 12:2.

Table 12:2. Highest Ranking Counselor Functions As Viewed By
Middle School Principals

Ranking	Percentage	Functions
1	98	Providing individual counseling for students with personal concerns.
2	96	Communicating the guidance programs and its services to students.
3	89	Organizing and administering the guidance program.
4	86	Identifying students in need of special services.
5	84	Communicating the guidance program to school personnel.
7	80	Interpreting standardized test results to students and parents.
7	80	Communicating the guidance program to parents.
7	80	Identifying and making referrals to other school personnel.
9	77	Consulting with teachers on developmental needs and concerns.
10	75	Conducting small groups counseling for selected student population.

As one can see from this data, the Michigan principals appear to agree with some of the guidelines established by the counselors' professional association. Pappas and Miller (1976) noted:

> Counselors and administrators have not always agreed on the appropriate role functions for the counselor. It is important, however, to identify and strengthen those functions where there is agreement. Thus, the basis for open communication and support in those areas of disagreement can be facilitated (p. 6).

In 1977 Miller and Pappas surveyed 120 middle school principals in South Carolina using the same instrument as in their 1976 research. Of the 120 middle schools, 64 reported having organized guidance programs.

The principals of South Carolina middle schools top ten ratings of counselor functions are presented in Table 12:3.

Table 12:3: South Carolina Principals' Rankings of Ten Highest
Counselor Functions

(N = 64)

Ranking	Percentage	Function
1.5	98	Communicating the guidance program and its services to students.
1.5	98	Providing individual counseling for students with personal-social concerns.
3	97	Organizing and administering the guidance program.
4	94	Developing and communicating the guidance program to school personnel.
5	88	Developing programs to prepare students in decision-making.
6	87	Identifying students in need of special assistance.
7	84	Conducting small group counseling for selected student populations.
8.5	81	Explaining and interpreting standardized tests to teachers.
8.5	81	Developing and communicating the guidance program to parents.
10	75	Participating in professional meetings and workshops.

The combined ratings of the Michigan and South Carolina middle school principals' top ten ratings are presented in Table 12:4.

Table 12:4. Combined Principals' Rankings of Ten Highest Counselor Functions

(N = 120)

Ranking	Percentage	Function
1.5	98	Communicating the guidance program and its services to students.
1.5	98	Providing individual counseling for students with personal-social concerns.
3	93	Organizing and administering the guidance program.
4	88	Developing and communicating the guidance program to school personnel.
5.5	83	Identifying students in need of special assistance.
7	81	Consulting with teachers on student development needs and concerns.
8	80	Conducting small group counseling for selected student population.
9.5	76	Interpreting standardized test results to students and parents.
9.5	76	Identifying and making referrals to other school personnel.

These combined data clearly indicate that the middle school principals in the two states agree with the ASCA role statement. In examining these combined data the authors concluded:

> This study represents a point of departure from which middle school educators can begin the examination of guidance programs.
> . . . .
> These results indicate support of such programs and emphasize the need for middle school counselors and their administrators to work together to develop and refine the guidance services offered to middle school children (Miller and Pappas, 1977).

Middle school counselors' views of their functions were also studied by Miller and Pappas (1978). Again, the entry level competencies (Geisler, 1974) were used as they surveyed 80 Michigan and 70 South Carolina middle school counselors. In this study, 54 of the Michigan and 56 of the South Carolina counselors responded. Results of the ratings of these 110 counselors are presented in Table 12:5.

Table 12:5. Combined Rankings of Ten Highest Middle School Counselor
Functions
(N = 110)

Ranking	Percentage	Function
1	98	Providing individual counseling for students with personal-social concerns.
2	94	Communicating the guidance program and its services to students.
3	89	Organizing and administering the guidance program.
4	87	Communicating the guidance program to school personnel.
5	85	Consulting with teachers on student development needs and concerns.
6	84	Identifying students in need of special assistance.
7	80	Conducting small group counseling for selected student populations.
8	78	Communicating the guidance program to parents.
9	76	Identifying and making referrals to other school personnel.
10	74	Interpreting standardized test results to students and parents.

In examining these results the three C's of counseling, consulting and coordinating were clearly evident. The counseling functions
of counselors were ranked first, seventh and tenth. Consulting functions were ranked fifth, sixth and ninth. Coordinating activities were
ranked second, third, fourth, and eighth.

From this study, Miller and Pappas (1978) identified some implications for middle school counselors. They suggested such data could
help middle school counselors in promoting their accountability and
further clarifying their roles in the schools. It was also suggested such
functions could be used for developing logs for keeping a record of
the counselor's professional activities.

Miller and Pappas (1978) also noted the need to clarify the
certification criteria for middle school counselors and the need for
counselor education programs to develop plans for pre- and in-service
preparation.

The studies presented in this section represent some of the initial data-based efforts to clarify the role of the middle school counselor. It is apparent throughout these studies that counselors and principals are able to clearly identify the functions counselors are to perform. It remains for counselor and principals to work together to facilitate the implementation of these functions.

Developing Middle School Guidance Programs

In this portion of the chapter some guidance model information will be presented along with some ideas for promoting counselor-principal interactions.

In 1976 Bohlinger described some research findings about middle school guidance programs and presented some information about the type of comprehensive guidance program most appropriate for middle schools. He surveyed 162 middle schools in Ohio. Results were gathered from 106 schools, and these results indicated what services the school counselors actually performed. Table 12:6 contains the results of this study. Ninety-seven of the 106 schools had a counselor component and each aspect of the counselor component with the appropriate percentage of each of the 97 schools having such a service is presented. In addition, the advising, peer counseling and exploratory components and their percentages are also presented.

Table 12:6. **Percentage of Middle Schools Reporting Components and Services**

	N	*%*
COUNSELOR COMPONENT	97	91
1. Information Service		93
2. Testing Service		95
3. Records Service		83
4. Referral Service		78
5. Conference Service		88
6. Consulting Service		67
7. Parent Education Service		23
8. Career Service		43
9. Orientation Service		87
10. Placement Service		84
11. Monitoring Service		83
12. Group Counseling		61
13. Personal, Individual Counseling		90
ADVISOR COMPONENT	24	23
PEER COUNSELING COMPONENT	3	3
EXPLORATORY COMPONENT	55	52

Allen, Splittgerber, and Ryan (1978) surveyed 800 teachers and counselors throughout the United States. The data collected from 569 of these people indicated the types of guidance services provided in the school in which these individuals were employed. As can be seen in Table 12:7 personal guidance was the first priority noted by the teacher and counselors.

Table 12:7. Middle School Guidance Services

N = 569

Service Provided	Frequency	Percentage
Personal Guidance	537	94.4
Vocational Guidance	348	61.2
Discipline	237	41.7
Testing	21	14.3
Group Work	20	13.6
Scheduling	19	12.9
Home Visits	11	7.5
Academic Advising	10	6.8
Attendance Duties	6	4.1

An interesting note from this study was that 85 percent of the teachers saw themselves as playing some role in the guidance functions of the schools.

Both the Bohlinger (1976) and Allen, Splittgerber and Ryan (1979) studies have highlighted some of the actual functions counselors are responsible for in a guidance program. In the discussion of a comprehensive guidance model, Bohlinger (1976) clarified essential components of such a program. As part of the counselor component, Bohlinger (1976) views the counselor as being responsible for coordinating such efforts as testing, referral procedures and parent education.

The advisory component (Bohlinger, 1976) consists of providing information and assistance to the student regarding specific school-related programs. This component is seen predominantly within the responsibility of the teacher. In addition to this information-providing function, the teachers are also responsible for developing appropriate educational experiences for the students and for reporting, in a systematic fashion on their progress.

Bohlinger (1976) also stresses the component of teacher-student interaction as being critical in a guidance program. Through daily student contacts in a positive environment, teachers can do much to promote positive self concepts in their students. Such interactions can also help students keep abreast of their educational progress within each class.

Peer counseling represents Bohlinger's fourth component. This approach of preparing students to act as helpers to their peers expands guidance services throughout the school. It can do much in encouraging students to talk over their concerns with someone whom they believe is concerned and understands them.

The final component Bohlinger suggests is an exploratory program. Such an effort capitalizes on the various interests of students and provides mini-courses based on students' interests. The purposes of these courses are threefold; (1) to promote new avenues of thinking, as students explore areas of their interest; (2) to help students increase their self awareness by exploring new activities and talents; and (3) to promote decision-making by students.

To develop such a model program the counselor may wish to consider the four stages developed by Bohlinger (1976) as well as the ideas presented by Duff (1978). Bohlinger (1976) suggests going through a search stage wherein people in the school become aware of the need for an expansion of the guidance program. The feasibility stage (Bohlinger, 1976) consists of developing efforts toward planned change. These include surveys of teachers and students, cost analyses, sampling community reactions and discussing such a program with one's superiors.

Bohlinger (1976) describes the next stage as the unfreezing stage. It is during this time that one promotes greater faculty awareness of the guidance program. In addition, task forces are developed to make suggestions for the program and their recommendations are considered. During this unfreezing stage budget decisions are made, materials are secured and in-service training programs are designed. Finally, members in the community are informed about the program and are invited to act as monitoring agents for the program's efforts.

The final stage is the pilot stage (Bohlinger, 1976). At this point the program is initiated and revised as needed. Evaluation is also conducted during this stage to ascertain how well the goals of the program have been developed.

By following these steps the counselor can develop a viable guidance program. In addition the counselor needs to verify to principals and teachers that as a counselor he or she is indispensable. Duff (1978) notes that counselors need to be fully prepared when meeting with principals and be able to clearly articulate their needs and the needs of their program. Duff (1978) also suggests making the principal a part of the program through direct involvement. Lastly, Duff (1978) encourages counselors to offer assistance to teachers whenever possible. Such help to teachers provides an indirect help to the principal, who as a result may form a more positive view of the guidance program.

The Detroit Program

The Department of Guidance and Counseling in the Detroit Public Schools (1979) has published a guidance model for use in Detroit's middle schools, which include grades six through eight. For each grade level the following services are provided: (1) counseling; (2) consultation; (3) coordination; (4) career guidance; (5) program selection and placement; (6) referral and information service; and (7) evaluation (Detroit Public Schools, 1979).

The complete program developed by the Detroit Public Schools is presented in Appendix D (Detroit Public Schools, 1979).

The objectives, activities, time lines and success criteria for the Detroit program are clearly presented for the counselor. Obviously, each school has its own specific needs which must be met for the unique population enrolled in that school. The Detroit model can easily be adapted and revised according to each school.

Conclusions

Throughout this chapter, some of the research about middle school counselors and their programs have been discussed. Ideas about guidance programs and a specific model for such a program have been presented. Hopefully, this information has provided some clear, concise ideas for the middle school counselor.

REFERENCES

Alexander, W.M. & Williams, E.L. Schools for the middle school years. *Educational Leadership*, 1965, *23*, 217-223.

Allen, H.A., Splittgerber, F.L. & Ryan, J.P. *The middle school as seen by teachers.* Unpublished manuscript, 1978 (Available from Harvey A. Allen, College of Education, University of South Carolina, Columbia, S.C. 29208).

Bohlinger, T. Middle school guidance: Problems in comprehensiveness and implementation. *Middle School Journal,* 1976, *7*, pp. 7; 22-23.

Brooks, K. The middle school — A national survey. *Middle School Journal,* 1978a, *9(1):* 6-7.

Brooks, K. The middle school — A national survey. *Middle School Journal,* 1978b, *9(2):* 6-7.

Compton, M.F. The middle school: A status report. *Middle School Journal*, 1976, 7, 3-5.

Cuff, W.A. Middle schools on the march. *The Bulletin of the National Association of Secondary School Principals*. 1967, 51, 82-83.

Department of Guidance and Counseling, Detroit Public Schools. *Guidance Program Model for Elementary, Middle, Senior High*. Detroit: Detroit Public Schools, 1979.

Duff, C.F. Creating effective counselor-principal interaction. *Middle School Journal*, 1978, 9, 14-15.

Geisler, J. Counselor education position statement on entry level counselor skills. *Michigan Personnel and Guidance Association Journal*, 1974, 6, 20-23.

George, P.S., McMillan, M., Malinka, R., & Pumerantz, P. Middle school teacher certification: A national survey. *Educational Leadership*, 1975, 33, 213-216.

Miller, G.M. & Ammons, J.M. Certification trends for middle school counselors. *Oregon Personnel and Guidance Journal*, 1980, 4, 26-27.

Miller, G.M. & Pappas, J.G. *Middle school counselor functions: The principals' views*. Unpublished manuscript, 1977 (Available from Gary M. Miller, College of Education, University of South Carolina, Columbia, S.C. 29208).

Miller, G.M. & Pappas, J.G. Middle school counselors view their priorities – in Middle/Junior high school counselors' corner edited by Judy Tindall in *Elementary School Guidance and Counseling*, 1978, 12, 289-293.

Pappas, J.G. & Miller, G.M. Middle school principals' perceptions of their counselors. *Middle School Journal*, 1976, 7, pp. 6; 22.

Pumerantz, P. Few states certify teachers for growing middle schools. *Phi Delta Kappan*, 1969, 51, 102.

APPENDIX

Appendix A
The Unique Role of the Middle/Junior High School Counselor

There is a unique role for the middle/junior high school counselor, and there has been an increasing need to develop a position paper to describe this role. This position paper was originally authored by Mary K. Ryan, Middle/ Junior High School Vice President for ASCA, 1972-73. The original paper has since been modified by incorporating suggestions and recommendations made by practicing school counselors. This position paper has now been officially recognized and accepted by the American School Counselor Association Governing Board.

The middle/junior high school counselor recognizes the commonalities of the role and function with those of the elementary and secondary work settings. However, since early adolescents or transcents have special physical, emotional, and social needs, services specifically related to middle/junior high school students must be established. To ensure the fullest development of each child's talents and capabilities, an effective guidance program must recognize the many physiological and psychological differences of adolescents in grades five through nine.

Counseling

In serving as a facilitator of self-development, the middle/junior high school counselor should provide an individual counseling environment for all students to help them gain an understanding of themselves and find an identity. Emphasis on individual counseling does not rule out the benefits obtained from group sessions or peer counseling. The capable middle/junior high school counselor will utilize all techniques in helping students objectively evaluate their present and future lives. The counselor recognizes that a successful developmental guidance program with such a learner-centered base depends upon cooperative efforts of the total learning team.

School Staff

To improve the educational climate and foster personal and social development of the counselee, it is incumbent upon the counselor to share his expertise with the teachers. Through individual conferences, case conferences, inservice training, and as an integral part of the team, the counselor can assist the staff in becoming increasingly aware of and sensitive to the needs of the early adolescent. The counselor should supply necessary personal data, interpret test results, and help resolve value conflicts.

Teachers, with their close, everyday student contact, have significant opportunities to affect the students' self concepts. Cooperation is not only essential but beneficial to the counselor and to the staff since both are working toward the same goal — i.e., enabling the student to reach his full potential.

The counselor may assist administrators in ascertaining that the curriculum is meeting the needs of all students, that discipline is a positive nature, and that quality integrated services are provided.

Parent Involvement

Maintaining open lines of communication with parents, in either individual or group settings, should maximize the students' social as well as academic adjustment. This counselor responsibility, applicable to all age groups, is particularly pertinent in the middle/junior high school, since adolescents are striving for independence and are reaching a level of maturity and socialization that causes them to question environmental pressures.

The counselor's role in parental consultation includes such activities as interpreting test results, acquainting parents with school policy and procedures, making parents aware of in-school and out-of-school referral agencies, as well as assisting through direct instruction in parental understanding of child growth and development.

Community Contact

Since the general public has been oriented to thinking of guidance counselors as means of obtaining college admissions and vocational information, it is mutually advantageous for the community to have an understanding of all guidance functions as they relate to this work setting.

Contact with community social, civic, and professional organizations is essential for maximizing student welfare. In order to facilitate community understanding of the middle/junior high school guidance program, the counselor has a responsibility to share the guidance program with the public through the newsletter, handbooks, newspaper articles, radio and television.

The citizens' involvement in defining community needs will ensure support for the counselor's endeavors in planning a complete guidance program. Untapped resources will be forthcoming from the public to assist the counselor in becoming a change agent in promoting improved human relations. Prevention of problems for the impressionable early-teenagers should be an outcome of the combined school and community interest.

Other Areas of Special Responsibility

Orientation to junior and senior high schools, educational placement, career development, and group activities to promote greater self-direction, particularly in value formulation and decision making, are all areas with special implications for the middle/junior high school counselor.

A well-rounded middle/junior high school guidance program addresses itself to the social, emotional, and physical uniquenss of the early adolescent and aims to promote a high level of self-understanding and self-direction in each individual student.

It is hoped that this position paper will assist in strengthening the position of the middle/junior high school counselors. Counselors are encouraged to make use of this position statement whenever appropriate.

This paper was approved by ASCA Governing Board, August 1977.

Appendix B
Letter to Parents

Hello,

You have received a letter from _____
School District seeking your approval of special evaluation of your child.
This letter explains why your child is to receive this special attention and other questions that you may have will be answered as you
read through this booklet.

Why My Child?

_____(Name)_____ , _____(Title)_____ ,

is concerned about _____(Child's Name)_____ for
the following reasons:

(Those with check marks)

____ His reading ability is unsatisfactory

____ His math ability is unsatisfactory

____ His behavior is unsatisfactory

____ He appears to have difficulty with his hearing, vision, or
physical health

____ It is felt additional evaluation may help us determine if
there is a more appropriate way to teach your child than
that of his present placement.

____ His abilities and talents appear to be superior, and we seek
more information in order to better help him realize his
potential.

____ Other _____

_____

_____

_____

197

What Will You Do For My Child?

_____(District)_____uses the following test instruments for evaluating students' abilities, aptitudes and strengths. Those checked will be given to your child.

Academic Performance

____ *Wide Range Achievement Test*

____ *Peabody Individual Achievement Test*

____ Other _____

Intellectual Ability

____ *Wechsler Intelligence Scale for Children*

____ *Wechsler Preschool and Primary Scale of Intelligence*

____ *Slosson Intelligence Test*

____ *Stanford-Binet*

____ Other _____

Additional Test Instruments

____ *Illinois Test of Psycholinguistic Abilities*

____ *Bender-Gestalt*

____ *Goodenough-Harris Drawing Test*

____ *Vineland Social Maturity Scale*

____ *Peabody Picture Vocabulary Test*

____ *Developmental Test of Visual Perception*

____ *Bender-Gestalt Test*

____ Other _____

What Do These Tests Test?

Wide Range Achievement Test (WRAT)

The purpose of the WRAT is to study achievement in reading, spelling and arithmetic computation. It does not measure reading comprehension, it measures pronunciation and word recognition. It is useful to evaluate achievement of persons from 5 years of age to adulthood.

Peabody Individual Achievement Test (PIAT)

The purpose of the PIAT is to provide a wide range screening measure of achievement in the areas of mathematics, reading, spelling and general information. Results of these subtests can be plotted on profiles according to age, grade placement, percentile and/or standard scores.

Wechsler Intelligence Scale for Children (WISC)

The WISC was established for use with children ranging from 5 to 15 years of age. It is a test which measures general intelligence. It will be administered by a competent examiner and when scored, will provide three I.Q. scores: the full scale I.Q.; the verbal I.Q.; and, the performance I.Q. All three scores are equally important and meaningful to the educator.

Wechsler Preschool and Primary Scale of Intelligence (WPPSI)

The WPPSI is designed to evaluate young children — 4 to 6 years of age. As is the case with the WISC, the WPPSI provides the educator with three I.Q. scores: full scale, verbal and performance. The location of problem patterns is probably one of the most valuable findings of this test. Careful review of the subtest scores is emphasized as further severe reading problems might be reduced with this understanding of related reading subtest areas.

Slosson Intelligence Test (SIT)

This intelligence test is administered in a relatively short amount of time. Its accuracy regarded as tentative. This instrument will let the educator know where the child is mentally in relation to his/her peer group. The SIT provides a mental age as well as I.Q., both of which give the educator insight into a student's academic abilities.

Stanford-Binet

This is a psychological tool for the measurement of mental abilities. The resultant mental age score ranges from two years to twenty-two years. The mental age and intellectual score (I.Q.) along with the six subtest scores are considered by the educator when planning an appropriate program for the child.

Illinois Test of Psycholinguistic Abilities (ITPA)
The ITPA is intended for use as comprehensive assessment of a child's psycholinguistic development. It is designed for children of 2½ years of age thru 9 years of age. The test is especially useful in planning remedial work for children with special language problems. The nine subtest scores provide indications of problem areas and remedial programs may be based on the test scores.

Goodenough-Harris Drawing Test
This test is designed as a measure of intellectual maturity – not personality assessment. It is designed for the five through ten year olds. The test reflects the child's concepts which develop with his/her mental level, experience, and general knowledge.

Vineland Social Maturity Scale (VSMS)
This instrument uses a checklist to measure successive stages of social competence from infancy to adulthood. The VSMS indicates a normal development schedule, a measure of individual differences and can be used to evaluate the influence of environment and/or handicaps.

Peabody Picture Vocabulary Test (PPVT)
The PPVT provides a verbal intelligence by evaluating the subject's auditory vocabulary. This test is excellent to use with nonreaders or remedial readers.

Developmental Test of Visual Perception
The test's purpose is to focus on the five visual perceptual abilities of children aged from 3½ to 7½ years. There is a specific remedial program designed for children with deficits in specific areas of visual perception.

Bender-Gestalt Test
The purpose of the Bender-Gestalt Test is a developmental test of visual motor functioning in children. Through the scoring the psychologist will be able to compare the student's scores with the scores appropriate at his age level. This test investigates retardation, organic brain damage, loss of functions and provides an index of school readiness and/or emotional disturbance.

Other tests(s) to be used:

Name _____

_____

_____

_____

_____

_____

_____

Will I Know About the Test Results?

_____(District)_____ invites you to visit
the office of the psychologist and examine the test instruments and results — or to get acquainted with the procedures we follow to assure
your child's best educational placement.

The results of the testing on your child will be reviewed by a staffing
committee (placement committee). This committee will review all pertinent records, results of psychometric testing, behavioral histories, adaptive behavior scales, etc. It will be the function of the staff committee
to recommend, describe, or suggest procedures designed to generate
written individual plans for all exceptional pupils. This group of professionals will outline *for you* the program plan which best suits your
child. _____(District)_____ wants you to be
fully informed of the evaluation results and program planning. We wish
to emphasize that until the district officially has invited you to participate in the decision making process and provided an opportunity for
the parent to present his/her view, there will be no change in your
child's educational placement.

What If I Do Not Think I Should Permit You
To Give My Child These Tests?

It is your right to refuse permission for this evaluation. As it is
our sincere interest in your child that prompts this evaluation request,
we do have the right to present our reasons through a hearing process in
an attempt to obtain your approval.

We feel that this evaluation is necessary in order for _ (District) _
_____ to provide for your child.

What Happens After You Test My Child? What Then?

Your child shall remain in the present educational program until such time as there is approval of the best, least restrictive placement for him/her. (In those rare emergency situations where health and safety of your child or others is endangered, placements will be quickly decided by an impartial third party.)

This placement of your child will be considered in light of the least restrictive alternative.

This chart indicates the progression of placement from least restrictive to most restrictive:

Regular Classroom

Regular Class With Itinerant Teacher

Regular Class With Resource Room

Self-Contained Class

Special Day School

Residential School

When Will My Child Return
To A Regular Classroom Setting?

Periodic reviews by _____ (District) _____ will evaluate your child's progress and the effectiveness of the program. At any time you may request such a review.

Before such a review you will be notified of the date and procedures to be initiated. We invite you to participate in this review.

If you cannot or choose not to participate, we will inform you of the results of the review within ten days of its completion.

This school program is protected by public law. The State Plan states that if a parent does not respond within 15 days to the school district's attempts to gain consent for evaluation, the district may request a hearing to obtain approval.

Of course, you will be informed and requested to attend the hearing.

You, as a parent, have the right to appeal the decision and for that reason we list free legal counsel agency(ies) available to you:

_____

_____

_____

An impartial third party, trained by the State Department of Education, will serve as the hearing officer. This hearing officer will preside at the hearing and conduct the proceedings.

This hearing will be private except to you and appropriate school personnel. However, if you wish to invite others, you may have an open hearing.

The hearing officer will decide the best placement for your child.

What If I Don't Agree With The Decision Of The Hearing Officer?

After the hearing officer's decision, you or ____ (District) ____ _____ may initiate a judicial appeal. This appeal would be conducted according to the statutes governing proceedings of judical appeals.

What If I Want Someone Else to Evaluate My Child?

_____ (District) _____ has listed those agencies in the state which evaluate students:

Summary

The model which has been developed provides a systematic approach in dealing with the complicated legal aspects of "due process". The basic rights guaranteed by "due process" have been identified and summarized as the following:

Rights of child under the age of majority
1. Right to have parent surrogate.
2. Right to request change of parent surrogate.

Rights of the Parent
1. Right to deny permission for evaluation or placement of child in special program.
2. Right to review all school records.
3. Right to request an alternative evaluation.
4. Right to request a hearing.
5. Right to be present at hearing, to request the presence of certain witnesses and to question all witnesses.
6. Right to request re-evaluation subsequent to placement.
7. Right to appeal decision of hearing officer.

Appendix C
Career Guidance and Occupational Information Systems
CAREER INFORMATION SYSTEM OF IOWA

Place a check by the letters that describe or pertain to this system. If it has additional components, add those.

1. This system is
   ____ A. a career guidance system
   _X_ B. an occupational information system

2. The content of this system includes
   ____ A. values exercises
   ____ B. a decision-making model
   _X_ C. occupational information
   _X_ D. college information
   _X_ E. vocational-technical schools
   ____ F. financial aids
   ____ G. military information
   _X_ H. an interest inventory
   ____ I.

3. The content is updated
   _X_ A. annually
   ____ B. biennially
   ____ C.

4. The content can be localized
   _X_ A. by the system
   _X_ B. by the user

5. The readability levels are
   ____ A. 1st - 6th grades
   _X_ B. 7th - 8th grades
   _X_ C. 9th - 10th grades
   ____ D. 11th - 12th grades
   ____ E. Above 12th grade

6. The content is designed for
   _X_ A. 7th - 8th grades
   _X_ B. 9th - 10th grades
   _X_ C. 11th - 12th grades
   _X_ D. Adults

7. For the occupational information content, this system uses the
   _X_ A. *Occupational Outlook Handbook*
   _X_ B. *Dictionary of Occupational Titles*
   _X_ C. State Employment Service Bulletins
   _X_ D. Department of Labor Bulletins
   _X_ E. Workers on the job

204

Criteria developed by and permission for reproduction granted by Ms. Delores McCord, Career Counselor, Valencia Community College, Orlando, Florida 32802.

8. The system groups occupations according to
___ A. D.O.T. numbers
___ B. Interests
___ C. Holland codes
_X_ D. "modified" USOE clusters (15)
___ E.

9. The system has in it the following number of occupations:
___ A. Fewer than 200
_X_ B. 201 - 300
___ C. 301 - 500
___ D. 501 - 1000
___ E. over 1000

10. The system can be accessed by the user within
_X_ A. 5 minutes   20-25 minutes average time/user
___ B. from 6-10 minutes
___ C. from 11-15 minutes
___ D. from 16-20 minutes
___ E.

11. This system sells
___ A. the program (software)
___ B. computer time
___ C. both
_X_ D. neither

12. This program can be used with the following computers:
___ A. an IBM _____
_X_ B. a Burroughs _B6700_____
___ C. a Univac _____
___ D. a Honeywell _____
_X_ E. a Digital Equipment Corporation _11/70, 11/60, PDP 11/03_____
_X_ F. Apple II; Hewlett-Packard 2000 Access; H-P 3000

13. This system is compatible with the following terminals:
___ A. IBM _____
_X_ B. Burroughs_____
___ C. Univac _____
___ D. Honeywell_____
_X_ E. HP-2600 series, TI, Teletype compatible terminals
_X_ F. Dec-writers

14. The average amount of time per week required for maintenance of this
system in the user's data processing department is
_X_ A. 1 - 5 hours
___ B. 6 - 10 hours
___ C. 11 - 20 hours
___ D. over 20 hours

15. This system provides the following as a part of the package:
_X_ A.   computer tape
_X_ B.   technical information
_X_ C.   counselor information
_X_ D.   user information
____ E.   A-V productions
_X_ F.   in-service training
____ G.
____ H.

16. Room space is needed for
_X_ A.   computer terminals
____ B.   modem
____ C.   control unit
_X_ D.   telephone
____ E.

17. This system requires
_X_ A.   dial telephones
_X_ B.   private telephone lines
_X_ C.   direct telephone lines
_X_ D.   direct line (hardwire)

18. The cost of the program package (software only) is
_X_ A.   Under $10,000
____ B. $11,000 - $19,999
____ C. $20,000 - $29,999
____ D.   over $30,000

19. The estimated monthly cost of this system for the hardware, i.e., computer time, phone lines, terminals, etc., is
____ A.   up to $500
____ B. $501 - $1,000
____ C. $1,001 - $2,000   Does not apply
____ D.   over $2,000

20. The hardware, i.e., computer, terminals, etc., can be purchased for
____ A. $100,000 or under
____ B. $101,000 - $200,000
____ C.   over $200,000   Does not apply

21. The hardware can be leased monthly for
____ A.   under $1,000
____ B. $1,000 - $1,999
____ C. $2,000 - $2,999   Does not apply
____ D.   over $3,000

22. The cost per student is estimated to be
____ A.   less than $1.00
____ B. $1.00 - $1.99
____ C. $2.00 - $2.99   Varies upon computer
____ D. $3.00 - $3.99
____ E.   over $3.99

23. This system can also be used for
____ A.   student records or information
____ B.

24. The number of staff necessary to supervise the usage of the system during the time of operation for two terminals is
_X_ A.   1
____ B.   2
____ C.   more than 2

25. The estimated number of terminal hours of material is
____ A.   1 - 2
____ B.   3 - 5
____ C.   6 - 10
____ D.   11 - 20
_X_ E.   over 20

Additional comments:

C.I.S.I. is a software system and we are not connected with any particular hardware or vendor.

COORDINATED OCCUPATIONAL INFORMATION NETWORK, INCORPORATED

Place a check by the letters that describe or pertain to this system. If it has additional components, add those.

1. This system is
____ A.   a career guidance system
_X_ B.   an occupational information system

2. The content of this system includes
____ A.   values exercises
____ B.   a decision-making model
_X_ C.   occupational information
_X_ D.   college information
____ E.   vocational-technical schools
____ F.   financial aids
_X_ G.   military information
_X_ H.   an interest inventory
_X_ I.   college file; school subjects file

3. The content is updated
_X_ A.   annually
____ B.   biennially
____ C.

4. The content can be localized
_X_ A.   by the system
_X_ B.   by the user

5. The readability levels are
  X   A.   1st - 6th grades
  X   B.   7th - 8th grades
  X   C.   9th - 10th grades
 ____ D.   11th - 12th grades
 ____ E.   Above 12th grade

6. The content is designed for
  X   A.   7th - 8th grades
  X   B.   9th - 10th grades
  X   C.   11th - 12th grades
  X   D.   Adults

7. For the occupational information content, this system uses the
  X   A.   *Occupational Outlook Handbook*
  X   B.   *Dictionary of Occupational Titles*
  X   C.   State Employment Service Bulletins
  X   D.   Department of Labor Bulletins
  X   E.   A variety of over 600 traditional and non-traditional sources

8. The system groups occupations according to
  X   A.   D.O.T. numbers
  X   B.   Interests
  X   C.   Holland codes
  X   D.   OVIS Scales
  X   E.   Career Clusters

9. The system has in it the following number of occupations:
 ____ A.   Fewer than 200
  X   B.   201 - 300
 ____ C.   301 - 500
 ____ D.   501 - 1000
 ____ E.   over 1000

10. The system can be accessed by the user within
  X   A.   5 minutes
 ____ B.   from 6-10 minutes
 ____ C.   from 11-15 minutes
 ____ D.   from 16-20 minutes
 ____ E.

11. This system sells
  X   A.   the program (software)
 ____ B.   computer time
 ____ C.   both
 ____ D.

12. This program can be used with the following computers:
  X   A.   an IBM
  X   B.   a Burroughs
  X   C.   a Univac
  X   D.   a Honeywell
  X   E.   a Digital Equipment Corporation
  X   F.   a Hewlitt Packard (2000 + 3000) Prime

13. This system is compatible with the following terminals:
 ___ A. IBM _____ The system can be _____
 ___ B. Burroughs _____ accessed by almost any _____
 ___ C. Univac _____ CRJ or teletype _____
 ___ D. Honeywell _____ terminal _____
 ___ E.
 ___ F.

14. The average amount of time per week required for maintenance of this system in the user's data processing department is
 _X_ A. 1 - 5 hours
 ___ B. 6 - 10 hours
 ___ C. 11 - 20 hours
 ___ D. over 20 hours

15. This system provides the following as a part of the package:
 _X_ A. computer tape
 _X_ B. technical information
 _X_ C. counselor information
 _X_ D. user information
 ___ E. A-V productions
 _X_ F. in-service training
 ___ G.
 ___ H.

16. Room space is needed for
 ___ A. computer terminals
 ___ B. modem
 ___ C. control unit
 ___ D. telephone
 ___ E.

17. This system requires
 ___ A. dial telephones
 ___ B. private telephone lines
 ___ D. direct telephone lines
 ___ D.

18. The cost of the program package (software only) is
 _X_ A. Under $10,000
 ___ B. $11,000 - $19,999
 ___ C. $20,000 - $29,999
 ___ D. over $30,000

19. The estimated monthly cost of this system for the hardware, i.e., computer time, phone lines, terminals, etc., is
 ___ A. up to $500
 ___ B. $501 - $1,000   Costs are totally depended on
 ___ C. $1,001 - $2,000   location of the data center
 ___ D. over $2,000

20. The hardware, i.e., computer, terminals, etc., can be purchased for
____ A. $100,000 or under
____ B. $101,000 - $200,000   Depends on user's configuration
____ C.   over $200,000

21. The hardware can be leased monthly for
____ A.   under $1,000
____ B. $1,000 - $1,999   N A
____ C. $2,000 - $2,999
____ D.   over $3,000

22. The cost per student is estimated to be for up to 1,000 students
____ A.   less than $1.00
____ B. $1.00 - $1.99
____ C. $2.00 - $2.99   Depends on local situation
____ D. $3.00 - $3.99
____ E.   over $3.99

23. This system can also be used for
____ A.   student records or information
____ B.

24. The number of staff necessary to supervise the usage of the system during
     the time of operation for two terminals is
_X_ A.   1   (System can be operated without direct supervision)
____ B.   2
____ C.   more than 2

25. The estimated number of terminals hours of material is
_X_ A.   1 - 2
____ B.   3 - 5
____ C.   6 - 10
____ D.   11 - 20
____ E.   over 20

GUIDANCE INFORMATION SYSTEM

Place a check by the letters that describe or pertain to this system. If it has additional components, add those.

1. This system is
_X_ A.   a career guidance system
_X_ B.   an occupational information system

2. The content of this system includes
____ A.   values exercises
____ B.   a decision-making model
_X_ C.   occupational information
_X_ D.   college information
_X_ E.   vocational-technical schools
_X_ F.   financial aids
_X_ G.   military information

    H.   an interest inventory
  X I.   off-line correlation to eight (8) standardized interest inventories

3. The content is updated
    A.   annually
  X B.   biennially
    C.

4. The content can be localized
  X A.   by the system
  X B.   by the user

5. The readability levels are
    A.   1st - 6th grades
  X B.   7th - 8th grades
    C.   9th - 10th grades
    D.   11th - 12th grades
    E.   Above 12th grade

6. The content is designed for
  X A.   7th - 8th grades
  X B.   9th - 10th grades
  X C.   11th - 12th grades
  X D.   Adults

7. For the occupational information content, this system uses the
  X A.   *Occupational Outlook Handbook*
  X B.   *Dictionary of Occupational Titles*
  X C.   State Employment Service Bulletins
  X D.   Department of Labor Bulletins
  X E.   Direct contact with employers

8. The system groups occupations according to
  X A.   D.O.T. numbers
  X B.   Interests
    C.   Holland codes
  X D.   U.S.O.E. Clusters
  X E.   U.S. Dept. of Labor Interest Areas

9. The system has in it the following number of occupations:
    A.   Fewer than 200
    B.   201 - 300
    C.   301 - 500
  X D.   501 - 1000
    E.   over 1000

10. The system can be accessed by the user within
  X A.   5 minutes
    B.   from 6-10 minutes
    C.   from 11-15 minutes
    D.   from 16-20 minutes
    E.

11. This system sells
___ A.   the program (software)
___ B.   computer time
___ C.   both
_*_ D.

12. This program can be used with the following computers:
_X_ A.   an IBM 370/370
_X_ B.   a Burroughs 2700
_X_ C.   A Univac 1100
_X_ D.   a Honeywell any having GECOS
_X_ E.   a Digital Equipment Corporation 10, 20, PDP11 w/RSTS-6C
_X_ F.   TSC 200/300; HP 200Q, 3000 access; Prime 400, CYBER series;
         BTI 4000

13. This system is compatible with the following terminals:
_X_ A.   IBM
_X_ B.   Burroughs
_X_ C.   Univac
_X_ D.   Honeywell
_X_ E.   any
___ F.

14. The average amount of time per week required for maintenance of this
    system in the user's data processing department is
_X_ A.   1 - 5 hours
___ B.   6 - 10 hours
___ C.   11 - 20 hours
___ D.   over 20 hours

15. This system provides the following as a part of the package:
_X_ A.   computer tape
_X_ B.   technical information
_X_ C.   counselor information
_X_ D.   user information
___ E.   A-V productions
_X_ F.   in-service training
_X_ G.   other materials as required by customer
___ H.

16. Room space is needed for
_X_ A.   computer terminals
___ B.   modem
___ C.   control unit
_X_ D.   telephone
_*_ E.

See additional comments

17. This system requires
___ A. dial telephones
___ B. private telephone lines
___ C. direct telephone lines
_X_ D. any phone

*18. The cost of the program package (software only) is
___ A. Under $10,000
___ B. $11,000 - $19,999
_X_ C. $20,000 - $29,999   *development costs*
___ D. over $30,000

*19. The estimated monthly cost of this system for the hardware, i.e., computer time, phone lines, terminals, etc., is
___ A. up to $500
___ B. $501 - $1,000
___ C. $1,001 - $2,000
___ D. over $2,000

*20. The hardware, i.e., computer, terminals, etc., can be purchased for
_X_ A. $100,000 or under
___ B. $101,000 - $200,000
___ C. over $200,000

*21. The hardware can be leased monthly for
___ A. under $1,000
___ B. $1,000 - $1,999
___ C. $2,000 - $2,999
___ D. over $3,000

*22. The cost per student is estimated to be for up to 1,000 students
___ A. less than $1.00
___ B. $1.00 - $1.99
___ C. $2.00 - $2.99
___ D. $3.00 - $3.99
___ E. over $3.99

23. This system can also be used for
___ A. student records or information
_X_ B. computer assisted instruction

24. The number of staff necessary to supervise the usage of the system during the time of operation for two terminals is
_X_ A. 1
___ B. 2
___ C. more than 2

25. The estimated number of terminal hours of material is
___ A. 1 - 2
___ B. 3 - 5
___ C. 6 - 10

* *See additional comments*

___ D.   11 - 20
___ E.   over 20
_X_ F.   On-line utilization will vary according to the needs of the user – not
         a lock-step program.

Additional comments:

*   Hardware needs and costs, software pricing, and access will vary greatly for
     each installation. Detailed information in all areas will be available during
     the technical session and presentations.

DISCOVER

Place a check by the letters that describe or pertain to this system. If it has additional components, add those.

1. This system is
_X_ A.   a career guidance system
___ B.   an occupational information system

2. The content of this system includes
_X_ A.   values exercises
_X_ B.   a decision-making model
_X_ C.   occupational information
_X_ D.   college information
_X_ E.   vocational-technical schools
_X_ F.   financial aids
_X_ G.   military information
_X_ H.   an interest inventory
___ I.

3. The content is updated
_X_ A.   annually
___ B.   biennially
___ C.

4. The content can be localized
___ A.   by the system
_X_ B.   by the user

5. The readability levels are
_X_ A.   1st - 6th grades   high school version
_X_ B.   7th - 8th grades   high school version
_X_ C.   9th - 10th grades   high school version
_X_ D.   11th - 12th grades   high school version and college version
___ E.   Above 12th grade

6. The content is designed for
_X_ A.   7th - 8th grades   high school version
_X_ B.   9th - 10th grades   high school version
_X_ C.   11th - 12th grades   high school version
_X_ D.   Adults

7. For the occupational information content, this system uses the
   X   A.   *Occupational Outlook Handbook*
   X   B.   *Dictionary of Occupational Titles*
   X   C.   State Employment Service Bulletins
   X   D.   Department of Labor Bulletins
   X   E.   Other printed resources and interviews if necessary

8. The system groups occupations according to
   ___   A.   D.O.T. numbers
   X   B.   Interests
   X   C.   Holland codes
   X   D.   Favorite subjects
   X   E.   Job characteristics
   X   F.   Values

9. The system has in it the following number of occupations:
   ___   A.   Fewer than 200
   ___   B.   201 - 300
   X   C.   301 - 500   major occupations plus 500
   ___   D.   501 - 1000   military occupations
   ___   E.   over 1000

10. The system can be accessed by the user within
    ___   A.   5 minutes
    ___   B.   from 6-10 minutes
    ___   C.   from 11-15 minutes
    ___   D.   from 16-20 minutes
    X   E.   immediate use

11. This system sells
    X   A.   the program (software)
    ___   B.   computer time
    ___   C.   both
    ___   D.

12. This program can be used with the following computers:
    X   A.   an IBM _____
    ___   B.   a Burroughs_____
    ___   C.   a Univac _____
    ___   D.   a Honeywell_____
    X   E.   a Digital Equipment Corporation Colorado Career Information
                              System (CCIS) uses parts of DISCOVER

13. This system is compatible with the following terminals:
    X   A.   IBM 3270 series with light-pen_____
    ___   B.   Burroughs _____
    ___   C.   Univac _____
    ___   D.   Honeywell_____
    X   E.   Other vendors with IBM 3270 compatible CRT's with *light-pen*
    ___   F.

14. The average amount of time per week required for maintenance of this
     system in the user's data processing department is
_X_ A.   1 - 5 hours
____ B.   6 - 10 hours
____ C.   11 - 20 hours
____ D.   over 20 hours

15. This system provides the following as a part of the package:
_X_ A.   computer tape
_X_ B.   technical information
_X_ C.   counselor information
_X_ D.   user information
_X_ E.   A-V productions
_X_ F.   in-service training
____ G.
____ H.

16. Room space is needed for
_X_ A.   computer terminals
_X_ B.   modem
_X_ C.   control unit
_X_ D.   telephone
____ E.

17. This system requires
____ A.   dial telephones
____ B.   private telephone lines
_X_ C.   direct telephone lines
____ D.

18. The cost of the program package (software only) is
____ A.   Under $10,000
____ B. $11,000 - $19,999
_X_ C. $20,000 - $29,999
____ D.   over $30,000

19. The estimated monthly cost of this system for the hardware, i.e., computer
     time, phone lines, terminals, etc., is
____ A.   up to $500
_X_ B. $501 - $1,000   per site (i.e. terminal) average
____ C. $1,00s - $2,000
____ D.   over $2,000

20. The hardware, i.e., computer, terminals, etc., can be purchased for
____ A. $100,000 or under
_X_ B. $101,000 - $200,00   A possible configuration for a DISCOVER site
____ C.   over $200,000

21. The hardware can be leased monthly for
____ A.   under $1,000
____ B. $1,000 - $1,999
____ C. $2,000 - $2,999
_X_ D.   over $3,000   Rental costs per month for the site specified
                              in item 20

22. The cost per student is estimated to be for up to 1,000 students
____ A.   less than $1.00
____ B. $1.00 - $1.99
____ C. $2.00 - $2.99
____ D. $3.00 - $3.99
_X_ E.   over $3.99

23. This system can also be used for
_X_ A.   student records or information
____ B.

24. The number of staff necessary to supervise the usage of the system during
the time of operation for two terminals is
_X_ A.   1 part time
____ B.   2
____ C.   more than 2

25. The estimated number of terminal hours of material is
____ A.   1 - 2
____ B.   3 - 5
____ C.   6 - 10
____ D.   11 - 20
_X_ E.   over 20

Appendix D

Guidance Program Model for Middle School
(Detroit Public Schools)

1. *Introduction to Middle School Guidance Program*

Sixth Grade Guidance Services

2. *Counseling*
   - Objective
   - Individual and Group Counseling
   - Reports
   - Role and Function of Guidance
   - Referrals
   - Counseling Students with Special Needs
   - Evidence of Success

3. *Consultation*
   - Objective
   - Parents
   - Guidance Advisory Committee
   - School Staff
   - In-Service Training
   - Evidence of Success

4. *Coordination*
   - Objective
   - Pre-School Orientation
   - School Rules and Procedures
   - Organization, Scope, and Counselor Functions
   - Planning and Orientation Program for Parents
   - Introduction of Other Pupil Personnel Services
   - Orientation for New Students
   - Evidence of Success

5. *Career Guidance*
   - Objective
   - Coordination of Career Guidance Program
   - Cooperation and Resource for Teachers
   - Career Awareness and Other Guidance Areas
   - Conferences with Students
   - Career Information
   - National Career Guidance Week
   - Guidance Service Centers
   - Evidence of Success

6. *Program Selection and Placement*
   - Objective
   - Seventh Grade Articulation
   - Alternatives for Students with Special Needs
   - Evidence of Success

7. *Referral and Information Service*
   - Objective
   - Cumulative Data
   - Referral Resources
   - Educational Information
   - Evidence of Success

8. *Evaluation*
   - Objective
   - Questionnaires
   - Reports
   - Program Modifications
   - Counselor Logs
   - Guidance Plan of Action
   - Evidence of Success

Seventh Grade Guidance Services

1. *Counseling*
   - Objective
   - Individual and Group Counseling
   - Self-Referrals
   - Records and Reports
   - Group Formation
   - Evidence of Success

2. *Consultation*
   - Objective
   - Teachers
   - Administrators
   - Parents
   - Evidence of Success

3. *Coordination*
   - Objectives
   - Improving Guidance Services
   - Guidance In-Service for Teachers
   - Case Studies for Students with Special Needs
   - Guidance Program Orientation of Students, Parents, Teachers
   - Guidance Advisory Committee
   - Evidence of Success

4. *Career Guidance*
   - Objective
   - Organization, Selection, Collection, Utilization of Career Guidance Materials
   - Evidence of Success

5. *Program Selection and Placement*
   - Objective
   - Courses
   - Alternative Educational Programs
   - Orientation of New Students
   - Intervention Strategies, Grade Failures
   - Evidence of Success

6. *Referral and Information Service*
   - Objective
   - Student Assessment
   - Information Sharing
   - Referrals
   - Evidence of Success

7. *Evaluation*
   - Objective
   - Questionnaires
   - Implementing Change
   - Evidence of Success

Eighth Grade Guidance Services

1. *Counseling*
   - Objective
   - Individual and Group Counseling
   - Orientation
   - Conducting
   - Evidence of Success

2. *Consultation*
   - Objective
   - Clarification, Guidance Goals and Objectives
   - Staff Planning
   - Parent Conferences
   - Guidance Advisory Committee
   - Consultant, Curriculum Planning
   - Evidence of Success

3. *Coordination*
   - Objective
   - Planning: Staff, Students, Parents
   - Guidance Advisory Committee
   - Visits; Feeder School Students
   - Visits; Middle School Students to High Schools

- Community Resources
- Counselor-Faculty Meetings
- Orientation; New Students
- Articulation with High Schools
- Orientation to High School Graduation Requirements and Sequential Programs
- Evidence of Success

4. *Career Guidance*
   - Objective
   - Speakers, Audio-Visual Materials, Group Guidance Activities, Classroom Activities, etc.
   - Interest Inventories
   - Area Vocation Centers
   - Specialized High School Programs
   - Test and Record Data
   - Guidance Service Center
   - Evidence of Success

5. *Program Selection and Placement*
   - Objective
   - Student Enrollment
   - Information: Ninth Grade Options
   - Pre-Employment Skills
   - Graduation Requirements
   - Four-Year Plan of Work
   - Evidence of Success

6. *Referral and Information Services*
   - Objectives
   - Students: Special Needs
   - Guidance Service Center
   - Group Guidance
   - Anecdotal Records
   - Decision-Making Skills
   - Newsletter
   - Evidence of Success

7. *Evaluation*
   - Objectives
   - Pertinent Data
   - Formal and Informal Tools
   - Follow-Up Study
   - Exit Interviews
   - Daily Schedule
   - Evidence of Success

INTRODUCTION

*Middle School Guidance and Counseling: Core Objectives, Activities,
and Expected Outcomes – Grades 6 - 8*

Such terms as "tween-agers," "transescents," and "emerging adolescents" are used in attempts to describe the unique needs and developmental stages of middle school youngsters. Characteristics of the age group (10-14) include physical, social, and emotional development ranging from that of *children* at age ten (10) to *adults* by age fourteen (14). Helping pupils to "bridge the gap" between childhood and adulthood is the primary concern of guidance at the middle school level. This concern places added emphases on the need for a strong personal-social guidance program, in addition to an effective academic and career guidance program.

Guidance Service Centers (GSC) are a recent middle school innovation in Detroit Public Schools. They are being established in middle schools to help provide a more comprehensive program of services. With the assistance of specially-trained Guidance Aides, counselors are making career guidance materials and other guidance services more accessible.

An effective middle school guidance program reflects not only the goals and objections of the school counselors, but also those of the total school-community. A structure must exist which will allow the school to identify local school needs and which will give assurance to pupils, parents, teachers and others, that such needs will be recognized and met. GUIDANCE ADVISORY COMMITTEES carry responsibility for linking schools with community concerns.

In twenty-three of the larger middle schools, Guidance Department Heads provide leadership and direction for the implementation of the Modified Counseling Program.

Immediately following are core objectives, activities, a time frame for activities, and expected outcomes of middle school guidance programs in the seven component areas. Timelines for activities at the local school level should be refined so that they will be workable and precise in each school setting.

COUNSELING (INDIVIDUAL & GROUP)
GRADE 6

Objective(s):

- to provide counseling services for individual students and for small groups of students,
- to inform students, parents, and faculty of the procedures to be used when one needs counseling services.

Activities: *Time Frame*

Counselors will:
- organize a schedule of guidance services and activities   Sept.-June
  that will provide for individual and group counseling

sessions; conduct counseling sessions,

— maintain and use adequate counseling records – records that reflect respect for the confidential nature of the counseling relationship,	Sept.-June
— report to administrator positive and negative aspects of the counseling program,	Sept.-June
— introduce students, staff, and parents to the roles and functions of all guidance personnel and inform them of appropriate methods of referrals,	Sept.
— form groups, as needed, for specific short-term counseling for those students who have special needs, interests, and concerns.	Sept.-June

Evidence(s) of Success:

Students will:

- — find the contacts with their counselors helpful,
- — know who their counselors are, where to find them, and some of the services they provide,
- — demonstrate productive behavior changes, i.e., improved attendance, interpersonal relationships, achievement, self-image.

CONSULTATION

GRADE 6

Objective(s):

- — to consult with principals re: program, referrals, and guidance needs,
- — to consult with teachers re: specific pupils, classroom management techniques, and child growth and development,
- — to consult with parents, individually and in groups, re: child growth and development and specific concerns relating to their children.

Activities: *Time Frame*

Counselors will:

— plan and conduct periodic meetings with parent groups to discuss guidance needs and concerns; invite in-put into the guidance effort,	Sept.-June
— schedule activities so that parents can have face-to-face contacts with counselors on a one-to-one basis if the need arises,	Sept.-June
— utilize the Guidance Advisory Committee (GAC) or a similar representative committee to assist in formulating school guidance goals, objectives, and plans of action,	Sept.-June
— prepare and distribute to staff, students, and parents current materials that describe the school guidance program and the role of the counselor,	Sept.

— meet regularly with staff – in large or small groups – to discuss student/teacher/counselor relationships; group test results; etc.	Oct. & Feb.
— confer regularly with principal or his/her designee regarding guidance needs and concerns,	Sept.-June
— attend scheduled inservice meetings for continuous professional growth and development.	Sept.-June

Evidence(s) of Success:

- Principals will be kept informed about the school program, guidance needs and concerns, and will actively support guidance.
- Teachers will understand the services of counselors and will be able to utilize the process for getting the counselor's services.
- Parents who need and/or seek guidance and counseling services will be served or appropriately referred.

COORDINATION
GRADE 6

Objective(s):

- to plan and coordinate local school guidance and counseling activities which will enhance the adjustment of students to the school and the adjustment of the school to the students,
- to carry primary responsibility for planning and coordinating an effective orientation program,
- to assist in the implementation of specially-funded guidance projects.

Activities: *Time Frame*

Counselors will:

— assist in planning and conducting pre-school orientation activities: (a) visits to feeder schools, (b) conferences with feeder school staff members, (c) arrangements for school tours and visits for students and parents, (d) enrollment procedures,	May-June
— meet with classroom groups and parent groups, and teachers to: (a) outline guidance services, (b) procedures for getting to talk with a counselor, (c) discuss student needs, (d) review school rules and procedures, (e) learn the location of facilities,	Sept.-Oct.
— prepare and distribute to students, parents, and staff members, materials related to the organization and scope of guidance services and the role and functions of the counselor,	Sept.-June
— assist the administration in planning and conducting an orientation program for parents new to the school,	Sept.-Nov.

	assist in coordinating the introduction of other pupil services personnel to the faculty,	Sept.-June
	meet regularly and periodically with groups of new students throughout the school year to help them adjust to their new school.	Sept.-June

Evidence(s) of Success:

Students will:
- participate in planned orientation activities,
- be introduced to school rules, procedures, and will be able to state why such rules exist,
- make satisfactory adjustments to school,
- receive added assistance from specially-funded projects.

CAREER GUIDANCE
GRADE 6

Objective(s):
- to plan and conduct a series of career guidance activities that is compatible with the total school career education program,
- to help students individually and in small groups – gain insight into their own career needs, abilities, and interests,
- to serve as resource for teachers in the infusing of career education into the instructional program.

Activities: *Time Frame*

Counselors will:
- plan a coordinated career guidance program taking into consideration the developmental needs of students in this age group and focusing on career development, values clarification, decision making, etc., — Sept.-Oct.
- cooperatively work with teachers to promote and encourage career guidance, serve as a resource to teachers, — Sept.-June
- maintain displays that focus attention on career awareness and on other guidance concerns, — Sept.-June
- confer with students – individually and in groups – about their career interests and help them make decisions, — Sept.-June
- teach students how to locate information related to careers, i.e., in the library, the Guidance Service Center, etc. — Sept.-June
- observe National Career Guidance Week, — Nov.
- help maintain and supervise the Guidance Service Centers (GSC). — Sept.-June

Evidence(s) of Success:

Students will:
- be involved in activities related to career guidance,
- be able to utilize a variety of materials and/or methods in getting information about careers,
- demonstrate some degree of competency in discussing their interests, abilities, and needs in relationship to their chosen career areas,
- understand the "what" and "why" of Guidance Service Center (GSC) and other career resource centers.

PROGRAM SELECTION AND PLACEMENT
GRADE 6

Objective(s):
- to cooperatively plan with principal, teachers, other counselors, and parents for articulation to seventh grade,
- to assist pupils in making educational, career, and personal-social decisions.

Activities:	*Time Frame*
Counselors will:	
— consult with the principal or his/her designee re: plans for articulation to seventh grade,	Nov.
— make and maintain contacts with seventh grade counselors and teachers; develop activities for transition that will enhance growth and development of students,	Sept.-June
— conduct group guidance activities for parents and students to help them understand all school options, and procedures in moving to the seventh grade,	Sept.-June
— assist in planning appropriate educational programs and alternatives for sixth grade students who appear to have divergent needs, i.e., summer school for grade failures.	Sept.-June

Evidence(s) of Success:

Students will:
- be provided with the necessary information for making a smooth transition into the seventh grade,
- be able to articulate what courses they have selected, why they have selected those courses, and any pre-requisitions for getting into them,
- be given school programs that are in their best interest and in the best interest of the school.

REFERRAL AND INFORMATION SERVICE
GRADE 6

Objective(s):

- to identify referral resources, both within and outside of the school, that can be utilized in the best interest of the students,
- to make available to students, parents, and staff members information about educational opportunities that may be available.

Activities: *Time Frame*

Counselors will:

— review cumulative data and identify students in need of special help and/or attention and/or programs,	Sept.-Oct.
— follow school policy in making referrals; make appropriate referrals,	Sept.-June
— organize an information service and periodically evaluate its usefulness,	Sept.-Nov.
— meet with students, parents, and staff to discuss and interpret the testing program and test results,	Oct.-Dec.
— articulate and publicize the scope and organization of the school's guidance program for each group: students, parents, staff,	Sept.-June
— maintain adequate counseling records; prepare needed reports; observe rules of confidentiality,	Sept.-June
— update information about referral resources and inform the school-community that counselors can assist them in getting service,	Sept.-June
— discuss with faculty the appropriate use of the Counselor Referral Form,	Sept.-June
— respond to referrals noting the action taken.	Sept.-June

Evidence(s) of Success:

Students will:

- show improvement in their interpersonal relationships,
- have access to appropriate educational information and will use that information effectively in career planning,
- be aware of their strengths and weaknesses as measured by standardized tests.

EVALUATION
GRADE 6

Objective(s):

- to develop and use evaluative instruments that will assess the extent to which the school guidance program meets the needs of students, staff, and parents,

   –   to plan modifications to strengthen the school guidance program,
        whenever appropriate.

Activities: *Time Frame*

Counselors will:
   –   obtain through the use of questionnaires the reac-   Sept.-June
        tions of parents, pupils, staff, and administrators to
        various aspects of the guidance services and activities,
   –   prepare and submit to appropriate superior reports on   June
        the total school guidance program and on various
        aspects of it, when requested or when appropriate,
   –   make available to staff, pupils, administrators, par-   Sept.-June
        ents, et al., data from follow-up studies, research,
        when appropriate, suggest program modifications,
   –   review with individual students cumulative data and   Sept.-June
        request missing records, if necessary,
   –   maintain counselor's log,   Sept.-June
   –   prepare local school guidance and counseling plans of   May-Sept.
        action which include goals, objectives, activities,
        timelines for conducting activities, and expected
        outcomes.

Evidence(s) of Success:

Students, Staff, and Parents will:
   –   be asked to evaluate the guidance services and/or program periodically
        and to make recommendations for improvement,
   –   be involved in the process of modifying the guidance program through
        participation in the Guidance Advisory Committee (GAC).

COUNSELING (INDIVIDUAL & GROUP)
GRADE 7

Objective(s):

   –   to counsel with individual students,
   –   to counsel with groups of students,
   –   to regularly inform pupils and parents of the process to be used in
        making self-referrals for counseling,
   –   to use test data and other information to help students benefit
        optimally from their school experiences.

Activities: *Time Frame*

Counselors will:
   –   devise an efficient system and timetable that will re-   Sept.-June
        flect a commitment to counseling services as being
        the most important of all the guidance services;
        inform all concerned persons of the schedule and
        processes,

— organize and conduct both individual and group counseling sessions that are developmental in their approach to child growth and development,	Sept.-June
— maintain appropriate records and prepare needed reports, in keeping with the confidential nature of counseling,	Sept.-June
— form groups, as needed, for specific counseling in such areas as: grade failures, attendance, career planning.	Sept.-June

Evidence(s) of Success:

Students will:
- have access to counseling services and know how to get to talk with a counselor,
- view the counselor as a person who knows him or her fairly well and can be an effective student advocate,
- have a better understanding of their own strengths and weaknesses and their educational opportunities,
- make self-referrals to the counselor, and be seen, when needs appear to warrant them.

CONSULTATION
GRADE 7

Objective(s):
- to provide consultative services to teachers, administrators, and parents in the best interest of the students,
- to confer with outside persons (alumni, drop-outs, employers, etc.) to determine the quality of existing school services and activities.

Activities:	*Time Frame*
Counselors will:	
— develop a plan for communicating regularly and frequently with parents and teachers — individually and in groups — verbally and in writing,	Sept.
— serve as the guidance consultant in classroom activities, etc., and in various administrative efforts,	Sept.-June
— provide input into the curricula that reflects good guidance principles and practices,	Sept.-June
— interpret test data to students, parents, and staff,	Sept.-June
— grow and develop professionally by continued participation in inservice programs,	Sept.-June
— confer periodically with the principal or his/her designee regarding the school guidance program.	Sept.-June

Evidence(s) of Success:

Students will:
- derive added benefits from available guidance services,
- experience fewer disruptions in their educational endeavors because of teacher-pupil or parent-child conflicts,
- teachers, administrators, et al., will: view counselors as helpful to them in their respective roles.

COORDINATION

GRADE 7

Objective(s):
- to be responsible for coordinating guidance and counseling services in the building,
- to conduct the local school guidance program within the framework established by the local school, regional, and central administration,
- to plan and conduct appropriate seventh grade orientation activities and procedures for articulation.

Activities: *Time Frame*

Counselors will:

develop specific strategies for improving comprehensive guidance services: counseling sessions, consultation, referral, record keeping, reports, and professional growth activities; inform all interested persons,	Sept.
plan and conduct programs of inservice for teachers in the area of guidance,	Oct.-May
conduct or participate in case studies for pupils with special needs,	Sept.-Oct.
meet with groups – students, teachers, and parents – to orient them to the guidance program and to the role and function of the counselor,	Sept.-Oct.
participate in the Guidance Advisory Committee and other school activities,	Sept.-June
orient "new" students regularly and periodically throughout the school year; provide for follow-up contacts.	Sept.-June

Evidence(s) of Success:

Students will:
- have access to the various components in a comprehensive guidance program,
- move to the next step on the educational ladder with increased ease.

CAREER GUIDANCE
GRADE 7

Objective(s):

- to make available comprehensive information which will help the individual make immediate choices, while also providing him/her with information for considering long-range alternatives,
- to provide, interpret, and relate information that will help the individual understand and accept himself/herself.

Activities: *Time Frame*

Counselors will:

- organize for systematic selection, collection, and utilization of career guidance materials by students, teachers, administrators, and guidance staff members, — Sept.
- make available for students, etc., appropriate guidance services, i.e., field trips, speakers, MOIS, — Sept.-June
- use announcements, newsletters, bulletin boards, etc., to inform others of the career guidance services, — Sept.-June
- develop plan for helping parents, students, et al., to become involved: (a) career night/day/week; (b) parent-teacher conferences; (c) study groups; (d) classroom units, — Sept.-June
- serve as a resource person in career development programs, — Sept.-June
- provide a variety of developmental group guidance activities to promote self-understanding, self-approval, career awareness, and career planning, — Sept.-June
- observe National Career Guidance Week with appropriate activities. — Nov.

Evidence(s) of Success:

Students will:

- be able to relate their current educational experiences, objectives, and their values to their life-career plans,
- have greater insight into the decision-making process,
- view the school guidance counselor as a prime resource for career guidance assistance.

PROGRAM SELECTION AND PLACEMENT
GRADE 7

Objective(s):

- to assist individuals in recognizing those opportunities most likely to enhance self-development,
- to strive to make each educational, social, and career decision the most appropriate one possible for the individual.

Activities: *Time Frame*

Counselors will:

- participate in the school's program selection process,   Sept.-June
  facilitating the selection of courses most appropriate
  for the student,
- plan and conduct group activities that will be broad-   Sept.-June
  ening and enriching experiences at the seventh grade
  level for achieving effective educational, social, and
  job-placement goals,
- design and use a variety of strategies to inform stu-   Sept.-June
  dents and parents of alternative educational pro-
  grams and job opportunities,
- enroll new seventh grade students; request records;   Sept.-June
  evaluate transcripts; and make necessary program
  adjustments,
- meet with all new seventh grade students in small   Sept.-June
  groups, to assist in their adjustment to the new
  school setting, and will follow up on "new" students
  by direct or indirect contacts,
- identify grade failures and employ intervention strat-   Sept.-June
  egies.

Evidence(s) of Success:

Students will:

- receive assistance from counselors in identifying opportunities or
  alternatives in course selection, in choosing curricula, and in post-
  school planning,
- be enrolled in courses and programs that are congruent with their
  interests, needs, and abilities,
- make a satisfactory adjustment to the seventh grade.

REFERRAL AND INFORMATION SERVICE
GRADE 7

Objective(s):

- to accept referrals from other people, and
- to make a referral whenever a counselee can benefit from working
  with another person,
- to provide an information service in guidance that includes a collection of occupational, educational, and personal-social materials for
  use by students, faculty, and parents.

Activities: *Time Frame*

Counselors will:

- assess student needs; review cumulative records, at-   Sept.-Oct.
  tendance records, counseling records, identify individuals with special needs/abilities,

— meet with parents and teachers — individually and in groups — to share information in the students' best interest,	Sept.-Feb.
— compile materials that will meet the guidance needs of students and staff,	Sept.-June
— devise a method for receiving and for making referrals; get administrative approval, inform concerned persons,	Sept.-June
— utilize a school periodical to inform the community of guidance activities.	Sept.-June

Evidence(s) of Success:

Students will:
- view their counselors as a primary source for current guidance information,
- have access to appropriate referral resources,
- find their contacts with guidance personnel satisfying and helpful.

EVALUATION

GRADE 7

Objective(s):
- to formulate an organized method of measuring the effectiveness and efficiency of the total guidance program or any part of it,
- to put into effect an evaluation plan or process,
- to collate data, make interpretations, modify programs.

Activities:	*Time Frame*
Counselors will:	
— assess needs of pupils, teachers, and other concerned persons using questionnaires and determine the extent to which needs are met,	Sept.-May
— establish criteria; proceed with evaluative plans,	Sept.-June
— outline procedures to be used in the implementation of recommendations, obtaining approval for such change.	Sept.-June

Evidence(s) of Success:

Students, Staff, and Parents will:
- have a basic understanding of the scope of the school's guidance program,
- know how to impact the guidance program,
- have available to them needed guidance and counseling services,
- have positive contacts with counselors,

COUNSELING (INDIVIDUAL & GROUP)
GRADE 8

Objective(s):

- to assist in integrating and interpreting information: (a) with individuals about themselves and their environments, and (b) with those who work with students – teachers, administrators, staff members, and parents.
- to facilitate the development of a course of action for an individual through the effective use of the counseling process.

Activities: *Time Frame*

Counselors will:

- determine and/or clarify for students, staff, and parents the scope of counseling services from the perspective of the: (a) functional role of the counselor, (b) individuals served, (c) kinds of information discussed or provided, and (d) counseling service components,   Sept.-June
- take necessary steps to assure availability of the counseling service and its components to those who have needs,   Sept.-June
- provide procedures for both individual and group counseling sessions; help students and faculty to understand the counseling relationship,   Sept.-June
- maintain adequate records and prepare reports that reflect the confidential nature of counseling,   Sept.-June
- form groups of students, as needed, for specific short-term counseling around such areas as: poor achievement, tardiness,   Sept.-June
- counsel individually with students who are self-referred or referred by staff or parent when needs appear to warrant such.   Sept.-June

Evidence(s) of Success:

Students will:

- report that they have had at least one face-to-face unhurried interview with their counselor,
- have access to on-going individual and group counseling services when self-referred,
- know and understand the educational options that are available to them.

CONSULTATION
GRADE 8

Objective(s):

— to confer with teachers, administrators, parents, support personnel, and others concerned with the growth and development of people, and
— to collaborate with parents and teachers in the best interest of the pupils.

Activities: *Time Frame*

Counselors will:
— meet at least once a year with the faculty to discuss   Sept.-June
  guidance goals and objectives and the role of the
  counselor,
— meet with smaller groups (new teachers, teachers   Sept.-June
  having difficulties, teachers involved in helping an
  individual pupils, etc.) as the need arises; invite in-
  put into the guidance program,
— conduct face-to-face conferences with parents of stu-   Sept.-June
  dents experiencing conflicts; conduct group conferences for parents on guidance services,
— use the Guidance Advisory Committee in a consulta-   Sept-June
  tive capacity in planning school-wide guidance programs,
— serve as a school guidance consultant in the area of   Sept.-June
  curriculum planning.

Evidence(s) of Success:

— Students will view counselors as significant persons in resolving school and home-school conflicts, and will make self-referrals.
— Teachers will be able to report the guidance and counseling services that make a positive difference in the learning process.
— Parents will support the efforts of the guidance and counseling department.

COORDINATION
GRADE 8

Objective(s):

— to coordinate a school-wide guidance program that reflects the needs and interests of pupils, parents, staff, and community persons, and
— to conduct inservice programs for faculty that will help to articulate and upgrade the guidance program.

Activities: *Time Frame*

Counselors will:

- plan guidance activities based on in-put from students,   Sept.-June
  parents, and staff and within the framework of the
  city-wide plans,
- participate actively as a member of the school Guid-   Sept.-June
  ance Advisory Committee (GAC) or other compar-
  able committee,
- assist in the planning of visits by feeder school stu-   April-June
  dents and of visits by middle school to various high
  schools and/or special high school activities,
- coordinate community resources including available   Sept.-June
  speakers, teaching aids, field trips, etc., and notify
  all concerned persons of the availability of such
  resources,
- develop a method of regularly communicating with   Sept.-June
  the school-community through newsletters, announce-
  ments, etc.,
- meet with faculty periodically to discuss guidance goals   Sept.-June
  and objectives,
- orient students new to the school,   Sept.-June
- participate in case conferences/studies,   Sept.-June
- meet with senior high counselor for articulating to   Sept.-June
  senior high and discuss graduation requirements and
  sequential programs.

Evidence(s) of Success:

Students will:

- be offered a variety of guidance-related activities and services,
- have access to community resources which will enhance their educational experiences.

CAREER GUIDANCE

GRADE 8

Objective(s):

- to plan and implement a career guidance program for pupils that will
  focus on: self-awareness and understanding, career awareness and
  exploration, career planning, and tentative career choices,
- to help pupils to identify their own areas of strengths, weaknesses,
  and/or interests.

Activities: *Time Frame*

Counselors will:

- identify career guidance needs and develop plans for   Sept.-June
  meeting such needs, i.e., speakers, audiovisual mate-

rials, group guidance activities, classroom activities,
field trips, career days, etc.

— coordinate and assist in the administration of the Cal-   Sept.-June
ifornia Occupational Preference (COP) or a similar
interest inventory to all eighth graders; interpret
results to pupils, parents, and teachers,

— use group guidance activities to introduce pupils to: Sept.-June
(a) area-vocational centers, apprenticeship programs,
etc., (b) specialized high schools, i.e., Cass, Murray-
Wright, Community, etc., (c) various high school
curricula, (d) work permits, (e) job applications,

— maintain a collection of school and college catalogues   Sept.-June
about educational and training opportunities,

— study and use available test and record data in pre-   Sept.-June
paration for conferences with individual students
and parents,

— utilize a variety of methods to encourage classroom   Sept.-June
teachers to become involved in the career guidance
effort,

— plan group orientations to the Guidance Service Center   Sept.-June
(GSC) and to the services of the Guidance Aides.

— orient students and parents to resources that are   Sept.-Dec.
available to them such as the Guidance Service Center, the medical careers club, the reading lab, etc.,

— involve students in group guidance activities which   Sept.-June
will enable them to develop their skills in getting
information and in using information,

— maintain and use anecdotal records,   Sept.-June

— assist students in developing decision-making skills,

— inform the school-community of guidance activities   Sept.-June
by using a newsletter.

Evidence(s) of Success:

Students will:

— be referred for special service whenever such service is deemed necessary and/or desirable,

— have access to information which they need in order to make fulfilling personal-social, academic, career decisions.

PROGRAM SELECTION AND PLACEMENT
GRADE 8

Objective(s):

— to help students get information about, make applications for, and
enroll in various classes, curricula, activities, and schools,

— to assist each student to "take the next step up the educational ladder" by maintaining articulation with senior high counselors.

Activities: *Time Frame*

Counselors will:
- enroll eighth grade students; arrange their programs,   Nov.-June
  and request appropriate records; evaluate transcripts;
  and make necessary program adjustments,
- inform students and parents — verbally and in writ-   Nov.-June
  ing — of the range of ninth grade program selection
  and placement opportunities, i.e., art classes, clubs,
  sports, vocational centers, special schools, high
  schools, scholarships, and work-study programs,
- whenever appropriate, meet with pupils and parents   Sept.-June
  on a one-to-one basis and review individual needs,
  strengths, weaknesses, and career plans,
- plan and use various strategies and techniques to   Sept.-June
  help prepare students in the method of applying for
  and adjusting to a job, i.e., resume writing, role-playing, etc.
- invite feedback from former pupils, informing the   Sept.-June
  administration of areas needing attention,
- meet with each eighth grade student in small group   Sept.-June
  sessions to discuss high school graduation require-
  ments, Four-Year Plan of Work, interest inventory
  results, and ninth grade registration,
- inform all potential grade failures of alternative   Sept.-June
  courses of action.

Evidence(s) of Success:

Students will:
- identify their tentative educational goals, determine what is to be
  done if those goals are to be achieved, and make appropriate choices,
  and
- view the school guidance counselor as a primary resource person for
  providing information about educational opportunities.

REFERRAL AND INFORMATION SERVICE
GRADE 8

Objective(s):

- to utilize available and/or appropriate referral resources — both within
  and outside of the school — to help pupils grow and develop to their
  fullest extent,
- to provide pupils and concerned others with information which will
  enable them to make wise and satisfying decisions.

Activities: *Time Frame*

Counselors will:
- examine cumulative records to identify students in   Sept.-June
  need of special attention and make appropriate referrals to school social work services, psychological
  services, tutorial programs, family services, etc.,

EVALUATION

GRADE 8

Objective(s):

- to utilize an organized process for periodically assessing the effectiveness of local school guidance and counseling services,
- to assist students to identify their strengths and weaknesses.

Activities: *Time Frame*

Counselors will:
- prepare guidance and counseling goals and objectives   May-Sept.
  annually,
- review cumulative folders with students and parents;   Sept.-June
  verify that test results and other pertinent data have
  been properly posted,
- use evaluative devices — formal or informal — to ap-   Sept.-June
  praise the various local school guidance and counsel-
  ing activities/services/programs; regularly report
  specific accomplishments to students, parents, staff,
  and administration; provide opportunities for in-put
  from each group into the guidance program,
- conduct follow-up studies of former pupils and make   Sept.-June
  appropriate recommendations to the administration,
- conduct exit interviews with all school leavers; help   Sept.-June
  them obtain suitable additional education or training,
- regularly inform parents and students of the process   Sept.-Oct.
  to be used when one wants to confer with his/her
  counselor; arrange a daily schedule that will allow
  for student self-referrals.

Evidence(s) of Success:

Students will:
- have ready access to counseling services, and
- be able to report that their contacts with their counselors have been
  reasonably satisfactory, and
- make educational decisions that are congruent with their needs, abilities, and best interests.

Evidence(s) of Success:

Students will:
- be able to identify their areas of greatest strength and weakness with the help of their counselors, and relate them to educational and career choices,
- select appropriate high school programs and courses, be able to tell why their selections are appropriate for them.

INDEX

Adolescence –
   and cognitive development, 18
   and emotional development, 26-27
   and physical development, 15-17
   and social development, 27-29
Adolescent behavior, 14
Aguilera, D., 82
Alexander, W.M., 5, 8, 9, 181
Alinsky, S., 124
Allen, H.A., 189
Alper, T., 111
American School Counselor Association, 11, 25-36, 183
Ammons, J.M., 182, 183
Anastasi, A., 152, 153
APGA Ethical Standards, 37
Armstrong, C.M., 25
Ayres, L.P., 2

Baird, L., 110
Baldwin, B., 82
Ball, G., 116
Ballou, M., 83, 85
Bardwick, J., 109
Barnes, E., 114
Barnette, E.L., 139
Baruch, G.K., 110
Bayley, N., 25
Behrens, H., 60
Binet-Simon Scale, 153
Blackburn, J.E., 8, 126
Blocher, D., 82
Bloom, B.S., 50, 81
Bohlinger, T., 188, 189, 190
Bohn, M.J., Jr., 177
Boocock, S.S., 177
Bookfinder, The, 118
Borow, H., 165
Bossing, N.L., 3
Bowsbey-Harris, 177
Bradway, K., 110
Broad, P., 6, 8
Brooks, K., 9, 181, 182
Brough, J.R., 167
Broverman, D.M., 109
Broverman, I.K., 109
Brown, D.E., 126
Brown, J., 34
Brown-Miller, S., 83

Callao, M.J., 114
Campbell, D., 111
Canfield, J., 116
Caplan, G., 81, 83, 84, 124
Career Awareness Program, 173
Career Guidance –
   and information retrieved, 177-178
   and personal growth, 165-167
   developing a program for, 167-168
   evaluating materials, 174-176
   model for, 169-171
   simulated materials for, 176-177
   strategies for, 168-174
Career Literature Evaluation Checklist, 174
Carlson, J., 124, 127, 135
Carmichael, C., 108
Cascade system of educational placement, 96
Cattell, J.M., 153
"C" Group, 135-136
Change –
   forces for and against, 147-148
Child abuse –
   and emotional symptoms of, 44-46
   and physical symptoms of, 40-44
   definition of, 32-33
Child and Family Services Act, 37
Childhood history of, 35
Children –
   influences on, 138, 140-145
Children's rights –
   a child's view, 34
   and American School Counselor
      Association, 35-36
   and standardization, 51
   list of from Massachusetts Advocacy Center, 35
   U.N. Declaration of the Rights of
      the Child, 33
Clack, S., 177
Clark, E., 32
Clarkson, F.E., 109
Committee of Ten, 1, 2
Committee on College Entrance Requirements, 2
Communication roadblocks, 133-134
Compton, M.F., 5, 6, 8, 181
Concrete operational thinking and
   transition to formal thinking, 25-26

241

242

The Middle School Counselor

Confrontation, 72
Connell, D.M., 110
Consultation —
and consultees, 128-129
and mental health and social work, 124
and the middle school, 124ff
four models of, 124-125
sample session, 129-133
systems of, 122-123
vs. counseling, 127
Cornell, E.L., 25
Council for Interracial Books, 119
Counseling —
and the multimodal therapy approach, 64-67.
See also Consultation
Counselor —
activities for working with minorities, 115-119
and children's rights, 36, 52
and disabled children, 97-100
and parents, 62-63
attributes for working with minorities, 112-115
characteristics of, 60-62
need for courage, 34
Counselor roles, 60
Cramer, R.V., 3
Cramer, S.L., 173, 177
Crisis —
a case analysis, 89-90
and approaches to intervention, 90-92
and counselor's role, 86-89
and growth, 85
definition of, 83
duration of, 84
factors causing, 83-84
literature on, 80-82
model of, 85
Crites, J.O., 166
Cuff, W.A., 8, 181
Curriculum —
latent, 50
manifest, 50
Curtis, T.E., 5
Curwin, G., 116
Curwin, R., 116

Davis, J.B., 10
Deaux, K., 111
Detroit Department of Guidance and Counseling, 191

Developmental task, 14
Dinkmeyer, D., 69, 124, 135, 137
Douvan, E., 109
Dubois, P.H., 152
Duff, C.F., 190, 191
Duncan, R., 148
Dworkin, A.L., 124, 125
Dworkin, E.P., 124, 125
Dyer, W.W., 69

Education for All Handicapped Children Act, 37, 95
Educational-Diagnostic Meetings, 77
Egocentrism, 29
Eichholz, G.C., 146
Eichhorn, D.H., 25
Eliot, C.W., 1
Elkind, D., 21, 29, 60
Emma Willard Task Force on Education, 118
Entwisle, D., 111
Epstein, H.T., 25
Erikson, E., 59, 82
Ethical Guidelines for Counselors, 77-78

Family Educational Rights and Privacy Act, 36-37
Farmer, H., 111
Faust, V., 127
Feedback, 72
Female socialization and conflict, 108-111
Fennema, E., 111
Fine, M.J., 126
Fink, S., 85
Fix, C., 97
Focus on Self-Development, 118
Formal operational thinking, 23-25
Free to Be You and Me, 118
Freed, A.T., 65
Friedman, S., 32

Galton, F., 152, 153
Gastwirth, P., 6
Geisler, J., 183, 186
Generalizations vs. stereotypes, 105-106
George, P.S., 182
George-Barden Act, 10
George-Dean Act, 10
George-Ellezey Act, 10
George-Reed Act, 10
Gersoni-Stavin, D., 118

Gil, D., 32
Glasser, I., 50
Glasser, W., 75, 76, 77
Glitzer, B., 109
Glossary of terms, 53
Gohn, M., 111
Golan, N., 81, 82, 83
Goldman, L., 157, 167
Goodstein, L., 60
Gordon, T., 133, 137
Gray, S., 110
Greenberger, E., 111
Greenleaf, B.K., 35
Greenwood, J., 109
Group counseling, 69-70
    and counselor's role, 72
    and forces of influence, 70-71
    skills needed for, 71ff
Guidance programs –
    and research of, 188-191
Guidette, M.J., 109
Guilford, J.P., 18, 20
Guillion, M.E., 137

Hall, G.S., 2
Handicapped children –
    and the regular classroom, 100
    definition, 95
    vs. disabled, 95
Hansen, L.S., 168, 172
Harmon, L., 111
Harris, J.A., 177
Harris, T., 60
Havighurst, R.J., 4, 5, 14, 15, 165
    and developmental tasks, 15
Heibrun, A., 110
Henry, S.A., 137
Herr, E.L., 173, 177
High intelligence –
    and performance, 26
Hill, G.R., 155
Hines, V.A., 5
Horner, M., 110, 111
Howe, L.W., 116
Huber, C.H., 97
Humes, C.W., 100
Hummel, R.C., 166
Hurlock, E.B., 27

Inhelder, B., 24, 60
Intelligence –
    Guilford's model of, 18-20

Iscoe, L., 81
Ivey, A.E., 72, 73

Jacklin, C.N., 109, 111
Jacobson, G., 82
Jakubowski-Spector, P., 116
Johnson, D.W., 72
Johnson, H.E., 110
Johnson, R.H., 177
Jones, H.E., 18
Jones, M.C., 18
Junior High School Movement, 1-4
    purposes, 3
    See also Middle School,
        Kagan, J., 110

Kadushin, A., 124
Kagan, J., 110
Kalish, B.J., 32
Kameen, M.C., 97
Kangas, J., 110
Kannenberg, G., 138, 144-145
Kealy, R.P., 8, 9, 181
Keat, D., 64
Kelly, J., 124
Kempe, C.H., 32
Kiil, V., 17
Kirschenbaum, H., 116
Klien, D.C., 81
Kline, D.F., 40, 41, 53-55
Koos, L., 2, 3
Kubler-Ross, E., 82
Kuchemann, D.E., 25

Lagsbrun, F., 118
Landers, A., 34, 40
Landon-Dahm, M., 117
Lange, A., 116
Lawson, A.E., 25
Lazarus, A., 64
Learning disabilities checklist, 100-102
Least restrictive environments, 96
Leavitt, H., 111
Lerner, H.E., 109
Light, R., 32
Lindeman, R.H., 177
Linndeman, E., 80, 81, 82
Lipman-Blumen, J., 111
Lippitt, G., 147
Lippitt, R., 124
Lipsett, L., 166, 167, 168
Lipsitz, J.S., 16

Listening, 72
Litwack, J., 83
Litwack, L., 83
Loesch, L.C., 51, 154, 157, 158, 163
Looft, W.R., 109

Maccoby, E.E., 109, 111
Madsen, C.H., 135
Madsen, C.K., 135
Malinka, R., 182
Martin, H., 32
Martin, R., 124
Mathewson, R.H., 10
Matthews, E., 111
Maynard, G., 60
McCall, R.B., 26
McClung, F., 123
McCord, D., 178
McFadden, J., 116, 138, 144-145
McKay, G., 137
McMillan, M., 182
Mead, M., 4
Mental Measurements Yearbook and Tests in Print, 156
Messick, J., 82
Meyers, J., 124
Michigan School Testing Service, 160
Middle school –
    and counselor certification, 182
    and minorities, 111-112
    and teacher certification, 182
    background, 4-8
    counselor's functions, 183-188
    extent of, 8-9
    growth in numbers of, 181
    purpose, 6-8
    trends, 9
Middle school counselor –
    rationale for, 10-11
Middle school students –
    and developmental characteristics, 58-60
Miller, C.H., 165
Miller, G.M., 154, 156, 162, 173, 182, 183, 184, 186, 187
Miller, K., 81
Minor, C.W., 172
Minuchin, P., 107
Mitchell, J.J., 28
Mizer, J.E., 37
Moni, L., 11
Moore, N.F., 113, 114

Morley, W., 82
Morrice, J.K.W., 82
Morse, C., 32
Moser, H.P., 166
Moss, H., 110
Muro, J.J., 77
Myers, D.D., 114
Myrick, R.D., 11, 177

National Defense Education Act, 11
National Educational Association, 1
National Vocational Guidance Association, 174
Neimark, E.D., 25
Nelson, R.C., 124, 126
Newman, B., 59, 60
Newman, P., 59, 60

Ohlsen, M.M., 70, 71
Olsen, L.C., 78
Open-ended meetings, 77
Otis, A.S., 153
Overstreet, P.L., 166

Palomares, U.H., 116
Pappas, J.G., 183, 184, 186, 187
Parad, H.J., 81
Parent/child study groups, 136-138
Parson, R., 124
Patterson, G.R., 137
Perrone, P.A., 58, 60
Piaget, J., 20, 22, 23, 24, 60
    and stages of thinking, 21-23
Poggio, J.P., 126
Powell, W.C., 126
Prescott, D., 5
Psychological assessment –
    and guidance programs, 154
    and interpretation, 162
    and the rights of the child, 163
    definition, 154
    historical background, 152-153
    list of achievement tests, 161
    origin of group testing, 153
    rationale for in middle school, 154
    standards for a program of, 155-160
Pumerantz, P., 9, 181, 182

Rapoport, L., 86
Rasbaum-Selig, M., 116
Rayman, J.R., 177

Reality therapy. 75-76
Rebich, C., 85
Rejection —
  forms of, 146
Renner, J.W., 25
Renshaw, H., 83
Rigler, D., 32
Robertiello, R., 66
Robinson, L., 50
Rogers, C.R., 11
Rogers, E.M., 146
Rosenkrantz, P.S., 109
Ross, 62, 63
Rotter, J.C., 98, 100, 116, 138,
  144-145
Rusk, T., 82
Ryan, J.P., 189
Ryan, M.K., 11, 195
Ryan, T.A., 58, 60

Sahler, O., 32
Scales, A., 114
School —
  as an agent of change, 106
  educational goals, 107
School Child Abuse/Neglect Checklist,
  46-48
Schools Without Failure, 77
Schowengerdt, R.V., 126
Seguin, E., 152
Sexism and Youth, 118
Sexism in Education, 118
Shayer, M., 25
Sherman, J., 111
Shertzer, B., 10, 11, 154
Sifncos, P.E., 81
Simon, S.B., 116
Smith, E.D., 177
Smith, G.S., 114
Social worlds of adolescents, 27
South Carolina Employment Security
  Commission and the Job Bank, 178
South Carolina Occupational Infor-
  mation Coordinating Committee,
  177-178
Spiegal, J.P., 84
Spinetta, J., 32
Splittgerber, F.L., 189
Sproles, J.A., 97

Stanford-Binet Scale, 153
Stickler, J., 82
Stone, S.C., 10, 11, 154
Strayer, G.D., 2
Structured exercise —
  and group counseling, 74-75
Stunden, A., 123
Sue, D.W., 105
Sund, R., 60
Super, D.E., 161, 166, 167

Tanner, J.M., 17
Terman, L.M., 153
Thompson, A.S., 177
Thornburg, H.D., 15
Thorndike, E.L., 2
Tiedeman, D., 111
Todd, D., 124
Toepfer, C.F., 25, 26
Tomlinson-Keasey, C., 111
Tracy, J., 32
Traxler, A.B., 10
Trickett, E., 124
Trotzer, J.P., 74, 75
Turnbaugh, R.E., 6, 8
Turner, D., 139

United States Office of Education,
  173

VanHoose, W.H., 36, 126
Van Riper, B.W., 155
Vars, G.F., 4
Vocational Information for Educa-
  tion and Work, 177-178
Vogel, S.R., 109
Vriend, J., 69

Waidley, J.W., 173
Warnath, C.F., 166
Watson, J., 124
Wehrly, B.L., 167
Weinrach, S.G., 174, 176, 177
Wells, H., 116
Werner, J.L., 127
Westling, D., 97
Westly, B., 124
Williams, E.L., 5, 59, 181
Williams, J.H., 109

Wilson, C.E., 113   Yerkes, R.M., 153
Wolleat, P.L., 111
Wylam, H., 25   Zaltman, G., 148
Wyne, M.D., 126   Zeran, F.R., 58, 60